Deaf Learners

DONALD F. MOORES AND
DAVID S. MARTIN, EDITORS

Deaf Learners

Developments in Curriculum and Instruction

GALLAUDET UNIVERSITY PRESS • *Washington, DC*

© Gallaudet University Press
Washington, D.C. 20002
http://gupress.gallaudet.edu

© 2006 by Gallaudet University

Library of Congress Cataloging-in-Publication Data

Deaf learners : developments in curriculum and instruction / Donald F.
Moores and David S. Martin, editors.
     p. cm.
   Includes bibliographical references and index.
   ISBN 1-56368-285-0
   1. Deaf children—Education—Curricula. I. Moores, Donald F. II. Martin,
David S.
   HV2440.D42 2006
   371.91'2—dc22

                                                                    2005055222

ISBN 1-56368-285-0

⊗ The paper used in this publication meets the minimum requirements of American National Standard
for Information Sciences—Permanence of Paper for Printed Library Materials, ANSI Z39.48-1984.

Text design and composition by John Reinhardt Book Design

This book is dedicated to the memory of David A. Stewart, a friend and colleague for more than 20 years. David died unexpectedly at the age of 50 during the preparation of this book, to which he contributed chapters on classroom communication and physical education. He played a leadership role in research on classroom communication and published some of the seminal work in our field. At the same time he was a leader in the Deaf community and made significant contributions to the field of deaf sport and physical fitness: a true Renaissance person. Just before his death he was discussing with one of the editors, Donald Moores, the development of a handbook for hearing parents of deaf children. He is sorely missed.

Contents

Part Three:
Instructional Considerations Across the Curriculum

Part Four: Final Comments

Preface

THE ORIGINAL IMPETUS for this book came from a PhD level course in curriculum and instruction for deaf learners that we co-taught. Each of us had taught undergraduate and graduate curriculum courses in general education, special education, and education of deaf learners, and we were aware of the ongoing confluence of education of deaf students with general education, along with the attendant challenges. The career goals of the students in the class primarily were to become college and university professors participating in research and preparing undergraduate and graduate students to be involved professionally with deaf learners. We were all aware that the requisite sets of knowledge and skills for teachers of deaf students were changing rapidly and that traditional paradigms were not satisfactory. Educational placement patterns for deaf students have been evolving during the past two generations, from predominantly residential and separate day schools in large cities to public school settings that range from complete integration (immersion) to partial integration to separate classrooms in schools with a majority of hearing students.

Concurrent with changes in placement, a variety of options in instructional modes of communication is now available, including oral-only instruction, English-based signing with or without speech, and American Sign Language. It is common now for deaf students to have a variety of educational placements and to be taught in different modes of instruction by the time they have completed their secondary education. This is a relatively new situation. The growing utilization of cochlear implants and increased sophistication of digital hearing aids has also presented new challenges and opportunities to educators.

In addition to these realities, deaf students represent the same geographic and ethnic diversity as the general school-age population. Added to this are educationally relevant variables such as age and extent of hearing loss, quality of communication in the home, and possible existence of disabilities concomitant with the cause of deafness itself in a particular child, such as premature birth or meningitis.

Traditionally, education of the deaf has been separate from general education and even what has been considered special education. The primary focus in many deaf education programs was the development of articulate speech and of English skills, predominantly through the spoken word but also to some extent through reading and writing. As we document in the opening chapters, the emphasis on preparing (predominantly) hearing teachers to concentrate on speech development resulted in neglect of traditional content areas such as math, science, social studies, and English.

The English or "language" instruction that deaf children received bore little resemblance to the general education curriculum. Rather, it was designed to teach deaf children the English skills that hearing children brought to the educational process. The field has been hampered by low expectations for students and inadequate training in subject matter for teachers.

We are at a point in American education where a number of complex factors intersect. There is a movement to increase academic achievement by strengthening the curriculum, improving teacher training, providing parents with more options, and requiring annual statewide assessments of educational progress. This movement toward what might be considered educational excellence occurs at the same time that there is a trend toward equity of access, or inclusion, for all children in the process. Historically, American education has swung back and forth between the ideals of equality and the ideals of excellence. The present situation combines, perhaps for the first time, a commitment to strive for high levels of achievement for all children with a federal mandate for rigorous coursework.

The goals of equity and excellence are not always compatible. In the case of deaf learners, beginning around 1975, access to the regular educational curriculum was emphasized. This has expanded in the present time to include demonstrated success in the regular curriculum, including, in most states, the same high-stakes testing necessary for promotion and high school graduation as is found for hearing students.

Although we talk of the regular educational curriculum, it is evident that there is no one curriculum in the United States. Despite growing federal influence, American education remains primarily under state and local control. Curricula vary across and within states, and, to a large degree, reflect the constituencies that they serve. Although we are aware of this, we use the terms "regular" or "general" curriculum as a convenience. In this text we address common issues and realities that deaf children, their parents, and professionals serving them must face in improving educational services and outcomes. Among these realities are the facts that most deaf children have the intellectual potential for high achievement but usually start the educational process without mastery over either a spoken or signed language. Our goal is to provide a developmental framework of child variables, particularly special characteristics of deaf children, from kindergarten through grade 12 within a framework of family, social, and educational contexts, in such a way as to maximize academic success.

No book of this scope would be possible without the rich contributions of the numerous authors of its chapters, all of whom lent their considerable expertise to this venture. The authors, individually and collectively, have a wide variety of knowledge, skills, and experience. We greatly appreciate their cooperation and professionalism. Brief biographical sketches of the chapter authors can be found at the back of this book. Several of the authors could have contributed more than one chapter to this text. In fact many, if not most, of the contributors have published or edited their own texts in the field. As the editors, we (Moores and Martin) have collaborated on several parts of the text and have provided individual chapters as well. The collaboration was seamless. One time, when we were teaching a doctoral course on curriculum development, a student commented that we were like a tag team, with each one picking up on the other's ideas effortlessly. We had a similar experience in producing this book, a feeling that extended to our collaborators.

Claudia Pagliaro is a recognized authority in the field of teaching mathematics to learners who are deaf or hard of hearing. Donald Moores provides information on curriculum in general and print literacy in particular. Harry Lang has carried out numerous studies related to the teaching of science. The late David Stewart's treatment of educational use of American Sign Language and English-based signing represents a significant contribution, and his chapter with Kathleen Ellis on physical education addresses an important area often neglected in our schools. John Luckner's expertise in the role of the itinerant teacher for deaf and hard of hearing children adds an important element to our understanding of the curriculum needs of growing numbers of deaf children in regular classroom placements. Claudine Storbeck and Lucas Magongwa, representing the international community, are a hearing-deaf writing team with unique perspectives in teaching about deaf culture. David Martin's knowledge of assessment issues, cognitive-strategy instruction, and the teaching of social studies provides useful directions for those interested in curriculum. Pamela Luft's extensive background in deaf education and teacher preparation enhances our understanding of curriculum selection issues. Thomas Jones, Julie Jones, and Karen Ewing have in-depth experience in the teaching of children with multiple disabilities, including but not limited to deafness. Barbara Bonds has carried out significant work on the school-to-work transition and shares that expertise with us. Harold Johnson and Donna Mertens provide a critical dimension through a focus on technologies, present and future, within the curriculum. Margery Miller includes a balanced approach to educational assessment, including the psychoeducational dimension that is so important to classroom applications. Marc Marschark, Carol Convertino, and Doni LaRock systematically discuss the special characteristics of deaf learners, characteristics of which all professionals must be cognizant if they are to instruct deaf students effectively.

Organization

The text is organized into four parts. In part 1 Moores and Martin begin by providing an overview of curriculum and instruction in general education and education of deaf learners, with concentration on access to and success with the general curriculum. This is followed by a short chapter by Martin, Moores, and Luft about the selection of appropriate curriculum and instructional techniques.

Part 2 addresses curriculum content, the primary focus of the book. Pagliaro examines the National Council of Teachers of Mathematics standards and presents ways in which the mathematics achievement of deaf students may be improved. Moores presents background information on the development of print literacy of deaf students and discusses conflicting elemental, "phonics"-based approaches and more holistic approaches within the context of the requirements of the No Child Left Behind legislation and the extant research. Lang reports that there is a growing body of knowledge within the science education field about tailoring instruction to deaf learners, although a basic theory of learning has not yet been developed. Similar to Pagliaro's approach in mathematics, Lang ties reform in science education for deaf students to the National Science Education Standards developed by the National Research Council. Martin traces the development of what is now commonly known as social studies over time from a concentration on history and geography to include fields such as economics, political science, and sociology. He relates the education of deaf learners to the goals established by the National Council for the Social Studies. Stewart and Ellis emphasize the need for physical fitness and report that physical education in our schools has been an "ugly duckling" during the past generation. They argue that deaf children fare worse than hearing children in many cases, and they recommend implementation of standards espoused by the National Association for Sport and Physical Education. Luckner traces the changes in educational placement of deaf students from predominantly self-contained environments to the present, where a majority of deaf children are educated in regular class settings at least part-time. Storbeck and Magongwa argue that deaf history and deaf culture are appropriate components of the curriculum for both deaf and hearing children, and they provide information on incorporating the teaching of deaf culture into the curriculum. Jones, Jones, and Ewing establish the framework for valid, cohesive, and effective curricula for students with multiple disabilities, and they stress the unique needs of children with more than one disability. Thus, a deaf student with mental retardation has learning needs that neither a typical curriculum for deaf children nor a typical curriculum for children with mental retardation would address. Bonds reviews the legislation, much of which is not implemented, that is designed to facilitate the progress of children from school to higher education and/or work and the implications for deaf individuals.

Part 3 includes instructional and assessment considerations across the curriculum. Miller analyzes the provision of meaningful individual assessment and educational planning for deaf students. She discusses issues about norms, test modifications, accommodations, and overall fairness as they relate to the demands of the standards-testing movement. Marschark, Convertino, and LaRock follow with a treatment of educationally relevant characteristics of deaf learners, and Martin addresses the importance of cognitive strategy instruction. Stewart then reviews the use of sign communication during a 40-year span and concludes that both American Sign Language and English-based signs can be effectively implemented in what he characterizes as instructional and practical communication (IPC). Johnson and Mertens explore a vision of a 21st-century learning environment, concentrating on web-based technologies, present and future, with specific applications for deaf learners.

In part 4 Moores and Martin briefly summarize developments in the field with an emphasis on the constant changes occurring and recent changes that had not been anticipated.

In any book of this type the editors are faced with decisions of what to include and what not to include, and the decisions on areas not to be covered may assume major importance. Such was the case with the present book. One major possible area of inclusion, in view of increased placement in regular classrooms, is the role of educational interpreters. The training, functioning, and effectiveness of educational interpreters varies greatly at a time when their roles are becoming more and more critical. Unfortunately, there is a current dearth of research in the area. Our hope is that this will be resolved by the efforts now under way, led by the work of Marschark, Convertino, and LaRock, who contributed to this book on another topic.

Another area of interest concerns the significant increase in the numbers of children receiving cochlear implants, numbers that are projected to increase with breakthroughs in efficiency and miniaturization. In this case, there is a growing body of research on cochlear implants that could be reviewed. However, at this point, we decided that the procedure itself had no direct effect on the delivery of curriculum to children; it might alter the numbers of deaf and hard of hearing children but not the ways they are taught.

We planned for the inclusion of a chapter on the arts in the curriculum for deaf and hard of hearing children. We consider this subject to be one of equal importance to other subject areas, but regrettably were unable to identify a willing author.

Audience

This book is designed for a wide range of readers and includes anyone with an interest in and commitment to facilitating the growth and achievement of young deaf children and youth. One primary audience consists of upper-level undergraduate students and graduate students preparing for careers working with deaf students as teachers, interpreters, school and rehabilitation counselors, child- and adolescent-development specialists, school and clinical psychologists, social workers, and speech and hearing specialists. An equally important audience includes parents of deaf children who, by law, have rights to participate in educational decision making and to guide the educational process. Another extremely important target of this book is all of the professionals in general education who in the past had no responsibility for education of deaf children but who now are expected to provide quality education to deaf children within a classroom context in which the majority of children are hearing. Currently, these teachers, secretaries, principals, and other personnel receive little or no training for their important roles. We are not sure of the current breakdown, but the day may not be far off when more deaf children may be educated by regular classroom teachers than by teachers of deaf children.

DONALD F. MOORES
DAVID S. MARTIN

Acknowledgments

As editors we owe a strong debt to many highly qualified individuals. First, we are indebted to our chapter authors whose strength and professional commitment will be obvious to any reader; without them, there simply would be no book. Second, we deeply appreciate the sensitivity of Ivey Wallace of Gallaudet University Press, who provided counsel throughout the book development process, and to Deirdre Mullervy, also of Gallaudet University Press, who saw it through to publication. Third, we also appreciate the assistance of Dina Raevsky, who, as a graduate student in education at Gallaudet University, provided important editorial help at various stages of the process. Finally, we express our appreciation to all of the deaf students we have met over the years and from whom we have learned so much.

PART ONE

The Context

DONALD F. MOORES

DAVID S. MARTIN

Overview: Curriculum and Instruction in General Education and in Education of Deaf Learners

THE FIELD OF EDUCATION of deaf children and youth has undergone major changes that have significant implications for curriculum and instruction. Traditionally, educators of deaf students have struggled with three important questions (Moores, 1991): (a) Where should deaf children be taught? (b) How should they be taught? (c) What should they be taught? Although many educators have addressed the questions separately, they are not discrete issues. In fact, they are complexly interrelated and decisions in one area have significant implications for the other two. There are no final answers, but there are definite trends that must be considered. Some of them have been developing over decades, even generations.

We should consider briefly some of the major changes in the three areas and their implications. First is the question of where to educate deaf children. Most readers are aware that the trend in recent years has been toward academic placement contiguous to hearing peers to the greatest extent possible, and the literature is full of terms such as *least restrictive environment, mainstreaming, integration,* and *inclusion* that in different ways reflect this orientation. Most readers, however, are not aware that the trend began more than half a century ago, shortly after the end of World War II (Moores, 2001). At that time most deaf children attended residential schools for the deaf or separate day schools for the deaf in large cities. The postwar baby boom produced an enormous increase in the number of children and, by extension, the number of deaf children. State legislators were reluctant to build additional separate facilities for an increase in the number of deaf children that was thought to be temporary, so there was a push for establishment of separate classes for deaf children within public schools serving predominantly hearing children. This movement was intensified by the rubella epidemic of the mid-1960s, which doubled the number of deaf children born during a short period of time, a time when the American school-age population was declining and classroom space was available. When Public Law 94-142—the

3

Education for All Handicapped Children Act of 1975—was enacted, enrollment in residential schools and day schools for the deaf had already dropped to less than half of the deaf school-age population. The impetus away from separate academic placement for deaf children continues to this day. Although there are differences of opinion about the benefits of this trend, it is a reality.

The question of how to teach deaf children in essence involves the centuries-old oral-manual "methods war." Some professionals advocate the use of oral-only instruction, with emphasis on speech, speechreading, and use of residual hearing. Others advocate the use of an American Sign Language (ASL) and English bilingual approach. There are numerous gradations between the two. The use of an English-based sign system—differentiated from ASL—either alone or in combination with speech, is common, as is an approach incorporating oral communication, English-based signing, and ASL depending on situational variables and child needs.

The question of what to teach deaf children has now assumed center stage. Traditionally, the curriculum in education of the deaf had little or no relation to the general educational curriculum. Residential schools established in the first half of the 19th century had a primarily vocational emphasis for deaf students, with some basic attention to English, math, and moral development. Instruction was conducted through either sign language (natural signs) or an English-based sign system (methodical signs). Beginning in the latter third of the 19th century, the emphasis shifted toward the development of vocal communication skills, especially in the newly established day schools, and reliance on any kind of signs (either natural or methodical) was either discouraged or repressed. The greater part of the school day was devoted to English, sometimes referred to as "language." Individual, small group, and class activities evolved around lessons in speech, speechreading, and English structure, with concentration on drill and practice. Content areas such as math, social studies, and science received minimal attention. Success was judged on fluency in vocal communication.

The original press toward use of the regular educational curriculum came because of the increasing tendency of deaf children to attend the same schools as hearing children, sometimes in separate classes and sometimes integrated into classrooms with hearing students for part or all of the school day. There was a need for consistency across the two systems. This occurred at the same time that state and federal agencies were promoting *access* to the general educational curriculum for all children, including those who were deaf. Over time the U.S. government and states have expanded the mandate from *access* to *demonstrated proficiency* in academic content. Proficiency is measured through standardized, grade-level, statewide testing of all children. In increasing numbers of states, the testing is of a high-stakes nature, meaning that children who do not reach a certain level of proficiency may not be promoted to a higher grade or may not receive a high school graduation diploma.

Programs for the deaf have responded to this initiative by adopting and adapting regular curricula. We should note that there is no one regular or general curriculum in the United States. Although federal influence has increased significantly, the Constitution does not mention education, and therefore state and local governments have ultimate responsibility for educating their children. Although there are commonalities, there is curricular variation across and within states. Typically, residential schools adopted the curriculum of a local or county school district and day schools, and other local programs for deaf students adopted the curriculum of the host district. A major challenge is how to provide access to and ultimately, demonstrated mastery of, the regular curriculum for deaf children who may not have complete proficiency in English. This is the purpose of this book. As we have noted, the traditional curriculum for deaf children was designed to help them develop English skills similar to those that hearing children brought to the learning process. Now, we are faced with the challenge of facilitating mastery of math, science, social studies, and literature while developing English and other communication skills to the greatest extent possible. We cannot allow English to be a barrier to learning.

To date, our record of success has been quite limited, partly because of the lingering effects of the traditional concentration on "language" and the lack of attention to academic subject matter. For example, the Council for Exceptional Children and Council on Education of the Deaf Joint Knowledge and Skills Statement for All Becoming Teachers of Students Who Are Deaf or Hard of Hearing (Joint Standards Committee, 1996) lists a total of 66 knowledge and skills standards for teachers of the deaf. The list contains many admirable standards, but only two statements of knowledge outcomes address academic content aside from communication (p. 222), as follows:

> Number 32. Subject matter and practices used in general education across content areas.
> Number 35. Research supported instructional strategies and practice for teaching students who are Deaf or Hard of Hearing.

No skill statements address academic content. "Communication" was mentioned in 17 of the 66 standards, but mathematics, social studies, science, and literature did not appear. We strongly support an emphasis on the importance of communication for deaf learners but believe that the standards reflect an imbalance. A review by Moores, Jatho, and Creech (2001) of all 130 peer-reviewed articles that appeared in the *American Annals of the Deaf* during a 5-year period further illustrates the lack of emphasis placed on academic content. Only 3 articles dealt with mathematics, 2 of which were contributed by Pagliaro (1998a, 1998b), who is the author of the chapter on mathematics in this book. There were no articles addressing science or social studies. This lack should astound the reader.

Although the situation is improving, the field is hampered by low expectations for deaf children. Many teachers of deaf children lack skill and training in the subject matter that they teach. There is evidence, for example, that teachers of deaf children spend less time on mathematics areas than regular classroom mathematics teachers with deaf children integrated into regular classes in the same school building. The regular classroom teachers provide higher level material, give and grade more homework, and ask higher level questions (Kluwin & Moores, 1987). We strongly believe that teachers of deaf children are as capable as any teachers in facilitating high levels of educational achievement and that deaf learners are capable of meeting rigorous standards of proficiency. This book is dedicated to help achieve those goals.

Overview of General Education

The landscape in our field has changed to the extent that any discussion of the curriculum for learners who are deaf must take place within the larger context of general education. In the past, that general education context was *not* considered important because deaf education was in large measure a thing apart from the general educational area. However, today, with the advent of inclusion and raised expectations for learners who are deaf, that context becomes highly relevant and serves as a backdrop against which deaf education trends are played out.

It is well recognized that the American educational system as we know it today, separate from whatever educational system was practiced by native peoples before the advent of the Europeans, had its roots in the early colonies. Some of the first schools were "dame schools" in which a woman of a village would give reading instruction using the Bible around the hearth of her home for children from nearby. This system evolved gradually into schools that were organized around local interests and needs; we know that when the colonies became states in a new nation, they reluctantly gave up some of their autonomy to the good of the new nation as a whole. However, they clung tenaciously to the right to make local decisions in relation to education (and in other matters) and to maintain local and then state control over education. It is true that we have never had a national system of education and probably never will, although a large federal "intrusion" into education occurred in 2001 with the passage of the national No Child Left Behind Act.

The foundations of the American school system, which also affect the roots of deaf education at least indirectly, rested on several important principles and beliefs. Freeman Butts, the historian of American education, provides a most helpful chart titled Triform Foundations of the American School System (Butts & Cremin, 1953). He proposed a three-dimensional model consisting of cohesive values, social characteristics, and segmented pluralisms. The cohesive values of America include liberty, equality, popular consent, and the public good; the social characteristics include secularization, industrialization, popular participation, and the central power of the state (not the federal government) in education; and the segmented pluralisms that characterize America include multiethnicity, multiple races, multiple localisms, and multiple religions. Today, we would add a fifth pluralism—that of multiple languages—and a sixth one—that of different kinds of disabilities that the schools must serve. Thus, taken together, the interaction of these different factors along the three dimensions serves as a means of understanding the complexities faced by the American school system in a national "experiment" that had never before been attempted by any country in the world.

Butts' view, then, provides us with a way of analyzing also what is at stake in deaf education as well—the same values, social characteristics, and pluralisms are the foundation within which the microsystem of deaf education must function.

The American educational scene has been buffeted by many different trends and fads during the years since its inception as a collection of numerous state school systems held loosely together by some national interests. It is not our purpose to trace those trends, which began in the late 18th century. They are treated with great skill in other works on the history of American education, and the interested reader is referred to them (e.g., Cremin, 1988; Farris, 1999).

However, it behooves us to consider the most recent cycles of change that began in the years immediately after World War I. These years were characterized in some ways by the need to consolidate and standardize the curriculum to deal with a school population that was more diverse than ever before—with the end of that war and thus the ending of the Great Depression, a greater percentage of children were in school than not, and more children stayed longer in school than ever before.

Then in the era of the 1960s, during which there was a significant change in social movements and technical innovation, we witnessed important curriculum reform. Some trace the roots of that era of change to the launching of the Russian spacecraft *Sputnik* in 1957, which shocked Americans into realizing that their country was no longer the leader in technology and that something had to be done with the American curriculum to remedy this problem. (It is interesting to note how frequently a national or world event refocuses attention on the schools as the problem or the solution, when in fact the situation is often far broader than merely the schools alone.) The federal government responded with the National Defense Education Act, which put federal funds into educational innovation. Among the professional innovations resulting from renewed attention to schools was the publication of *The Process of Education* (Bruner, 1960), which called for important curriculum reform and a number of exciting curriculum projects in social studies, mathematics, and sciences.

In these projects, for the first time, subject matter scholars, psychologists, and teachers collaborated to produce new elementary and secondary curricula. We note that these significant changes had little influence on the majority of deaf children, who at that time were still taught primarily in residential schools and separate day schools. Developments in social studies, mathematics, and science in general education had little effect on the curriculum in most programs for deaf students.

In the 1970s, however, a clear retrenchment was evident in general education, labeled as the "back to basics" movement. There was a renewed focus on basic skills in mathematics and literacy that to some extent eclipsed many of the innovations of the 1960s. To some extent this was a reaction to the perceived "permissiveness" of American schools and American society. Many of the innovations of the 1960s were deemed failures; in truth there was little evidence of failure. Schools had become more inclusive of all segments of the American population and academic levels had risen in general.

The 1980s saw the renewal of some educational experimentation, but at the same time, criticism of the schools increased and culminated in 1983, "the year of reports." The most influential of these was *A Nation at Risk* , the well-known national report (National Commission, 1983), which found fault with various aspects of the public schools. The condemnation of American education is exemplified by the second paragraph of the report (p. 5):

If an unfriendly foreign power had attempted to impose on America the mediocre educational performance that exists today, we might have viewed it as an act of war. As it stands, we have allowed this to happen to ourselves. We have even squandered the gains in student achievement made in the wake of the Sputnik challenge. Moreover, we have dismantled essential support systems which helped make those gains possible. We have, in fact, been committing an act of unthinking educational disarmament.

These are powerful statements. In our opinion, they are also overstated and overly emotional, although there is enormous room for improvement in our educational system. The nation was able to survive the "risk" and even prosper.

During that same time period several important programs for the teaching of higher-order problem-solving strategies began to make their mark, thus providing an alternative to the exclusive focus on "basic skills." For example, Gardner's *Frames of Mind* was also published in 1983, in which Gardner established the basis for the argument that intelligence is not a single, unchangeable property, but that there are multiple intelligences, which could and should be fostered throughout the life span.

The 1990s were a time of continuing calls for reform and was marked by a spate of continuing national reports criticizing elementary, secondary, higher, and teacher education. Small wonder that educators have felt besieged from many sides. Yet during the same era, the parallel interest in higher-order thinking skills somehow survived as demonstrated by the publication of numerous commercial programs designed to help students acquire creative and critical thinking strategies. During this time also, however, schools were increasingly required to adhere to national curriculum standards promoted by national professional associations, which in turn became the basis for mandated state curriculum frameworks in nearly every state. That trend was followed predictably by the development of high-stakes examinations for students in those states, which would determine their promotion and/or graduation based on the curriculum standards.

At the start of the 21st century, as previously noted, the massive federal law, No Child Left Behind, built upon the trend toward state-mandated high-stakes testing and required that states implement additional testing at those grade levels where testing was not already mandated; it further required the comparative public ranking of school successes on such tests together with penalties for low-performing schools and imposed strict requirements about the preparation of teachers in subject matter. The focus was clearly on demonstrable student outcomes as the key criterion for judging school quality; the problem, of course, has been how to best and most fairly measure that success without oversimplifying a definition of success and tying it to whatever is easily measured. Later in this book, we discuss the problem of equitable testing for deaf learners.

The Quest for Excellence

The 1980s were a time when the goals of equity of access to education and excellence in education first came together; we continue to feel the effects today. Walberg and Shanahan (Walberg, 1980; Walberg and Shanahan, 1984) analyzed thousands of studies to identify "alterable" factors that could enhance achievement. For example, family socioeconomic status or student gender would not be alterable. The authors identified reinforcement, accelerated programs, and reading training as having significant effects. They also found graded homework, class morale, and school-parent programs to improve academic conditions in the home to be effective. The finding about graded homework deserves special mention; homework that is graded or commented on was shown to be three times as effective as homework that was merely assigned but not graded. This is especially important given the previously cited research by Kluwin and Moores (1987) that showed mathematics classes with all deaf students received less homework that was graded than deaf students in predominantly hearing classes with interpreters.

Bloom (1984) reported what he labeled the "2-sigma problem." In essence he argued that the child functioning at the 50th percentile of his or her reference group could, under ideal conditions, achieve at the level of the top 2% of students. This suggests that excellence essentially can be achieved by all children and is not limited to a select few. Because the ideal situation entailed individual tutoring, Bloom concentrated on group instruction and alterable variables such as quality of teaching, use of time, and cognitive and affective characteristics. Bloom identified instructor variables such as appropriate reinforcement and positive feedback, mastery learning (the addition of testing, feedback, and corrective procedures to enhance learning), graded homework, time on task, and concentration on improved reading and study skills.

In a sense Bloom, Walberg, and Shanahan identified simple ways to enhance learning. The answers may be simple, but they are not easy to implement. There must be a conscious effort to improve instruction and a teacher's continuous self-evaluation of his or her effectiveness as well as an evaluation of the students themselves. We are committed to the proposition that deaf children can achieve excellence, and we believe it will be achieved through the efforts of parents, teachers, and other professionals dedicated to the learning to deaf children.

Reading and Writing Across the Curriculum

The emphasis on academic content increases the importance of reading and writing for all children, especially for deaf students. Reading requires not only the ability to decode words but also to decipher meaning. As is reported in the chapters on academic content, the standardized tests that are being used are in reality tests of reading as well as of science, math, and social studies knowledge. It is not sufficient today, for example, for a student to know how to perform addition or subtraction tasks or solve quadratic equations. A student must read a problem, decide what function is required, and then solve the problem. A student without mastery of English will not succeed, regardless of computational skills. The relationship between reading and subject matter should be reciprocal; reading should provide access to content areas at the same time that content areas such as social studies and science provide a foundation for reading. It is our responsibility to build reading skills in conjunction with academic subject matter.

The school environment also calls for more writing skills than in the past, when writing did not receive the attention it deserved either in general education or in education of deaf learners. This added emphasis is because of increased reliance on electronic print and the need for clear expression. Once again, standardized tests call for answers to be given in narrative form. Our students must not only have knowledge but also be able to express that knowledge literately. Teachers must devote more time in the school day to teaching a systematic way of writing.

The Challenge of Placement

Our present educational system provides a variety of academic placement options for deaf students including residential and day schools serving only deaf children, separate classes for deaf students within schools where the majority of children are hearing, resource rooms for deaf children where they may be integrated with hearing students for one or more subjects, and full-time inclusion with hearing students in conjunction with services from itinerant teachers of the deaf on a "pull-out" basis. In reality these four options do not reflect the complexity of the entire range of possibilities, but they do encompass the placements for most deaf children. Children who receive itinerant services represent the fastest growing segment of the deaf school-age population.

Given the diversity of the deaf school-age population, the placement options represent a positive response to the needs of the children. In some cases these options are not available, especially in view of the decline in residential school enrollment and the closing in some states of state-supported residential schools for the deaf. That is a disturbing trend, but, in general, deaf children and their parents can make choices from among different placement options.

Regardless of placement, the Individuals With Disabilities Education Act (IDEA) expects deaf children to have access to the regular educational curriculum. Residential schools adopt a county or school district curriculum and other programs for deaf students usually adopt the curriculum of the local school district. However, the presentation of curriculum can be quite different. Teachers of the deaf instruct children in residential schools, public day schools, and separate classrooms for deaf students. Both teachers of the deaf and regular education teachers instruct children in resource rooms, and teachers of the deaf often provide additional support for the regular classroom subject areas. Regular classroom teachers instruct children who are integrated full time, with an itinerant teacher of the deaf providing support and advice to the regular classroom teacher and individual tutoring to the deaf child.

Each type of placement requires different skills for the teacher of deaf learners. It is beyond the scope of this book to provide in-depth information for each of the placements, but there are general principles that can be applied. In the past, most professional preparation programs concentrated on developing the skills to work with deaf children in separate settings on a full-time basis, but only a few have addressed the preparation of itinerant teachers of the deaf (Luckner & Howell, 2002). Luckner and Howell's book takes into account the complete range of placement.

Styles of Learning

For more than a century scientists have conducted studies on the intelligence and cognitive functioning of deaf individuals. In many cases investigators approached the issue with an implicit "deficiency" model, assuming that a lack of hearing would have negative effects on the development of intellectual or cognitive skills. In a review, Moores (2001) identified three stages in research with deaf individuals; (a) deaf people as inferior, (b) deaf people as concrete as opposed to abstract thinkers, and (c) deaf people as normal. The third stage reflects the present time. Those of us who have interacted with deaf children and adults are aware from the research literature and from our personal observations that deaf individuals have the same cognitive potential as anyone else. Deafness sets no limits.

Because of the negative nature of past research, there has been some reluctance to consider the possibility that deaf individuals, with more of a visual orientation, may perceive, organize, structure, and interact with the environment in some ways differently than that of hearing individuals. In fact, Marschark (2003) reports that research involving cognition and memory among deaf and hearing individuals consistently shows both similarities and differences in their performance. Marschark stresses that a difference does not imply a deficiency; in some tasks deaf subjects have an advantage. By further investigating and understanding relationships between cognition and deafness, we can improve educational instruction of deaf learners.

Disabilities

Many of the causes of deafness, for example, premature birth and meningitis, can also be related to a range of disabilities. As a result, the incidence of disabilities such as attention deficit disorder, visual impairment, learning disabilities, and developmental disabilities is somewhat higher in the deaf school-age population than in the general population. All professionals should be alert to this fact. Deaf students with multiple disabilities have had limited access to educational opportunities available to their deaf and hearing peers (Ewing & Jones, 2003). The need for person-centered planning for deaf students with multiple disabilities is even more imperative than for other students. There is a need for a complete text in this area.

Summary

There is a clear and present need to improve the academic achievement of deaf learners in elementary and secondary school settings. Deaf students now are expected to have access to the general curriculum and to master it. This calls for effective presentation of material and organization of opportunities for learning to close the gap in educational outcomes for deaf and hearing learners, bearing in mind the special characteristics of deaf students. The context in which deaf education interacts with the larger school framework is replete with challenges for teachers, curriculum, students, and schools in general. It is possible for the field of deaf education to learn a great deal from the experiences of general educators while avoiding some of the pitfalls that they have encountered.

This book analyzes many aspects of the curriculum, appropriate instructional options, and issues related to student assessment because they all affect deaf learners. Let us bear in mind these larger contexts while educators of deaf and hard of hearing students make the case for an accessible and equitable quality education.

References

Bloom, B. (1984). The 2-sigma problem: The search for methods of group instruction as effective as one-to-one tutoring. *Educational Researcher, 13*(2), 4–16.

Bruner, J. (1960). *The process of education.* Cambridge, MA: Harvard University Press.

Butts, R. F., & Cremin, L. (1953). *A history of education in American culture.* New York: Holt, Rinehart, and Winston.

Cremin, L. A. (1988). *American education: The metropolitan experience, 1876–1980.* New York: Harper Row.

Ewing, K., & Jones, T. (2003). An educational rationale for deaf students with multiple disabilities. *American Annals of the Deaf, 148*(2), 267–271.

Farris, P. J. (1999). *Teaching: Bearing the torch* (2nd ed.). Boston: McGraw Hill.

Gardner, H. (1983). *Frames of mind: A theory of multiple intelligences.* Cambridge, MA: Harvard University Press.

Joint Standards Committee. (1996). CEC-CED joint knowledge and skills statement for all becoming teachers for students who are deaf or hard of hearing. *American Annals of the Deaf, 141*(3), 220–230.

Kluwin, T., & Moores, D. (1987). The effects of integration on the mathematics achievement of deaf adolescents in different placements. *Exceptional Children, 55*(4), 327–335.

Luckner, J., & Howell, J. (2002). Suggestions for preparing itinerant teachers: A qualitative analysis. *American Annals of the Deaf, 147*(3), 54–61.

Marschark, M. (2003). Cognitive functioning in deaf adults and children. In M. Marschark & P. Spencer (Eds.), *Deaf studies, language, and education* (pp. 464–477). Oxford: Oxford University Press.

Moores, D. (1991). The great debates: Where, how and what to teach deaf children. *American Annals of the Deaf, 136*(1), 35–37.

Moores, D. (2001). *Educating the deaf: Psychology, principles, and practices.* Boston: Houghton Mifflin.

Moores, D., Jatho, J., & Creech, B. (2001). Issues and trends in instruction and Deafness. *American Annals of the Deaf, 146*(2), 72–76.

National Commission on Excellence in Education. (1983). *A nation at risk: The imperative for educational reform.* Washington, DC: U.S. Department of Education.

Pagliaro, C. (1998a). Mathematics preparation and professional development of deaf education teachers. *American Annals of the Deaf, 143*(1), 22–28.

Pagliaro, C. (1998b). Mathematics reform in the education of deaf and hard of hearing students. *American Annals of the Deaf, 143*(4), 285–292.

Walberg, H. (1980). Improving the productivity of America's schools. *Educational Leadership, 41*(8), 19–30.

Walberg, H., & Shanahan, T. (1984). High school effects on individual students. *Educational Researcher, 12*(7), 4–9.

D A V I D   S .   M A R T I N

D O N A L D   F .   M O O R E S

P A M E L A   L U F T

Selection of Curriculum: A Philosophical Position

THE SELECTION OF APPROPRIATE CURRICULUM for deaf learners is a topic of some argument in the present context of American education. On the one hand, educators in general and teachers in particular should retain the decision about what is best for students to study; on the other hand, they are not in complete control. The mandates of state curriculum frameworks, as well as the requirement that students pass high-stakes examinations, conspire to remove some of that autonomy from teachers' control. However, considerable latitude still exists in terms of using subject matter as the vehicle for various skills that can be learned through a variety of content. As a result, this chapter provides guidelines for how those decisions may be made thoughtfully and in the best interests of deaf learners. In this chapter we review a number of critical philosophical issues in education before proposing some criteria for curriculum selection. Every educator must first take a position on these philosophical issues before making intelligent decisions on curriculum choices.

Definition

The term *curriculum* did not enter common parlance in American education until well into the 20th century. It comes from the Latin meaning "a course to be run" and this origin implies exactly what a stream of study should be in the schools—a course in the sense of a river, flowing through the school years, with, it is to be hoped, some logic and sense.

Through the years "curriculum" has been defined in various other ways. One of the better known ones is a "series of planned events that are intended to have educational consequences for one or more students" (Eisner, 1997). We use the term, therefore, to refer to the content and teaching methodology for the material students are to master in the school years; assessment is not formally a part of curriculum but is critical to understanding what outcomes have been achieved. In a general sense, therefore, the curriculum can encompass the projected outcomes, the materials and media to be used, the procedures for learning, and the assessments to determine to what extent the outcomes have been achieved. When a curriculum is in written form for a year of study or a subject area, it should contain not only these elements but also a strong rationale for the study of that topic.

Conceptions of Curriculum

Eisner defined six different conceptions of curriculum, which are somewhat in conflict with each other (1997); it is important for educators to take a position on which conception or combinations of conceptions they espouse. Eisner's conceptions are:

1. Religious orthodoxy, which refers to the influence of some dogmatic beliefs on the ways in which schools function—influence that is not strictly religious in the church-related sense.
2. Rational humanism, focusing on scientific method, reasoning, and dialectic; this approach is not widespread in America at this time.
3. Progressivism, which will be familiar to many readers, as rooted in the nature of human experience and in social reform, exemplified first by the works of John Dewey; in this conception, the learner is not a vessel to be filled, but one who acts on the environment. In curriculum, problem-centered foci become important, and individualization is emphasized, with the primary responsibility for curriculum selection resting upon the classroom teacher.
4. Critical theory, which focuses on how schools can undo the unconscious promotion of an unjust social order; it focuses on the shortcomings of schooling and proposes allowing children to define their own educational ends to be implemented at least partially within the community through the study of controversial issues.
5. Reconceptualism, which emphasizes how personal purposes and lived experiences should affect students' understanding of the world; it also emphasizes getting away from an overdependence on measurable objectives (Eisner, 1997).
6. Cognitive pluralism, which underlines humans' unique ability to create and manipulate symbols and the decoding and encoding of information in any of the forms that humans use to convey meaning (Eisner, 1982).

Choosing from among these six ideologies, or other ideologies identified by other writers in the field of curriculum, is a largely intellectual task, but it also has consequences for the kind of curriculum that we desire for our students, and thus it is important to consider which combination of ideologies a school or a teacher chooses to adopt as the basis for whatever curriculum content is selected. We urge educators to review these conceptions and consider which elements constitute their own considered approach to curriculum. Once this process has been carried out, educators can then proceed to determining the content of their curriculum.

Position

Where, then, does this book fit among these six ideologies? Clearly, it does not fit squarely within any one of the ideologies in totality; it is, rather, somewhat eclectic in that it builds upon some elements of several of the ideologies as follows.

1. We propose that a strong curriculum for deaf and hard of hearing (and any other) students gives opportunities for learners to exercise reason in depth (borrowing from the rational humanists).

2. At the same time, we strongly hold the notions that intelligence is dynamic rather than fixed and that a child is a growing organism that develops in interaction with the environment (owing a debt in turn to the progressivists). Next, although chapters in part 3 outline important ideas for all of the major content areas of the curriculum, we see curriculum as based on a constantly changing body of knowledge; thus, we have strong concern about nationally imposed standardized expectations for all learners, which is characteristic of the current climate in American education. Thus, when the authors of the subject matter chapters in part 3 outline their curriculum content, they are recognizing at the same time that this content must be constantly adapted and that the learner must help to create the curriculum at the same time.

3. From the critical theorists, we believe that educators must make explicit what is frequently implicit in the value system of many schools today: we can only produce learners for the next generation who will successfully attack social injustice if we are able to make students consciously aware of social injustice in the world that surrounds them while they are still learners.

4. From the reconceptualists, we endorse the deep respect for the life of the imagination; creative and exciting curricula must appeal to the "life."

5. From the cognitive pluralists, we take the notion that, among other things, a balanced education must broaden literacy to include encoding and decoding many kinds of information; one of the longstanding problems in deaf education has been the focus on a narrow definition of literacy, which prepares students (especially deaf and hard of hearing students) for a life with low horizons; we favor instead a broad approach to decoding and encoding all kinds of information.

Thus, our approach freely borrows from several of these ideologies.

Balance

Achieving a balance among these various ideologies is an enormous conceptual challenge. In addition to balance among those ideologies is the need to find a balance for deaf and hard of hearing students between enabling them to achieve well on examinations that are based on a particular view of curriculum and enabling them to become lifelong learners who remain excited about the learning process. Creating that balance is the challenge for classroom teachers in this environment, and all too often the administrative and legal pressures to achieve certain scores on externally administered tests (which in many cases are inherently unfair to deaf students because they were developed by hearing people for hearing people) cause teachers great angst.

Somehow we must continue to prepare teachers and to support practicing teachers who will keep alive that vital balance. Successful teachers in our view also allow for the creative act in learners, as well as allow space for their own creativity as classroom teachers; such space for creativity is all the more difficult because of those external expectations.

Principles of Teaching

We know that all instruction should be exemplary, but what exactly does that mean? Several professional organizations have emphasized the need for high teaching standards (Interstate New Teacher Assessment and Support Consortium, 1992; National Academy of Sciences, 1995; National Board for Professional Teaching Standards, 2004). The emphasis on standards has also been defined to incorporate state standards and outcomes-driven learning that incorporates depth of understanding as well as reasonable breadth (Wiggins & McTighe, 1998; cf. National Center for Educational Statistics, 2003).

We also know that poor instruction can occur, even when using standards and outcomes-driven learning. For example, regardless of the standards or outcomes, teachers can present information or skills in a way that alienates or even confuses their students. Instruction must be well organized as well as clearly and effectively delivered, and must include learning activities that are appropriate in length, depth, and focus.

However, instruction is more than just clear links and observable outcomes. The ultimate goal of an education is to provide the skills and tools that students will need for the rest of their lives. For deaf and hard of hearing students this goal is particularly important. Instruction should provide the following:

1. An inquiry-based and problem-solving focus: Students need to be engaged in their own learning. Higher-order cognitive and problem-solving skills (see chapter about cognitive strategies later in this book) are needed for a successful adulthood, and employers increasingly require these of their employees (SCANS, 1991).
2. Depth of understanding: The Trends in International Mathematics and Science Study (TIMSS; National Center for Education Statistics, 2003) report has

compared math and science achievement among the countries of the world. Much to Americans' embarrassment, the United States is not near the top. Those countries that do score well offer much greater depth of instruction. We in the United States try to have broad curriculum coverage (including the overwhelming lists of content standards that states expect schools to cover in 1 year). Rather than an effective strategy, enormous breadth of coverage leads to less than exemplary outcomes. Instead, depth of coverage for a few key skills would leave students better able to retain information and to apply it to new situations; this approach would reflect that taken in some of the countries (such as Japan) with which the United States likes to compare itself in education.

3. Clear relationships and interrelationships among broad and lifelong concepts: We learn and remember well when we can add new information and skills into an existing link in our mental schemata of the world. Instruction can make explicit the multiple links and relationships among information and can facilitate students in weaving new information into multiple links. Obviously, this latter approach has a high probability of leading to better retention and better abilities to generalize and to use this information in new ways. These multiple relationships support the inquiry-based, problem-solving, and higher cognitive functions that employers need our students to bring to the workplace.

It is difficult enough to provide good instruction; to link it to standards may seem unattainable. Standards themselves often are broad and vague, and encompass a near-overwhelming number of individual and discrete skills or knowledge areas (Popham, 2001). However, several new publications offer educators some assistance in working with standards. These include *Linking IEPs to State Learning Standards* by Miller and Hoffman (2002), *Connecting Standards and Assessment Through Literacy* by Conley (2005), and *Aligning Transition and Standards-Based Education* by Kochhar-Bryant and Bassett (2002). These books all provide excellent information on the importance of standards and tips for using each within their differing contexts or subject areas.

However, another set of materials focuses on instructional design, beginning with content standards, is *Understanding by Design* (Wiggins & McTighe, 1998), as well as subsequent works by Wiggins and McTighe. A number of resources and guides are available online as well at www.ubdexchange.org/resources.html. The process they describe is specific and focuses on developing exemplary instruction that is both standards-based and outcomes driven. This process is accomplished by focusing on thematic units based on overarching, inquiry-based questions. The design process uses three stages in what the authors term the "backward design process." Rather than starting with a lesson plan or activity, these authors recommend starting with the standards and outcomes—a process that feels "backward" at first.

In Stage 1, teachers identify authentic, lifelong student needs and connect these to external standards. These standards are "unpacked" into meaningful and teachable chunks by reviewing the standard for those elements that are worth being familiar with, that are important to know and understand, and that are authentic and relevant and of lifelong value to the student.

Standards that incorporate all of these elements are those most helpful in focusing the unit. These are compiled across the content areas and reviewed to identify overarching and enduring understandings—those that will last the students' lifetime. These remain at the focus of the unit across the next two stages and are used to develop inquiry-based unit questions for the students to explore.

Stage 2 plans the assessment of the outcomes that prove the students' thorough understanding of the unit as well as achievement of state standards. These assessments typically reflect culminating activities rather than paper-and-pencil activities or tests. To ensure depth of understanding, six facets are identified, across which students should demonstrate each key understanding. These were developed from research, including use of Bloom's taxonomy of cognitive objectives (Wiggins & McTighe, 1998).

Figure 1 identifies a rubric for scoring such assessments, which includes specific unit descriptions according to the assessment task. Several of the facets can be effectively combined in a broader culminating activity. For example, a clear and thorough explanation (Facet 1) also can include examples and interpretations from real-life situations (Facet 2); this fact can be expanded through description of multiple perspectives (Facet 4) and demonstrating empathy (Facet 5) for the multiple perspectives; these knowledge and skills are demonstrated through an application project (Facet 3) after which the student evaluates his/her own self-knowledge (Facet 6), including his or her own emotional prejudices and cognitive "blind spots."

Stage 3 develops the lessons and instructional activities that prepare the students for successful demonstration of the overarching and enduring understandings (Stage 1) across the six facets (Stage 2). These activities must be of sufficient length and depth to ensure successful demonstration of the understandings and skills. When well done, all three stages support each other and lead to documentation of standards and lifelong outcomes for deaf and hard of hearing (and other) students. Further information is available at the UbD Exchange website at www.ubdexchange.org/resources/html, and a number of teaching units designed specifically for deaf and hard of hearing students can be found at www.educ.kent.edu/fundedprojects/TSPT/units/teaching%20units.htm. These latter units utilize a transitional focus to ensure authentic, lifelong, enduring understandings.

Critical Curriculum Ideas

Jerome Bruner (1960) led the way for much modern thinking in curriculum. One of his primary precepts that influenced curriculum innovation heavily during the 1960s and thereafter was the notion that it is possible for any child at any age to learn something "honest" about any subject—with "honest" meaning intellectually viable and not watered down. That notion led directly to the incorporation of sophisticated subject matter in elementary curricula, using methodology appropriate for the age group. Another important principle that he promoted (1966) was the concept of the "spiral" curriculum, in which significant ideas were repeated with increasing sophistication and different content throughout the school years; hence, in social studies the concept of "belief system" would be visited in a study of Native American culture in

Figure 1 Rubric for six facets of understanding						
FACET LEVELS	Explanation	Interpretation	Application	Perspective	Empathy	Self-Knowledge
	sophisticated explanations and theories	interpretations, narratives, and translations	uses knowledge in new situations and contexts	critical and insightful points of view	ability to get inside another person's feelings	to know one's ignorance, prejudice, and understanding
(high)	Sophisticated:	Profound:	Masterful:	Insightful:	Mature:	Wise:
	In-depth:	Revealing:	Skilled:	Thorough:	Sensitive:	Circumspect:
	Developed:	Perceptive:	Able:	Considered:	Aware:	Thoughtful:
	Intuitive:	Interpreted:	Apprentice:	Aware:	Developing:	Unreflective:
(low)	Naïve:	Literal:	Novice:	Uncritical:	Egocentric:	Innocent:

(Wiggins & McTighe, 1998).

the first grade, again in the third grade within the study of urban culture in American cities, and again later in still another context—building new understandings on these critical concepts that transcend particular subject matter. Both of these principles can easily form a philosophical basis for an approach to curriculum.

The idea of curriculum mapping has been explained by Jacobs (1997), building on the work of English (1983), in which she emphasizes that the teacher is the most important person to determine the three major elements of the curriculum map for the class: (a) the processes and skills to be emphasized, (b) the content of essential concepts and topics, and (c) the products and performances that are assessments of learning. Teachers, she says, should as much as possible merge concepts from two or more fields to ensure a powerful and lasting experience of learning, making linkages among subject matters (1997). Thus, she makes the case for interdisciplinary study at *all* age levels—a powerful notion that the subject area specialization of some schools actually militates against. In deaf education, we have the opportunity to reintroduce the advantages of interdisciplinary studies; the world outside of school today is linked in many different ways.

Research-Based Teaching

If we could somehow enable teachers to base their teaching on research evidence by encouraging administrators to recognize the value of a research-based pedagogy, then we could free teachers to make curricular decisions on what has been demonstrated to be worthy through collected evidence. Educators are fond of making comparisons between education and medicine, and those comparisons have serious limitations because of the large differences in the way the two professions actually operate. However, an analogy from the medical community is apt at this point—would the reader ever seek the services of a physician who practiced on the basis of only the requirements of some external board (composed largely of laypeople) rather than on the basis of research evidence for the most successful treatment and medications? Clearly not, and we should not require teachers to behave any differently in this respect.

We could begin by requiring that all future teachers in teacher preparation programs plan and carry out their lesson plans only when there is a research base for any instructional decision; a few teacher preparation programs have moved in this direction, and this movement bears close watching.

Curriculum Integration

The American curriculum, divided as it is into the subject matter categories of mathematics, science, social studies, language, and so forth, is at least in part the product of the visit by 19th-century American educator Horace Mann to Europe, from which he brought back concepts from the German curriculum, which was subject matter oriented. Although in some ways Mann advanced American education, one definitely negative result has been the fragmentation of the curriculum into "boxes" that are convenient for educators and scholars but that do not reflect the way a learner views the world. The learner sees the world as one, and it is the educators who have divided it up into the categories. Although the problem is not as serious in elementary education (for deaf or hearing children) because elementary education is sometimes interdisciplinary, the problem is indeed serious in American secondary education. The learner goes from subject to subject, and, unless the school is actively committed to preplanned team teaching, connections among the subjects in general do not occur for the learner because of this compartmentalization.

Thus, education in general, and deaf education in particular, would do well to reintegrate the curriculum by facilitating cross-disciplinary connections throughout the entire school career of deaf learners; in this way, the multiple rich connections that exist across subject matters would become clear, and learners could be in a position to make their own connections as well.

Criteria for Selection

On what bases, then, should a teacher select a curriculum? We can identify at least two dimensions of this question: (a) the criteria for making an intelligent choice about content, and (b) the criteria for purchasing or adapting externally prepared curricula for one's own classroom use.

Let us look at the first dimension. Others have proposed that the major considerations in choosing curriculum content would be (a) the nature of the society in which students are going to live; (b) the nature of the students themselves, including the ways that they learn; and (c) the nature of knowledge. If we look at each of these three elements, they illuminate the path for us.

1. The nature of society today is highly technological and multidimensional, with many kinds of diversity for which students need to be prepared; the world has

truly become a small place as a result of rapid communication and electronic interaction—the old boundaries of time and space have been largely dissipated.

2. The nature of the learners is something that teachers know best; for today's deaf education classrooms, we have a diverse gathering of students—diverse special needs, ethnicity, home background, and aspirations, to name only some. America has always been a diverse society, but today's classrooms are frequently microcosms of that diversity, whereas in the past, the diversity existed amid pockets of homogeneity. We also know from psychology and the wisdom of experience that learners need at least some of the time to *construct* their own knowledge and view of the world, which has clear implications for how we should teach.

3. The nature of knowledge in some ways appears to be the easiest challenge of the three, but even subject matters are changing rapidly. The World Future Society projects that by the year 2020, the knowledge in the world will double every 73 days, and so what is true today may be different next week or next year. Thus, an emphasis on the timeless concepts that transcend particular items of information is at least as important as factual knowledge, even though factual knowledge is a basis for lasting concepts. In addition, as mentioned previously, with the rapid increase in knowledge comes new interrelationships among knowledge areas—implying exciting possibilities for interdisciplinary studies.

The second dimension includes criteria for selecting or adapting published curricula or curricula developed by sources outside the classroom teacher; not all curriculum can be developed by the teacher or created by the teacher together with this year's students. These criteria imply that a teacher has a free choice in this matter, which is not the case in an era of state-mandated curriculum frameworks. However, even within such frameworks, a school or school district or teacher still has the latitude to choose some of the particular curriculum to carry out the state framework for that subject. Teachers should critically review externally developed curricula and would do well to consider at least the following quality indicators:

defensibility of the rationale presented for the curriculum by the publisher,
clarity of the specified outcomes,
relevance of the specified outcomes to students and society,
selection of significant concepts from the subject,
factual correctness of materials for students,
logic of the sequence of recommended teaching steps,
sufficient use of multiple media,
attractiveness and engaging quality of the presented materials,
depth of the assessment tools recommended,
breadth of the assessment tools recommended,
availability of additional orientation for teachers to the curriculum, and
general fit with the objectives of the mandated state or local curriculum
    framework.

One might add other criteria to this list, but any curriculum that is rated highly on most of these should be a strong candidate for adoption or adaptation. Such critiquing is best performed by groups of teachers working together rather than teachers working alone.

A final criterion applies particularly to educators of deaf and hard of hearing students, and that is the importance of *visual* presentation inasmuch as these particular learners must learn much through their eyes. Although not many published curricula have been developed *only* for deaf learners, we can nonetheless apply the criterion of adaptability to visual representation as a means of determining which general educational curricula may be most usable in a classroom of deaf students.

An Important Resource

An important national resource in the general field of curriculum for teachers and other educators is the Association for Supervision and Curriculum Development (ASCD). This national professional organization produces a monthly professional journal and numerous books on curriculum and instruction every year. Traditionally, educators of deaf and hard of hearing students have affiliated themselves only with deaf-related organizations, such as the Convention of American Instructors of the Deaf (CAID) and the Alexander Graham Bell Association. However, with the infusion of the regular curriculum into deaf education and of deaf students into inclusive classrooms, it is essential that educators of deaf learners take advantage of such resources as ASCD. The organization can be accessed through their website at http://www. ascd.org.

A Final Word

It is difficult to predict when the present emphasis on externally mandated curricula assessed with mandated high-stakes examinations will subside or be moderated; it is certain, however, that in some way, it will be moderated because the story of American education is the story of trends. However, each passing trend leaves some legacy behind and is never turned completely aside. The present movement will probably leave a legacy of greater attention to coordination among teachers and within school districts on what students should learn, and such a legacy would probably be positive. We must, then, keep that goal in mind while being wary of the tendency to fragment the curriculum as the result of external testing—children do not see the world as divided into small tasks or even separate subject areas; they see the world as one interdisciplinary whole. To the extent that we can ensure that our curriculum reflects this holism, we can assure that their view of the world is intact while it is at the same time ever-growing.

References

Adler, M. (1982). *The paideia proposal.* New York: Macmillan.

Bruner, J. (1960). *The process of education.* Cambridge, MA: Harvard University Press.

Bruner, J. (1966). Toward a theory of instruction. Cambridge, MA: Harvard University Press.

Conley, M. W. (2005). *Connecting standards and assessment through literacy.* Boston: Pearson.

Dewey, J. (1902). *The educational situation.* Chicago: University of Chicago Press.

Eisner, E. (1982). *Cognition and curriculum: A basis for deciding what to teach.* New York: Longman.

Eisner, E. (1997). *The educational imagination.* New York: Macmillan.

English, F. (Ed.). (1983). Fundamental curriculum decisions. Alexandria, VA: Association for Supervision and Curriculum Development.

Gardner, H. (1983). *Frames of mind.* Cambridge, MA: Harvard University Press.

Interstate New Teacher Assessment and Support Consortium. (1992). *INTASC's Model standards for beginning teacher licensing, assessment and development: A resource for state dialogue.* Washington, DC: Author. Retrieved November 3, 2004, from www.ccsso.org/content/pdfs/corestrd.pdf

Jacobs, H. (1997). *Mapping the big picture: Integrating curriculum and assessment, K–12.* Alexandria, VA: Association for Supervision and Curriculum Development.

Kochhar-Bryant, C., & Bassett, D. S. (2002). *Aligning transition and standards-based education: Issues and strategies.* Arlington, VA: Council for Exceptional Children.

Miller, L., & Hoffman, L. (2002). *Linking IEPs to state learning standards: A step-by-step guide.* Austin, TX: Pro-Ed.

National Academy of Sciences. (1995). *National science education standards.* Retrieved from http://www.nap.edu/readingroom/books/nses/html/

National Board for Professional Teaching Standards. (2004). *Standards and national board certification.* Retrieved from www.nbpts.org/standards/nbcert.cfm

National Center for Educational Statistics. (2003). *Trends in international mathematics and science study.* Washington, DC: Author. Retrieved [date] from http://nces.ed.gov/timss/

Popham, W. J. (2001). *The truth about testing: An educator's call to action.* Alexandria, VA: Association for Supervision and Curriculum Development.

SCANS: Secretary's Commission on Achieving Necessary Skills. (1991). *What work requires of schools: A SCANS report for America 2000.* Washington, DC: U.S. Department of Labor.

Wiggins, G., & McTighe, J. (1998). *Understanding by design.* Alexandria, VA: Association for Supervision and Curriculum Development.

PART TWO

The Content

CLAUDIA M. PAGLIARO

Mathematics Education and the Deaf Learner

Mathematics: the science of numbers and their operations, interrelations, combinations, generalizations, and abstractions and of space configurations and their structure, measurement, transformations, and generalizations

—Merriam-Webster On-line (2004)

THIS DEFINITION REPRESENTS what most of us would describe mathematics as—the science, the discipline, the "noun." What this definition does not capture, however, is the essence of mathematics—its importance, its practicality. It does not capture the "verb," the use of mathematics as an everyday tool—something that has been, is, and will continue to be indispensable not only to those who make it their profession, such as engineers, contractors, and of course mathematicians, but also to average people going about their daily lives. Without mathematics and the ability to use it, we would cease to function effectively and efficiently in life as we know it. Would we know how early to rise to arrive at work on time, given traffic? Would we have enough money to buy the appropriate amount of food for our family? Would we be able to schedule bus, snow removal, or garbage collection routes in a cost-efficient way? Even our very bodies run on a delicate mathematical balance of temperature, heart rate, and blood pressure.

The Essence of Mathematics

As mentioned, mathematics is more than the manipulation of numbers and symbols to obtain one right answer. Mathematics is about relationships and the use of those relationships for a purpose. Its goal is not simply the answer but also the search for the answer—product and process together.

Mathematics is "doing." It is active and ever-changing—full of life as much as life is full of it. It is thinking and communicating about patterns and interrelationships found everywhere from nature to art to technology. Truly understanding mathematics is to know these relationships and to be able to use them to resolve a question, ease a difficulty, or further an understanding. Thus, the goal of mathematics education is to provide guidance to the conceptual understanding of these relationships and the labels by which we can communicate that understanding.

How Does One Learn Mathematics?

According to the constructivist paradigm, learning is a process of constructing one's own image of the world whereby prior knowledge acts as a foundation on which new information and skills are built (Fosnot, 1989). The learner interacts with new experiences, forming relationships or connections between these experiences and previously formed cognitive structures or networks called schemata (Skemp, 1987). These networks begin in the earliest stages of life with initial encounters. Each new experience is then compared to the previously established representation, either supporting it (assimilation) or modifying it (accommodation) as necessary. This process of assimilation and accommodation of schemata is "learning." The more experiences with which one meaningfully interacts, the more complex and in depth the person's understanding and knowledge will be (Davies, 1984).

As we acquire language, these constructs and their properties are labeled, and a system is set by which a second level of learning takes place, that is, through the communication and sharing of our knowledge. As we continue to enrich our constructs, we also learn through our own personal reflections, using our abilities to reason, formulate ideas, and hypothesize, creating logical derivations that further our understanding (Skemp, 1987). We learn mathematics in the same way. Through exploration, communication, and reflection, students are led to a *conceptual understanding* of mathematical ideas, rich in schematic relationships.

According to research, children begin their mathematical development almost immediately as infants. Sensitivity to numbers and ordinality (counting), and even to addition and subtraction, has been documented in children younger than 1 year. As the child develops cognitively, linguistically, and socially, higher-order concepts take shape. By 7 years, the child has mastered counting and can use it to solve simple arithmetic problems including those involving measuring and division (Geary, 1994).

Children approach mathematics in developmental stages as well. First, the child begins solving problems by using modeling strategies where each quantity is represented and acted upon according to the context or story. The child then uses counting strategies where one quantity is used as the starting point from which to count up or back while the other quantity is kept track of or marked. Next, the child uses "derived facts" where a known fact is used to find the answer to an unknown one. Finally, the child uses known, retrievable facts, but now has the understanding of the concepts behind those facts, having gone through the stages of development. Naturally there is overlap between these developmental stages, depending on the difficulty of the problem, the quantities involved, and the context.

The key point is that mathematical concepts are *developed*, not memorized, as appropriate schemata come together to represent the concepts and procedures of mathematics. In general, children must accurately understand lower-order, more concrete concepts before they can understand higher-order, more abstract concepts. Thus, just as infants cannot be expected to walk before they crawl, so too children cannot be expected to understand facts and apply them to different situations without having first developed an understanding of number and the relationships between numbers through active engagement with hands-on, meaningful activities. It is the teacher's responsibility to create such a learning environment.

Mathematics Education

Before the late 1980s, educators approached the teaching and learning of mathematics from a behaviorist approach, where information was passed from teacher to student in a structured, stimulus-response sequence. Instruction was teacher directed and computation driven, dominated by worksheets and practice exercises. Students were instructed to memorize facts, formulas, and algorithms, often without the benefit of having understood the conceptual relationships behind them, and were expected to apply their newfound "knowledge" to scripted story problems.

Toward the end of the 20th century, however, in response to *A Nation at Risk*, the National Council of Teachers of Mathematics (NCTM) published three documents outlining a new approach to mathematics education based on the constructivist philosophy of learning (National Council of Teachers of Mathematics, 1989, 1991, 1995). Together, these documents changed mathematics education dramatically and spurred one of the most extensive and influential reforms of modern education. In 2000, the NCTM refined its original standards document to better reflect classroom instruction and student learning. This current document, *Principles and Standards for School Mathematics* (National Council of Teachers of Mathematics, 2000), establishes 6 principles (equity, curriculum, teaching, learning, assessment, and technology) and 10 standards (5 content standards: number and operations, algebra, geometry, measurement, and data analysis and probability; and 5 process standards: problem solving, reasoning and proof, communication, connections, and representation) that together are intended to guide mathematics education in schools today.

Reform-Based Curriculum

In a reform-based curriculum, instruction is student centered, based on conceptual development, not grade or age. Frequent opportunities exist for students to engage in meaningful, true problem solving: making use of a synthesis of various knowledge and ideas, furthering their understanding of concepts, and communicating their thought processes and conjectures to others, while actively reflecting on their learning. Problem solving is emphasized throughout the curriculum, not only in the application of known constructs, but more importantly as the impetus for constructing new knowledge. Limited use is made of drill and practice, rote memorization, and direct instruction, and increased use is made of open-ended questions and real-world problems. Manipulative materials are used at all levels to assist in the teaching of concepts and the solving of problems.

Assessment in a reform-based curriculum is an ongoing, formative process that informs instruction and enhances learning. It is problem based and includes true mathematics, where the thinking process involved in obtaining an answer to a problem is just as important, if not more so, than the correct answer. Students are required to justify and support their thinking—the strategies they choose and the plan that they make. Data on student learning are obtained through multiple sources of evidence throughout the learning process and are interpreted in relation to the student's cognitive development.

Although no specific mathematics curriculum for deaf and hard of hearing students exists, regardless of placement or approach, a committee of mathematics educators and deaf education professionals in and out of mathematics met in 1993 to discuss issues related to mathematics instruction for deaf and hard of hearing students. The result was a document titled *Moving Toward the Standards: A National Action Plan for Mathematics Education Reform for the Deaf* (NAPMERD) (Dietz, 1995). The plan stressed the critical need for change in mathematics education with deaf and hard of hearing students toward one that parallels the direction used in general education as outlined in the Standards documents of the NCTM. It also provided specific recommendations for preservice and in-service teacher support, formal assessment, and research, including focused attention on the unique linguistic and experiential needs of deaf and hard of hearing students.

Problem Solving

The cornerstone of a reform-based curriculum is problem solving. True problem solving is defined as a task for which the solution method is unknown. Students must therefore work toward the goal using a synthesis of their own knowledge based in context.

Although not exclusive, the primary way in which problem solving is included in the mathematics curriculum is through story problems (although traditionally called word problems, they will be referred to here as story problems because they may be given in a signed mode). These problems begin as simple one-step arithmetic story problems, but as students get older and more mathematically mature, they take the form of multiple-step tasks that are project based. Extensive research in mathematics education indicates that story problems play a fundamental role in students' conceptual development by linking informal knowledge and experiences that children learn outside of school with the more formal mathematics concepts and algorithms that they learn in the classroom (Carpenter, Ansell, Franke, Fennema, & Weisbeck, 1993; Heibert et al., 1996). In addition, they provide teachers access to their students' thought processes and enhance overall mathematics performance (Carpenter, Fennema, Peterson, Chiang, & Loef, 1989). Students who are frequently given a variety of story-problem types and who are allowed to think about them logically with the freedom to devise strategies to solve them, and who are then encouraged to share their thinking about those strategies, develop a conceptual understanding of problem solving and perform better in mathematics than do others who do not have such opportunities. Those who are not given such opportunities but rather are taught to seek out key words, for example, maintain only a procedural understanding of problem solving and have difficulty applying their knowledge from one context to another.

Mathematics Performance

Hearing Students

Since the onset of a reform-based curriculum, we have seen a positive trend in mathematics performance by students. Although there is certainly room for improvement, the results from the 2003 National Assessment of Educational Progress (NAEP) report indicate that fourth and eighth grade students continue to show increases in their average mathematics scores under a reformed curriculum. Seventy-seven percent of fourth graders were found to be at or above "basic" understanding of mathematics concepts, including 32% performing at the "proficient" and "advanced" levels. Among eighth graders, 68% scored at the "basic" level or above, with 29% scoring at the "proficient" and "advanced" levels. This result is a marked increase from 1990 (prior to mathematics reform) when just 50% of fourth graders and 52% of eighth graders scored at or above the "basic" level.

Deaf and Hard of Hearing Students

Unfortunately, the mathematics performance of deaf and hard of hearing students has not changed significantly during this same period. These students continue to lag behind their hearing peers by several grade levels in mathematics. According to the most recent data available from the Standard Achievement Test-9 (Traxler 2000), more than 80% of both deaf and hard of hearing fourth graders and of eighth graders score below the "basic" level in procedural performance (computation), with half falling below a third grade level and below a fifth grade level respectively. In problem solving, the situation is equally as bleak. Again, results show that 80% of fourth graders and 80% of eighth graders alike score at a "basic" or "below basic" level, with half of fourth graders scoring just above a second grade level and half of eighth graders at only a fourth grade level. Further, the results show that 50% of deaf and hard of hearing students perform at just below a sixth grade level in procedures (computation) and only a fifth grade level in problem solving upon graduation (Traxler, 2000).

Reasons for Poor Performance in Deaf and Hard of Hearing Students

Naturally, the question that begs to be answered is, "Why do deaf and hard of hearing students perform so poorly in mathematics?" Evidence shows that there is no difference in cognitive abilities between deaf and hearing students and that deafness itself is not a factor (Barham & Bishop, 1991; Nunes & Moreno, 1998); however, experiential deficits, language difficulties, and a traditionally based instruction do negatively affect deaf students' building of schemata (Nunes & Moreno, 1998). Let us now examine each of these factors.

Experience

First, deaf and hard of hearing children's poor performance in mathematics may be linked to their limited informal learning experiences. They do not have the opportunities that hearing students do for incidental mathematics learning. They do not overhear the talk about the 50% off sale at Macy's for shoes and whether that is better than the "buy one, get one free" promotion at Payless. They do not "catch" the news story on TV about the number of electoral votes needed to win by a presidential candidate while they are at play. In addition, for various reasons (overprotective parents, no transportation, no interpreter, etc.) the child may not be able to participate in extracurricular activities at school or home. Limited experiences (the primary level of learning) can lead to immature or incorrect schemata and, hence, poor mathematics learning. Therefore, it is critical that teachers of deaf and hard of hearing students present appropriate experiences on which to build mathematical knowledge. These experiences must be based on an accurate and true assessment of the student's current understanding and conceptual development, not an assumption of what that understanding should be.

Language

A second factor that may be involved in the poor mathematics performance of deaf students is related to language. Successful communication—the ability to understand and be understood—between teacher and student is critical. Because communication is another mode by which we develop schemata, lack of full access to a complete language and/or delays in language development can limit the learning of mathematics concepts. NAPMERD stresses the importance of clear and accurate communication of mathematics concepts for teachers and interpreters, including the use of appropriate technical sign vocabulary, and various ways of communicating mathematical meanings. In addition, certain aspects of the language of use itself (both English and American Sign Language [ASL]) may affect mathematics learning.

Researchers in the mathematics education of deaf and hard of hearing students often attribute students' poor performance in mathematics, particularly problem solving, at least in part to difficulties with English (Barham & Bishop, 1991; Kelly & Mousely, 1999; Kidd & Lamb, 1993; Kidd, Madsen, & Lamb, 1993). It is well documented that deaf and hard of hearing students experience difficulty in the reading and comprehension of written English text (Allen, 1995; Traxler, 2000). Aspects of English (whether spoken, written, or signed) within mathematics, such as the use of conditionals, comparatives, negatives, and inferentials; the use of words with meanings that differ inside and outside the classroom; the existence of multiple ways to express a single idea; and varied forms, abbreviations, and symbols, all combine to create a barrier to the mathematical concepts presented in this form.

In an effort to by-pass these obstacles, teachers may choose to translate the problems from written English to sign language; however, no standardized signs exist for many mathematics concepts. This circumstance creates great variety in the ways in which mathematics concepts are signed by teachers and interpreters, which in turn may cause great confusion for students as they build their knowledge.

Other issues related to ASL may hinder or help with mathematics learning in general and problem solving in particular, depending on the accompanying instruction. Factors related to ASL, such as the ease with which counting can be done and the cardinality of number signs, can lead the student to a procedural understanding of numbers if not accompanied by proper conceptually based instruction (Frostad, 1999; Pagliaro & Ansell, 2002). This situation is exemplified by young deaf students who overwhelmingly use counting strategies before (and instead of) modeling strategies or who use the procedure whereby they, starting with the sign for one quantity on one hand, continue counting on the raised fingers of the sign for the second quantity on their other hand, regardless of problem context and number (using this procedure without a conceptual understanding of numbers, the child will obtain an answer of 9 or 10 for the equation 7 + 6, depending on the quantity the child uses at the start of the procedure) (Pagliaro & Ansell, in preparation).

Teachers need to recognize and capitalize on the benefits of language, particularly ASL, in the conceptual understanding of mathematics, much like those in Asian cultures do with elements of place value and number understanding. (In Chinese, Japanese, and Korean, for example, the word for 12 is "ten two" and 63 is "six ten three." This clarity in language has afforded students from these countries an earlier, more meaningful understanding of place value, as compared with students from the United States, where English does not include a regular named-value system.) In addition, teachers themselves must understand the salient elements of mathematics and problem solving, including the mathematical semantic structure of story problems, to *properly* present problems to their students in ASL (Ansell & Pagliaro 2001). If they do not have this understanding, students will once again be limited in the types of problems they experience and in their conceptual development of mathematics.

Instruction

This point leads us to the third and most influential factor in the poor performance of deaf students in mathematics—instruction. Although NAPMERD called for reform in the mathematics education for deaf and hard of hearing students in the mid-1990s, teachers continue to make infrequent use of suggested Standards-based activities (Kelly, Lang, & Pagliaro, 2003; Pagliaro, 1998b; Pagliaro & Kritzer, 2005) and instead encourage rote memorization of facts, formulas, and algorithms through drill and practice, and worksheets filled with computation exercises. Instruction is teacher-directed and dominated by lecture, particularly in the higher grades, and includes little opportunity for open-ended investigations and real-world problem solving. Students are not given frequent opportunities to engage in reform-based learning opportunities, including challenging problem solving where they would make use of higher-order cognitive functions and thinking skills, such as analyzing, synthesizing, and evaluating information in response to an authentic problem. Instead, much of their time is spent doing simple calculations and lower cognitive functions—defining, labeling, and application. Assessment, too, often follows a traditional approach with students given problems where they apply the most recently learned algorithm without any understanding of origin or purpose and no opportunity for communication of thought processes.

Problem Solving

In particular, problem solving in the deaf education mathematics classroom appears to be lacking. Although most deaf education teachers claim to include problem solving as part of their instruction, the frequency and quality of the problems is questionable. At the elementary level, teachers make instructional decisions that can lead to limitations in their students' problem-solving experience. Individual teachers may choose to skip story problems altogether because of the linguistic difficulties that they believe hinder their students' mathematics performance and learning (Goodstein, 1994). Hoping to reduce confusion and frustration in their students, some may focus on the identification of cues (e.g., key words) rather than the mathematics and context within the problems. In the higher grades (secondary education), the majority of teachers make use of practice exercises rather than true problem solving and emphasize problem setup rather than in-depth analysis of solution strategies (Kelly, Lang, & Pagliaro, 2003). To improve problem solving, teachers need to provide opportunities for students to work with true problems, not exercises, which include analyzing and representing data and synthesizing knowledge to logically solve problems.

Reasons for Lack of Reform-Based Instruction

There are several reasons that contribute to the lack of reform-based practices in deaf education mathematics instruction, including teachers' lack of preparation, a curriculum that undervalues mathematics, and low expectations for students.

Teacher Preparation

It is not surprising that teachers may not have a true understanding of mathematics in general or the benefit of the suggested changes in instruction. Few deaf education teachers hold degrees or certification in mathematics or mathematics education (Kelly, Lang, & Pagliaro, 2003; Pagliaro, 1998a). Although research has shown that teachers who have preparation in mathematics tend to make use of reform-based practices in their instruction, including giving more "true problems" to their students (Kelly, Lang, & Pagliaro, 2003; Pagliaro & Ansell, 2002), most preparation programs in deaf education do not require preservice teachers to take even one course specifically in mathematics education. Without preparation, teachers cannot be expected to understand the content, pedagogy, or conceptual development of mathematics instruction and learning. The result is teachers who encourage students to memorize facts and algorithms and who focus students on key words and quantities instead of the logical solution strategies based on the context of the problem. Instructors who, albeit with good intentions, try to move students along forfeit conceptual understanding, resulting in detrimental effects on performance.

Deaf education teachers need to be sufficiently and appropriately prepared in mathematics and mathematics education. They need to know the developmental relationships among mathematical concepts. They need to know how to evaluate students' understanding of mathematics concepts in order to make instructional decisions and determine subsequent lessons. They need to have a sense of not only where the students are in their mathematics development but also of where they are going and how to guide them into making appropriate schemata.

Curriculum

Having a curriculum that focuses on reading to the exclusion of, rather than integration with, content areas may also contribute to the lack of reform in mathematics instruction in deaf education. The primary focus of teacher preparation, curriculum, and research in the field of deaf education has long been on reading and language to the practical exclusion of mathematics and other content areas, thus devaluing these other disciplines. Mathematics is not thought of as worthy of the time and attention that a reform-based curriculum takes. Although reading and language arts are without doubt a significant problem for deaf and hard of hearing students, their mathematics education cannot be ignored if they are to succeed in the 21st century. In fact, the thinking skills inherent in mathematics problem solving may actually help increase the deaf child's reading and language skills. Integrating reading and mathematics, for example, may enhance the student's schemata necessary to both areas. Higher-order thinking skills traditionally kept in the mathematics classroom can transfer to the reading process, adding depth and breadth to story comprehension and expanding the student's repertoire of reading strategies. At the same time, discussing mathematics through literature (at any level) provides a natural contextually based setting for presenting mathematical concepts, away from the procedural instruction of key words and algorithmic processes (Pagliaro & Roudybush, 1999).

In addition, as the previous paragraph alludes, reform-based instruction takes time and attention. Students must be allowed to work with problems, at times for more than one class period. They need to be allowed to collect data and think about various strategies for solving one problem, to use manipulatives at all grade levels, and to discuss their thinking with one another. Teachers, too, need to take the time to assess students' current understanding and develop appropriate experiences to guide the students along in their conceptual development. The long-term effect, however, will be students who know mathematics and use it well, teachers who understand their students' learning and can instruct them to further understanding, and citizens who contribute positively to society.

Expectations

Finally, low expectations of deaf and hard of hearing students' abilities in mathematics may be a factor in the lack of reform-based teaching approaches. Educators who do not believe in the success of their students or in their ability to develop appropriate schemata approach mathematics instruction from a procedural, rather than conceptual, perspective. They teach the students "the rules" for mathematics, having them memorize facts and procedures and practice them again and again. They focus students on cues within a problem to "move the students along" and get them to the right answer quickly and easily, but with no conceptual understanding. No conceptual understanding, of course, will lead to poor performance, thus beginning the cycle all over again.

Summary and Recommendations

As the NCTM *Principals and Standards* states, "Excellence in mathematics education requires equity—high expectations and strong support for all students.... [M]athematics can and must be learned by *all* students" (National Council of Teachers of Mathematics, 2000). The deaf or hard of hearing student is no exception, and the cycle of poor performance must be reversed. The first step is a change of attitude toward mathematics. We, as professionals who have an interest in the successful education of deaf and hard of hearing students, must give time and attention to true mathematics in the curriculum, showing its value explicitly and implicitly not only in academics but also in everyday life. Mathematics should be integrated throughout the curriculum, as it is integrated in our everyday world, with purpose and with meaning.

Teachers, both preservice and in service, need to be prepared in mathematics content, pedagogy, and cognition (student learning) so that they will understand "mathematics" (the noun *and* the "verb") and be able to appropriately and accurately provide the experiences and guidance that their deaf and hard of hearing students will need to develop mathematical skills and schemata.

Mathematics instruction within deaf education should be reform based (as outlined in the NCTM *Principles and Standards*), particularly in light of the specific and unique linguistic and experiential needs of deaf and hard of hearing students. Included should be frequent opportunities for students to actively engage in challenging, open-ended, authentic problem solving from which they can make use of and further develop higher-order cognitive functions. Assessment should reflect and inform instruction.

Finally, deaf and hard of hearing students need to realize their own potential in mathematics. With the help and support of well-prepared teachers and an appropriate curriculum and pedagogy, students can be empowered to reflect upon and build their own conceptual understanding of mathematics, using this power to succeed in the 21st century.

References

Allen, T. E. (1995). Demographics and national achievement levels for deaf and hard of hearing students: Implications for mathematics reform. In C. H. Dietz (Ed.), *Moving toward the standards: A national action plan for mathematics education reform for the deaf* (pp. 41–49). Washington, DC: Pre-College Programs, Gallaudet University.

Ansell, E., & Pagliaro, C. M. (2001). Effects of a signed translation on the type and difficulty of arithmetic story problems. *Focus on Learning Problems in Mathematics*, 23(2–3), 41–69.

Barham, J., & Bishop, A. (1991). Mathematics and the deaf child. In K. Durkin & B.

Shire (Eds.), *Language in mathematical education: Research and practice* (pp. 179–187). Philadelphia: Open University Press.

Carpenter, T. P., Ansell, E., Franke, M., Fennema, E., & Weisbeck, L. (1993). Models of problem solving: A study of kindergarten children's problem-solving processes. *Journal for Research in Mathematics Education, 24*(5), 428–441.

Carpenter, T. P., Fennema, E., Peterson, P., Chiang, C. P., & Loef, M. (1989). Using knowledge of children's mathematics thinking in classroom teaching: An experimental study. *American Educational Research Journal, 26*(4), 499–531.

Davies, R. B. (1984). *Learning mathematics: The cognitive science approach to mathematics education.* Norwood, NJ: Ablex Publishing.

Dietz, C. H. (Ed.). (1995). *Moving toward the standards: A national action plan for mathematics education reform for the deaf.* Washington, DC: Pre-College Programs, Gallaudet University.

Fosnot, C. T. (1989). *Enquiring teachers, enquiring learners: A constructivist approach for teaching.* New York: Teachers College.

Frostad, P. (1999). Deaf children's use of cognitive strategies in simple arithmetic problems. *Educational Studies in Mathematics, 40,* 129–153.

Geary, D. (1994). *Children's mathematical development: Research and practical applications.* Washington, DC: American Psychological Association.

Goodstein, H. (1994). Teaching mathematics and problem solving to deaf and hard-of-hearing students. In D. F. Robitaille, D. H. Wheeler, & C. Kieran (Eds.), *Selected lectures from the 7th International Congress on Mathematical Education* (pp. 137–145). Sainte-Foy, Canada: Les Presses de l'Universite Laval.

Hiebert, J., Carpenter, T., Fennema, E., Fuson, K., Human, P., Murray, H., Olivier, A., & Wearne, D. (1996). Problem solving as a basis for reform in curriculum and instruction: The case of mathematics. *Educational Researcher, 25*(4), 12–21.

Kelly, R. R., Lang, H. G., & Pagliaro, C. M. (2003) Mathematics word problem solving for deaf students: A survey of perceptions and practices in grades 6–12. *Journal of Deaf Studies and Deaf Education, 8*(2), 104–119.

Kelly, R. R., & Mousely, K. (1999, February). *Deaf and hearing students' transfer and application of skill in math problem solving.* Paper ED440501 presented at the 25th Annual Conference of the Association of College Educators for the Deaf and Hard of Hearing, Rochester, NY.

Kidd, D. H., & Lamb, C. (1993). Mathematics vocabulary and the hearing-impaired student: An anecdotal study. *Focus on Learning Problems in Mathematics, 15*(4), 44–52.

Kidd, D. H., Madsen, A. L., & Lamb, C. S. (1993). Mathematics vocabulary: Performance of residential deaf students. *School Science and Mathematics, 93*(8), 418–421.

Merriam-Webster On-Line. (2004). Retrieved April 2, 2004, from www.m-w.com/

National Center for Education Statistics. (2003). *The nation's report card: Mathematics highlights 2003.* National Assessment of Education Progress. Washington, DC: U.S. Department of Education Institute of Education Sciences.

National Council of Teachers of Mathematics. (1989). *Curriculum and evaluation standards for school mathematics.* Reston, VA: Author.

National Council of Teachers of Mathematics. (1991). *Professional standards for teaching mathematics.* Reston, VA: Author.

National Council of Teachers of Mathematics. (1995). *Assessment standards for school mathematics*. Reston, VA: Author.

National Council of Teachers of Mathematics. (2000). *Principles and standards for school mathematics*. Reston, VA: Author.

Nunes, T., & Moreno, C. (1998). Is hearing impairment a cause of difficulties in learning mathematics? In C. Donlan (Ed.), *The development of mathematical skills: Studies in developmental psychology*. Hove, Britain: Psychology Press.

Pagliaro, C. M. (1998a). Mathematics preparation and professional development of deaf education teachers. *American Annals of the Deaf, 143*(5), 373–379.

Pagliaro, C. M. (1998b). Mathematics reform in the education of deaf and hard of hearing students. *American Annals of the Deaf, 143*(1), 22–28.

Pagliaro, C. M. & Ansell, E. *Deaf and hard of hearing students' mathematics problem solving success and strategies with signed arithmetic story problems*. Manuscript in preparation.

Pagliaro, C. M., & Ansell, E. (2002). Story problems in the deaf education classroom: Frequency and mode of presentation. *Journal of Deaf Studies and Deaf Education, 7*(2), 107–119.

Pagliaro, C. M., & Ansell, E. (2005). *Deaf and hard of hearing students' mathematics problem solving success and strategies with signed arithmetic story problems*. Unpublished manuscript.

Pagliaro, C. M., & Kritzer, K. (2005). Discrete mathematics in deaf education: A survey to determine knowledge and use. *American Annals of the Deaf, 150*(3) 251–259.

Pagliaro, C. M., & Roudybush, K. (1999). Math tales: Using mathematics to enhance and encourage literacy. *Proceedings of the 59th Biennial Meeting of the Convention of American Instructors of the Deaf* [CD-ROM].

Skemp, R. R. (1987). *The psychology of learning mathematics*. Hillsdale, NJ: Lawrence Erlbaum Associates.

Traxler, C. B. (2000). The Stanford Achievement Test, 9th edition: National norming and performance standards for deaf and hard-of-hearing students. *Journal of Deaf Studies and Deaf Education, 5*(4), 337–348.

DONALD F. MOORES

Print Literacy: The Acquisition of Reading and Writing Skills

THIS CHAPTER ADDRESSES ISSUES of print literacy among deaf children. We expressly use the term "print literacy" in the title because the concept of literacy, by itself, has expanded to encompass a variety of domains. We encounter references, for example, to "computer literacy," "ASL literacy," and "cultural literacy." These are all quite valid and, for our purposes, are related. All children and adults, both hearing and deaf, must be computer literate to function effectively in today's world. For many, probably most, deaf individuals, ASL literacy is a major aspect of their daily lives. Because ASL does not have a commonly accepted written form, ASL literacy is meant to indicate a more general competence than only reading and writing. Cultural literacy is necessary if we are to bring our world knowledge and expectations to the processes of reading and writing. The reader should keep this in mind while we address issues of reading and writing instruction for deaf children. For the purposes of this chapter we use the terms "literacy" and "print literacy" interchangeably.

As with so many areas covered in this book, we are able to provide only a brief overview of a very complex topic that legitimately calls for a book-length treatment. Several excellent texts are available for further study. Among those are the following: *Language Learning in Children Who Are Deaf and Hard of Hearing* (Easterbrooks & Baker, 2002), *Language Across the Curriculum* (Luetke-Stahlman, 1998), *Literacy and Deafness* (Paul, 1998), *Language and Literacy Development in Children Who Are Deaf* (Schirmer, 2000), and *Literacy and Your Deaf Child* (Stewart & Clarke, 2003).

The Essence of Human Language: A Misconception

For a long period of time educators of the deaf labored under some seriously flawed assumptions. Underlying the concentration on developing oral language skills of deaf children was the belief that speech and language were equivalent and that the goal of educating deaf children was essentially that of "normalization," which could be achieved by training deaf children to speak like hearing children. Success was measured primarily by an individual child's approximation of spoken English. Other accomplishments were secondary, at least in the view of many leading educators. From our present perspective, this philosophy was flawed. Deaf children are normal regardless of spoken language proficiency. To argue otherwise is to denigrate the worth of a child. Also, we all know now that speech is not language but is a manifestation of a language in the same way that signs are a manifestation of a language. The primary functions of the mechanisms to produce speech involve breathing, tasting, chewing, and swallowing. Human language is not a product of our tongues, teeth, and lips; it is a product of our minds. Spoken language is an imperfect representation of our real inner competence and written language is an imperfect representation of spoken language.

The confusion of speech with language was further confounded by equating language solely with spoken English. Frequently, teachers would categorize children as having "poor" language skills, which, in translation, meant that their articulation was not clear. Children might be adept with print English or proficient in American Sign Language (ASL), a signed form of English, or another spoken language, but these accomplishments were considered irrelevant. In fact, ASL in many cases was not considered to be a real language. This confusion of speech, language, and English often worked to the detriment of deaf children.

Learning to Read and Write: Some General Considerations

Although reading and writing are closely related, most educators have paid much more attention to reading, and in most classrooms time on task for reading is greater than for writing. There are many reasons for this. Even though prereading and prewriting activities should begin early in life, it is clear that writing is more time consuming, even for proficient users. For example, it will require far less time for a person to read this chapter than it did for the author to write it. There is also the factor of passive control. To a large degree literate individuals understand more than they can express.

The relationship between reading and writing in a language is similar to but not precisely the same as hearing and speaking a language. Speaking is not consciously a laborious process. The same might be said for ASL or any sign language. Signing also is not consciously a laborious process. Contrast this to when a child begins to learn to write and even to use a computer.

This leads us to a fundamental distinction between language and print literacy, which is one manifestation of language. Language is *learned* by a child in an active, creative way, whereas print literacy to a much greater extent is *taught*. Parents do not set out to teach English or ASL or any other home language to a child. It is acquired quite rapidly within a social context in very complex ways that are not completely understood. The child is a language acquisition device who has mastered the home language by the beginning of formal schooling around age five or six. In the case of spoken English, this includes the 43 or 44 phonemes or basic sounds of American English, although there may still be a lag with pronunciation of some phonemes such as /l/, /w/, or /y/. It also includes the basic syntax and morphology of English, although again there might not be complete mastery of some more complex forms. Syntax refers to word order, and morphology refers to word meaning, which includes free or root morphemes that can stand alone (girl, run, house) and bound morphemes such as prefixes (in-, mis-, pre-), suffixes (-s, -ed, -ly), and infixes (men, mice, ran). The child does not possess the complete vocabulary, or lexicon, of an adult but does have a strong vocabulary base, including the most commonly used words of English (typically function words or interstitials), which establish the structure of the language and connect the more meaningful content words in discourse (Moores, 1997). The most commonly used interstitials include articles (a, an, the), conjunctions (and, but, or), prepositions (to, for, on), and pronouns (he, her, their). Although we may add content vocabulary, especially nouns, during our lifetimes, our corpus of function words remains relatively stable.

Children use language in a pragmatic way. They can use it to express emotions (I love you), obtain information (Why is the sky blue?), request help (I can't reach the milk), or provide information designed to get action (Mary won't share). Thus, the child begins school with an almost fully developed home language. If this language is the same as the language of instruction in school, it is a tool to acquire more knowledge and skills, including print literacy. If the child does not have the same language as the language of instruction, or if the child has not had access to any language, then the situation is complicated. We return to that problem in a later section.

Theoretically, for a child who has mastered spoken language, the process of learning to read and write should be a straightforward one. Reading has been described as training the eye to do the work of the ear. By extension, writing might be described as training the hands and fingers to do the work of the mouth and tongue. Following this line of thought, the development of reading skills would involve matching the phonemes, or sounds, of English to the graphemes, or letters, of the alphabet. Because alphabetic print, in English and other languages, was designed to reflect spoken language, decoding print should entail learning phoneme/grapheme (sound/letter) correspondence, assuming the child has already developed proficiency in phonology, morphology, syntax, vocabulary, and pragmatics.

There is substantial slippage between theory and practice. Many children do acquire print literacy in this way. Typically, they learn to read during the first 4 or 5 years of school, and after that they read to learn. Learning to write proficiently takes more time. Unfortunately, many children do not achieve success under this model. One reason for this is the complex relationship between a spoken language and its print code. Decoding print does not involve a simple one-to-one match. Print is one of the greatest, if not the greatest, inventions of humanity, and our civilization would be impossible without it. Still, any alphabetic system is an imperfect code for a spoken language: it is presented through a different channel and has different physical attributes. It cannot completely represent spoken language.

To compensate for its deficiencies, the English writing system makes use of such strategies as capitalization, commas, colons, semicolons, parentheses, quotation marks, periods, and so forth to convey meaning and structure. It also visually separates out streams that are combined in everyday speech ("imana" may appear as "I am going to"). Another complication is the fact that we use the 26 letters of the English alphabet to represent 43 or 44 phonemes, depending on geography, and many of the phoneme/grapheme relations are inconsistent. There are endless examples. To cite one, an item for the hair (bow) and the bending of the body (bow) are different words that are pronounced differently but are spelled the same way, whereas the bending of the body (bow) and a branch of a tree (bough) have identical pronunciations. By extension, the "gh" in ghost, rough, through, sigh, and bough are all pronounced differently.

Print Literacy: The Great Debates

Despite the surface simplicity, the acquisition of print literacy often is difficult, even for children who have already mastered the spoken language. As might be expected, failure promotes concern, debates, and conflict. There have been trends, claims, and counterclaims for more than a century in American education. One approach has been characterized as elemental, building block, and basal and has been described as a bottom-up approach. One aspect of this has been the phoneme/grapheme matching discussed previously, a step-by-step process often involving memorization, drill, and practice. Variations of a bottom-up approach were dominant in the United States for roughly the first two-thirds of the 20th century. As evidence mounted that large numbers of children were not achieving literacy through this approach, concern arose that it was not tied to real-life situations, and that the stress on drill and memorization decreased motivation to read and write and detracted from the pleasure of print literacy. There was growing support for a more holistic, top-down emphasis that was characterized as a whole language philosophy. The emphasis shifted from decoding the text to understanding the content, with the idea that if children read and wrote for meaning and were involved in meaningful relevant activities, they would develop literacy in a more natural way. Reading was viewed as an exercise in which the reader constructed meaning from print rather than as a decoding exercise. Similarly, writing could develop in a holistic manner without emphasis on structure and little or no need for practice in spelling and grammar, per se, doing away with the practice of returning papers to students full of corrections in red pencil. Reading would include group reading and would involve stories of interest. The effect would be closer to that of acquisition of spoken or signed language in the home, particularly to the extent that concentration shifted from structure to functions of language.

Whole language instruction, in theory, dominated American education for the last third of the 20th century, although there was always criticism that it ignored the basics of spelling and grammar (syntax and morphology) and did not provide a sound foundation for literacy. By the end of the century reaction had set in and the pendulum had started to shift back to an elemental approach, with renewed attention to "phonics" or "phonological awareness." This movement gained impetus from federal mandates, such as those contained in the No Child Left Behind legislation, which specified that instruction should be scientifically based and in the case of literacy should focus on phonics. There is no strong research evidence, from my perspective, that unequivocally supports either a bottom-up or top-down system for all children. To me the results seem mixed, but the government has provided money specifically for support of research on phonics-based instruction.

As might be expected, teachers generally do not adhere to either a completely top-down or bottom-up philosophy but tend to be eclectic in their instruction, especially because individual differences among children suggest that there is no one model that is appropriate for all and that effective instruction should incorporate the strong points of bottom-up and top-down instruction in a more balanced system of instruction. This perspective was presented succinctly in a seminal article by Stanovich (1980), titled "Toward an Interactive-Compensatory Model of Individual Differences in the Development of Reading Fluency," that has had a significant effect on instruction. One component of this model is the idea that weakness at one level of the complex process of reading can be compensated for by strengths in other levels. This interactive model represents a balance between top-down and bottom-up models and is particularly attractive for teachers of deaf children. Even if many deaf children have not completely mastered English syntax, morphology, and semantics, they can compensate by greater application of their cognitive skills.

Although we separate reading and writing to some extent in this chapter, it should be stressed that they are not separate entities but are components of a larger and more complex process involving production, mediation, and reception. This larger process may be considered print literacy.

Print Literacy and Deaf Students

Deafness, per se, has no effect on the acquisition of literacy skills. A deaf child has the same intellectual capacity as a hearing child. A deaf child who has access to a language, either signed or spoken, from birth, who has no educationally relevant disability, who has ample opportunity for incidental learning, and who grows in a supportive environment that nourishes literacy as part of everyday life is a strong prospect to develop effective literacy skills (Miller, 2004a; Moores, 2001). There are numerous examples of deaf students who go through school reading and writing at grade level or higher on standardized tests.

Unfortunately, this is not the norm for deaf children at present. Despite progress, serious obstacles remain. One key factor is early identification and service. Most states now have laws for screening for hearing loss at birth and providing services to families and children. There are states where the systems for identification and service function well and there are clear benefits for families and children. However, all too often children are not identified with a hearing loss for years, and there may be an inexcusably long lag between identification of a hearing loss and the start of services. Any time lost is precious. Children from poor families, from racial minorities, and from immigrant families may not be identified until they enter school. Any child who is not identified close to birth is at a disadvantage. A child who misses 5 or 6 years of normal interaction faces a daunting challenge. A second factor is that even with early identification, deaf children and their families may not be getting appropriate advice, training, and support to help them establish effective communication and facilitate literacy skills. A third factor is evidence that a large percentage of deaf children have educationally relevant conditions that may be related to some of the etiologies of deafness. These would include premature birth, meningitis, and mother-child blood incompatibility. The final responsibility rests on teachers. We must develop better ways to instruct deaf children.

From the opening of the American School for the Deaf in 1817, educators have made the development of reading and writing skills in deaf individuals a major focus of education of the deaf. In today's highly technical society, literacy has assumed an increasingly important status, especially in consideration of the fact that effective expression and electronic reception of information is requisite for growing numbers of occupations. In fact, Stewart and Clarke (2003) argue that that acquisition of proficient literacy skills is the most important educational task facing deaf children. An individual without both expressive and receptive print literacy skills has severely limited career opportunities. At present, there is an increased mandate for literacy because deaf children are now expected both to receive instruction through the general educational curriculum and to be evaluated through state-level standardized tests. These tests are, at their base, tests of reading regardless of whether they address content in science, mathematics, or history. For example, in the past, many math tests would have a selection on computation that would require no reading skills. At present, tests usually present story problems. The student must read a problem, decide what is being requested, and then solve the problem by applying the requisite math skills. If the student does not understand the question presented in English, she will fail the item even if she was capable of performing the required mathematical task.

With the possible exception of the oral-manual controversy, no area in education of the deaf has received more attention than reading. Writing has received less attention, possibly because it is more difficult to measure and quantify writing skills than it is reading skills. At least, there are more standardized tests in existence for reading than for writing. The extent to which these tests are valid for deaf students is debatable.

Although some deaf children achieve high levels of print literacy, there is no doubt that on the average many deaf children lag far behind their potential. For purposes of this chapter we concentrate on the majority of deaf children who, at present, encounter difficulty with print literature. To a large extent, the use of the term "lag" is misleading. It implies that deaf and hearing children follow the same developmental path in literacy acquisition. As noted previously, this may be true for deaf children who have access to a language, either spoken or signed, from birth, who have access to incidental learning, have no disabilities, and grow up in an environment that nourishes literacy as part of everyday life. For them the standardized scores may be valid, although there may still be some differences in syntax, morphology, and vocabulary.

Most readers probably have already come across the statement several times that the average deaf 17-year-old reads at the fourth grade level. That statement is only partly correct. It is true that the average score on a standardized reading test for a 17-year-old deaf student may be the same as for a fourth or fifth grade hearing child, but this does not mean that that they are reading at the same level or that they read in the same way. It simply means that they are responding correctly to the same number of items on a particular test, but they may have taken different paths to arrive at the same score. This is a concept that requires careful consideration.

Remember that a hearing child typically begins kindergarten and elementary school with mastery of the phonology, morphology, syntax, vocabulary, and pragmatics of the language of instruction, in this case English, and probably has had home experiences that provide a foundation for formal literacy instruction. The hearing child can utilize this background as a tool to acquire knowledge and skills, including the acquisition of literacy. Despite recent improvements in education of deaf children and the fact that increasing numbers of hearing parents are joining deaf parents in providing some form of sign communication to their deaf children, the typical deaf child today does not begin kindergarten and elementary school with the same level of English proficiency as the hearing child. Whereas English proficiency is a tool for learning that has been acquired without conscious effort for a hearing child, it is far too often an obstacle to learning for a deaf child, an obstacle that must be overcome with conscious effort as part of the educational process (Moores, 2001). Because deaf children possess the same intellectual potential as hearing children, they are capable of high academic achievement even when they do not have full command of all aspects of English (Miller, 2004b). However, extra effort may be required to achieve at high levels.

Research matching deaf and hearing students' performance on standardized reading tests, usually involving high school deaf students and fourth or fifth grade hearing students, indicates that in reality the deaf students have inadequately developed English syntax, morphology, and vocabulary (Moores, 2001). There is evidence that the problem may continue through college, at least in regards to morphology. Gonter Gaustad, Kelly, Payne, and Lylak (2002) compared the ability of deaf and hearing college students and deaf and hearing middle school students to segment morphemes within printed words and to recognize meanings associated with various printed morphemes. The hearing college students scored significantly higher than the other three groups, the deaf college students and hearing middle school students had similar performances, and the deaf middle school students were significantly lower than the other three groups. The authors concluded that deaf college students were required to read college level texts with middle school levels of word analysis skills and that time was running out to develop beyond basic morphological and reading skills.

The point I want to stress is that it may take more cognitive power for a deaf child to achieve the same score as a hearing child on a test of reading because the deaf child often must compensate for imperfectly developed grammatical skills and a limited vocabulary. Common types of errors by deaf students have been documented for more than a century in the United States and other countries in both English and other spoken languages. In English, these include reading a passive sentence (The cat was chased by the dog) as active (The cat chased the dog), reading a negative sentence (He did not read the book) as positive (He did read the book), and reading a distal reference (The woman who helped the man went to the store) as a proximal reference (The woman helped the man; the man went to the store).

The Place of ASL and English-Based Signing

I have taught using oral-only, Rochester Method, Simultaneous Communication (SimCom), and voice-off sign instruction, both English based and ASL based. I believe that deaf children have achieved success, in my classrooms and in general, under all different approaches, but that the number of successes through oral-only instruction has been too small, even with developments in digital hearing aids and cochlear implants, to support its exclusive use in fostering print literacy skills in deaf children. The Rochester Method, developed at the Rochester School for the Deaf, entails the use of the American Manual Alphabet, or fingerspelling, in coordination with spoken English. Theoretically, every letter of every word is spelled during instruction. The benefit is that the system follows English word order and provides a one-to-one match: the 26 letters of the manual alphabet represent the 26 letters of English print. A similar system, called neo-oralism, was used in Russia, with the exception that the Russian manual alphabet has 43 letters to represent the 43 letters of Russian print. Research suggests that children taught through the Rochester Method had reading achievement superior to children taught through oral-only instruction.

In recent years the popularity of the Rochester Method has declined. In my opinion, there are several reasons for this. Among these are processing and production issues and the restrictiveness of the method. Many children, especially those with disabilities, have difficulty in understanding long series of rapidly spelled English words and are even more limited in their ability to express themselves efficiently in English spelling. Because the system did not allow the use of either ASL or English-based signing, children were denied the opportunity for more free and easy communication. Philosophically, I am opposed to any approach—oral only, sim-com only, fingerspelling only, ASL only—that denies children access in a flexible way to all aspects of communication.

I am in agreement with the position expressed by Stewart in the chapter on instructional and practical communication in this book that for a majority of deaf children a mix of ASL and English-based signing is the most effective mode of communication in the classroom. It provides clarity and efficiency as well as the ability to respond flexibly to individual needs. I believe such an approach is particularly salient in development of print literacy. Most educators would agree that ASL, per se, is much more powerful than any English-based sign system. It is a fully developed language in its own right. Any English-based sign system is a code on spoken English just as English print is a code on spoken English. As such, compromises must be made to adapt a manual system to the constraints of oral communication.

Given the power of ASL, the question arises as to why we should not concentrate completely on ASL, by-pass English-based signing, and teach children to read and write English as a second language. In fact, this is an approach that is espoused by some of the bilingual-bicultural (Bi-Bi) programs, an approach that began in the 1980s and grew in the 1990s. Readers should consult two resources that covered the development (Walworth, Moores, & O'Rourke, 1992) and continuation (Andrews, Leigh, & Weiner, 2004) of Bi-Bi programs.

The rationale for including English-based signing in addition to ASL in the development of print literacy is the fact that ASL is a separate language and the reality that print literacy in the United States calls for proficiency in English. Science, math, literature, history, and social studies texts from elementary school through graduate school, with the exception of foreign languages, will be in English. All federal and state mandated testing will be in English, regardless of subject matter. English-based signing, despite its limitations, can be a bridge to English literacy. Obviously, English-based signing has the benefit of following English word order, or syntax. It also has implications for decoding print morphemes or morphographic associations by deaf students who, as argued by Gonter Gaustad et al. (2002), evince developmental delays in the area. The authors argue that direct instruction in morphographic analysis should be a systematic component of reading instruction. In support of their own findings they cite a study of reading and writing achievement of deaf adolescents with deaf and hearing parents in relation to 31 variables (Moores & Sweet, 1990) that found high correlations for both reading and writing with a written test of English syntactic abilities and a manual English test of morphology. In addition, for both groups, Moores and Sweet found significant correlations of reading and writing with English-based signing proficiency interviews but not with ASL proficiency interviews.

The lack of correlation between reading and writing with ASL proficiency deserves some discussion in view of our position that ASL is a powerful tool for instruction of deaf students. It is a powerful tool, but it is a different language so it is not surprising that it has low statistical correlations with measures of English.

The American Manual Alphabet

The American Manual Alphabet is an integral part of both ASL and English-based signing and can be effective in the development of print literacy. Although a sign may not have any clear relationship to a printed word, for example the sign for "psychology" or "America," the manual alphabet can mediate between the sign and print by allowing the instructor to use the sign, fingerspell it, and then relate it to the printed word. The bridge can work both ways. The manual alphabet also can be used to develop word analysis skills to show relationships among phonemes (sound), graphemes (print), and dactemes (fingerspelling).

The American Manual Alphabet has the advantage for deaf children, who by definition either cannot hear the spoken word or hear it imperfectly, that it was developed to express the printed word directly so that it can by-pass spoken English. It has a relation to spoken English, but it is an indirect one. Readers should be aware that the manual alphabet is not an exact representation of English print. It does not differentiate upper-case and lower-case letters and does not employ commas, colons, italics, and so forth, although there are signs for many of these print characteristics. Print English is a code on spoken English and the manual alphabet is a code on print English.

Phonics and Phonological Awareness

Lichtenstein (1983) reported that proficient deaf readers had well-developed phonological awareness skills superior to those of less skilled deaf readers. Since that time there has been extensive discussion of the necessity and/or sufficiency of phonological skills for deaf readers and the very real question of what is meant by the term for deaf individuals. The issue has assumed greater importance since the passage of the No Child Left Behind Act of 2002, which calls for all children to be taught using proven research-based methods instruction and which in the case of literacy calls for an elemental, sound-based "phonics" approach to teaching print literacy in general education. Responding to the lead of the U.S. Department of Education, there has been interest in developing phonological awareness or knowledge of the systematic relationship between speech and print. Following is a bare outline of the issues.

As educators of deaf children we must address the issue of the importance, if any, of phonological awareness in developing print literacy in children who cannot hear. Nielsen and Luetke-Stahlman (2002) provide basic operational definitions of some key concepts. *Phonological awareness* is defined as sensitivity to the sound patterns of a spoken language. *Phonics* is the understanding of how sounds are mapped onto letters, and *phonological recoding* is the translation of letters and letter patterns as they are produced in the mouth, palate, and nasal area into sounds or kinesthetic feelings.

Nielsen and Luetke-Stahlman argue that proficient readers cannot merely rely on visual memory for words; they must have word analysis skills to break the code or unlock the meaning of a word. Although they do not state so explicitly, the authors' position is that a whole language approach to reading and writing is insufficient for either deaf or hearing children to master the code. Because print words are sound based, they raised the question of whether there is a *causal* (emphasis added) relationship between phonological awareness and reading achievement in deaf readers. They conclude that phonological awareness is a necessary but not sufficient condition for the development of reading proficiency and recommend that phonological awareness should be taught to deaf children, with instruction and practice addressing sound to print relationships.

From my perspective Nielsen and Luetke-Stahlman have made their case effectively but did not go far enough. Some readers have interpreted the research on phonological awareness to mean that we should return to an oral-only system of instruction, a position not advocated by Nielsen and Luetke-Stahlman. Reading achievement is better now than in the days when all instruction was oral only and the teaching of English was completely sound based, at least up to age 12. Nielsen and Luetke-Stahlman, and others, stress that phonological awareness can encompass not only sound but an integration of sound, articulation, writing, and speechreading. I agree with this up to a point. Many of the researchers on phonological awareness refer to the work of the great Russian psychologist, Lev Vygotsky, and his work on *inner speech*. Vygotsky himself was responsible for the development of the curriculum for deaf children in Russia. He incorporated the Russian Manual Alphabet into the curriculum and would have included signs also, which were excluded for political reasons (Moores, 2001).

I know many deaf professionals who are excellent readers who do not have phonological awareness, as rigidly defined as limited to the English phonemic system, but do have sophisticated systems for decoding and encoding English print at the letter and morpheme level. This might be interpreted as having phonemic awareness, but I believe the term is too limiting. Throughout this book, we emphasize the importance of flexibility and responding to the strengths of individual children. This is especially important in reading and writing. Techniques for mastering codes for literacy may involve a range of integrated activities from phoneme/grapheme correspondence to articulation to speechreading to fingerspelling to English-based signs to ASL, but no individual child need require all of these components.

Writing

As noted previously, there is a complex interaction between reading and writing, which are the two components of print literacy. There are greater demands on written communication today than at any time in our history. Even if there is less reliance on some forms of writing, the ubiquitous nature of computers demands clear, effective written communication to function well in society. Writing is fundamentally a creative, functional, interactive process. We write for others, not ourselves. The competent writer must possess mastery of the building blocks and structure (graphemes, morphemes, syntax) of a language. He must also be sensitive to the requirements of a particular communication episode (a letter to a loved one, a business letter, an application for a job, a memo to fellow workers, a term paper) and take into account the nature of the audience as part of the process. In many cases this involves planning, writing, reviewing, and revising. We use different styles in face to face communication depending on whether we are in a classroom, at a football game, eating a family dinner, having an informal group conversation, having a job interview, or meeting people for the first time. The same is true for writing. Different styles must be cultivated.

There is a substantial research literature dating back to the work of Thompson (1936) on the writing of deaf individuals, although it does not match that on reading. The reader should refer to the work of Paul (1998) and Schirmer (2000) for in-depth treatments. For the most part, research on the writing of deaf individuals has concentrated on structural, technical aspects of the process. The results, in general, have been disappointing. We find such descriptors as *limited vocabulary, concrete, lack of function words, bland, poor mastery of verb inflections and plurals, repetitive, limited,* and *simple structure.*

We do know that some deaf children do develop effective writing skills and that deafness per se does not limit the potential of children to express themselves clearly in print. As a teacher of deaf undergraduate and graduate students, I am well aware of the high levels of print literacy within the grasp of deaf individuals. The goal is to bring all children to this level.

Given the close relationship between reading and writing, it is not surprising that approaches to writing may be characterized into three categories; bottom-up, top-down, and compensatory-interactive. The bottom-up, elemental, analytical approach was used throughout the history of educating deaf children, until a shift toward a more holistic top-down process approach started to have an influence about 30 years ago. Despite strong advocacy for both philosophies, and often strong disagreements, there is no evidence that either system, per se, has brought deaf children to parity with hearing children in writing. Advocates for a bottom-up approach argue that the top-down system ignores the essential building blocks for print literacy. Advocates for a top-down approach argue that the bottom-up system ignores that fact that print literacy involves a social constructive process and concentration on structure is too simplistic. Again, I believe that an interactive-compensatory model is most effective for meeting the individual needs of all children while developing essential structural and process skills. This includes instruction on sign to print, fingerspelling to print, sound to print, and morphological awareness as well as on functional, pragmatic aspects.

Kluwin and Kelly (1992) modified a traditional process approach to the writing process involving planning, translating, reviewing, and revising and expanded it for deaf children to include prewriting, organizing, writing, feedback, and revising. The system provides the opportunity for more feedback throughout the process.

Staton (1984) reported on the effectiveness of dialogue journals with deaf children. Dialogue journals have been used for generations with hearing children, usually involving written conversations between a teacher and a child. The basic premise is that the teacher will concentrate on the context of the communication and respond to the content, with little or no attention to grammar or spelling unless there is a problem in communication. There are few restrictions on the content and the student has practice in gearing her communication to an audience.

The concept of dialogue journals has evolved over time to include peers as well as teachers, with increasing use of computers. Batson (1993) developed the English Natural Form Instruction (ENFI) program, which enabled students in a classroom to work on computers with the teacher at the same time on a document. The concept has been extended significantly in recent years, with the model Secondary School for the Deaf playing a leadership role in developing content in subject matter areas and providing simultaneous access to students in different schools.

There has been a move to infuse print literacy across all school subjects, a movement that has attained critical status with the emphasis on state mandated standardized testing. In fact, several "Writing Across the Curriculum" programs have been developed.

Summary

The need for print literacy—reading and writing—is more important for deaf individuals today than it ever has been, and, with our increasing reliance on technology, the need will increase. It is clear that deaf children have the cognitive ability to master print literacy. Additional requirements include early access to clear communication, an environment fostering literacy, and flexible programs that can identify special strengths of individual deaf children and adapt the learning environment. Although there are numerous examples of success, the results to date demonstrate that the ideal has not been achieved for a majority of deaf children.

Research during the past several generations in the United States and elsewhere has found that deaf children and adults have difficulty with numerous aspects of reading and writing in the language being taught. These range from the smallest units (phonemes and graphemes) to morphemes, syntax, vocabulary, and pragmatics. Bound morphemes, function words, complex grammatical constructions, and verb tenses pose special challenges. In essence, most hearing children starting kindergarten and first grade have already mastered those aspects of a language, and learning to read and write involves building upon an already acquired mastery. For too many deaf children formal schooling must be designed to teach deaf children some of the skills that hearing children bring to the educational process. Because of the differences in English skills between hearing students and many deaf students, reports of grade level reading scores for deaf children may be misleading and should be interpreted with caution. Quite simply, a deaf child might have to bring more cognitive power to bear to achieve the same number of correct answers as a hearing child.

Infant screening and provision of services to families and deaf children have improved the situation in recent years, especially in those cases where, in coordination with early educational programs, parents have been encouraged to learn to sign and fingerspell, read to their deaf children, encourage the children to take beginning steps to reading and writing, and provide an overall environment conducive to literacy. Unfortunately this is not the norm.

Part of the problem experienced in helping deaf children acquire print literacy may be attributed to some misconceptions about the nature of language. Although the situation is improving, educators of the deaf traditionally have confused speech with language, when in fact language is a product of the human mind, not the tongue. As previously noted, it should be emphasized that spoken English is a code on English and print English is an imperfect code on spoken English. Signed English systems also represent imperfect codes on spoken English. Furthermore, the American Manual Alphabet is an imperfect code on print English. Finally, ASL is a fully developed language that has coexisted with English for almost two centuries but is independent of it. As a complete language, ASL is more powerful than manual codes on English.

Following the lead of general education, educators of deaf children have followed three basic approaches to develop print literacy. The first has been categorized as a bottom-up system of instruction. This may be thought of as an elemental, building block model concentrating on the structure of a language and involving drill and practice. Bottom-up instruction fell out of favor in the last third of the 20th century but has come back into prominence recently and has received strong support from the No Child Left Behind legislation, which calls for the use of phonics with concentration on phoneme/grapheme correspondence in reading instruction.

A second approach has been categorized as a top-down or whole language model that approaches literacy from a process, not a structural, orientation. The concentration is on literacy as a social, communicative construct, with expression and reception of meaning far more important than drills on subject/verb agreement or spelling. This approach was dominant in general education for most of the last third of the twentieth century, until a reversion to a bottom-up model began. It remained a predominant part of education of the deaf for a longer period, until the push for access to the general curriculum and standardized state mandated testing.

In reality, most teachers of deaf children have been eclectic in their classroom instruction and have included elements of both top-down and bottom-up instruction. Instruction could be improved with more systematic training and application of what has been described as an interactive-compensatory model of literacy instruction. Based on the acceptance of the importance of both top-down and bottom-up components of print literacy, this model also emphasizes that the strengths of a particular child in some areas may provide the foundation to compensate for gaps in other areas. This philosophy has particular salience for a population as diverse and the deaf American school-age population.

Deaf children should have at their disposal a complete range of options for the development of print literacy—ASL, manual codes on English, the American Manual Alphabet, speechreading, and speech—but individual children need not make use of all of them. As a general rule, the greater the hearing loss, the more reliance there should be on ASL, manual codes on English, and the American Manual Alphabet. The concentration should be on print literacy as a social communicative process. There should be meaningful direct teaching involving drill and practice in areas that traditionally have provided obstacles for deaf children. These include function words, prepositions, subject/verb agreement, bound morphemes, phonemic awareness (broadly defined to include signs and the manual alphabet), and complex grammatical structures. For most deaf children, ASL, manual codes on English, and the manual alphabet should be integral parts of both bottom-up and top-down aspects of literacy training.

In summary, deaf children are capable of developing high levels of literacy. We must find systematic ways to help them achieve this goal and strive for new insights. In no other area is the need for carefully developed effective individual education plans more critical than in fostering print literacy in deaf children.

References

Andrews, J., Leigh, I., & Weiner, M. (2004). Evolving perspectives on deafness from psychology, education, and sociology. Coleford, U.K.: Forest Books.

Batson, T. (1993). ENFI research. *Computers and Composition, 10*(3), 95–100.

Easterbrooks, S. R., & Baker, S. (2002). *Language learning in children who are deaf or hard of hearing.* Boston: Allyn and Bacon.

Gonter Gaustad, M., Kelly, R. R., Payne, J.-A., & Lylak, E. (2002). Deaf and hearing students' morphological knowledge applied to printed English. *American Annals of the Deaf, 147*(1), 5–21.

Kluwin, T., & Kelly, A. (1992). Implementing a successful writing program in public schools for children who are deaf. *Exceptional Children, 59*(1), 41–53.

Lichtenstein, E. (1983). *The relationship between reading processes and the English skills of deaf college students. Parts I and II.* Rochester, NY: National Technical Institute for the Deaf Communication Program.

Luetke-Stahlman, B. (1998). *Language across the curriculum.* Hillsboro, OR: Butte Publications.

Miller, M. R. (2004a, June). *Family issues related to language, literacy, and high stakes testing.* Keynote address presented at the Intermountain Special Study Institute on Deafness, Idaho State University, Pocatello.

Miller, M. R. (2004b, July). *Developmental variations in deaf children's language and thought patterns.* Paper presented at the Preconference on Developmental Psychopathology of the Biennial Meeting of the International Society for the Study of Behavioral Disorders, Ghent, Belgium.

Moores, D. F. (1997). Psycholinguistics and deafness. *American Annals of the Deaf, 142*(30), 80–89.

Moores, D. F. (2001). *Educating the deaf: Psychology, principles, and practices.* Boston: Houghton Mifflin.

Moores, D. F., & Sweet, C. (1990). Factors predictive of school achievement. In D. F. Moores & K. P. Meadow-Orlans (Eds.), *Educational and developmental aspects of deafness*. Washington, DC: Gallaudet University Press.

Nielsen, D. C., & Luetke-Stahlman, B. (2002). Phonological awareness: One key to the reading proficiency of deaf children. *American Annals of the Deaf, 147*(3), 11–19.

Paul, P. (1998). *Literacy and deafness*. Boston: Allyn and Bacon.

Schirmer, B. R. (2000). *Language and literacy development in children who are deaf*. Boston: Allyn and Bacon.

Stanovich, K. (1980). Toward an interactive-compensatory model of individual differences in the development of reading fluency. *Reading Research Quarterly, 16*, 32–71.

Staton, J. (1984). *Student attitudes toward dialogue journals*. Washington, DC: Gallaudet University Linguistics Laboratory.

Stewart, D. A., & Clarke, B. R. (2003). *Literacy and your deaf child*. Washington, DC: Gallaudet University Press.

Thompson, W. (1936). An analysis of errors in written composition by deaf children. *American Annals of the Deaf, 81*(2), 95–99.

Walworth, M. A, Moores, D. F., & O'Rourke, T. J. (1992). *A free hand: Enfranchising the education of deaf children*. Silver Spring, MD: TJ Publishers.

HARRY G. LANG

Teaching Science

A S TEACHERS WE USUALLY DEFINE science for our students as an accumulation of knowledge, based on observation and experimentation. We use the term "science" in this chapter to refer to systems of knowledge dealing with the physical or material world. The disciplines often have been referred to as "natural" sciences or "hard" sciences such as biology, chemistry, and physics as differentiated from social studies or history. Because of the overwhelming amount of knowledge available to us, science is organized into discrete fields, as mentioned, and theories have been developed to guide us in comprehending the complex phenomena in our world. Similarly, in science education, experts have developed national standards for curriculum and teaching. These leaders have developed a list of underlying concepts and principles that constitute the "big ideas" in science.[1]

More specifically, in the field of science education for deaf students, we have only recently begun to develop a body of knowledge, based on observation and experimentation (i.e., educational and psychological research). However, a basic theory of instruction for deaf learners has not yet been defined. Knowledge gained from research has yet to be organized in a manner that convincingly defines underlying principles and concepts to which we should adhere in teaching deaf students. In fact, a review of instruction-related articles appearing in the *American Annals of the Deaf* during a 5-year period from 1996 to 2000 (Moores, Jatho, & Creech, 2001) found that not one article was concerned with science. Mangrubang (2004) noted that elementary school teachers are responsible for introducing students to language arts, social studies, mathematics, and science and that, of these four, science gets the least attention. This chapter, then, summarizes some research findings from general education and draws implications for teaching and curriculum development in science. In effect, the underlying principles derived from research lead to certain tenets that may one day be the building blocks of a theory of instruction for deaf learners, regardless of the educational environment in which they study.

---

[1] In this chapter the term *deaf* is used to include both deaf and hard of hearing students.

Science Teaching: Challenges in the Field

One of the most profound social movements of the past three decades has been induced by the federal mandates to mainstream students with disabilities. "Inclusion" efforts have resulted in a wider diversity of students in the public school classrooms. A majority of deaf students are now receiving their education in mainstream environments. On the one hand, educational researchers have stressed that deaf learners should not be viewed simply as hearing students who cannot hear (Marschark, Lang, & Albertini, 2002): deaf students demonstrate many unique learning characteristics, and a teacher in any environment should make an effort to understand deafness as an educational condition. On the other hand, many dedicated teachers are enthusiastic about teaching deaf students, but they lack effective guidance, training, and resources based on sound educational research.

Training in the use of best practices with deaf learners is one of the most serious challenges to the provision of high-quality science education to deaf students on the K–12 level. The lack of teacher content knowledge is another challenge. The problem of underqualified, unprepared teachers is serious in both public schools and special education programs. This problem is, of course, also found in the science education of hearing students. Many teachers either have not met minimum requirements established by their states or have acquired basic credentials but are not receiving the support they need to grow in their profession (National Science Teachers Association, 2000).

In addressing this issue of teacher content knowledge in public education for hearing students, Ingersoll (1999) writes that the effects of being taught by a teacher without a strong background in a field may be just the kind of outcome not captured in student scores on standardized examinations. Teachers who are not well trained in science content also often resort to lectures over which they have more control. Like their hearing peers, deaf adolescents have identified content knowledge as one of the most important characteristics of an effective teacher (Lang, McKee, & Conner, 1993). Thus, a teacher should make every effort to be well prepared in the content area. This effort will increase the effectiveness of activity-based learning strategies and will lead to teachers being continuously ready to answer students' questions.

Cognitive Engagement of the Deaf Learner in Science

In reviewing research with deaf learners in science, one powerful overarching emphasis repeatedly emerges in the literature—cognitive engagement. Hands-on activities are effective. "Minds-on" activities are even more so. The traditional lecture, with its high percentage of teacher talk time, is often accompanied by passive student "listening." Although the same may be said for hearing peers, minds-on instructional emphases are especially effective with deaf learners. Such terms as "active," "interactive," "participative," and "engaged" have been found to be associated with enhanced academic achievement in research, whether the studies have examined reading in science

(Dowaliby & Lang, 1999), learning styles (Lang, Stinson, Kavanagh, Liu, & Basile, 1999), manipulative materials (Boyd & George,1973), or multimedia approaches to learning science (Lang & Steely, 2003).

Cognitive engagement of deaf learners is dependent on many factors. In mainstream classes, deaf students are often challenged to interact effectively with hearing peers and the instructor and to be able to participate on an equitable basis in classroom activities (Lang, 2002). (See also the chapter in this book on cognitive strategies for deaf learners.) Factors inhibiting full participation include pace (rate of presentation by instructor), the number of speakers involved, language and cultural difference, and the use of space (physical arrangements in the classroom). Communication methods may also influence participation. Some students may be more readily engaged when an instructor uses sign language as compared to presenting by voice only with a sign language interpreter translating the information (see Lang, 2002). When interpreters are not available, not familiar with the content, not visible from where the student is sitting, or not using a mode of signing that is similar to the student's, participation may also be impeded (Foster, Long, & Snell, 1999).

Reading Comprehension

Reading comprehension ability is another important factor influencing both access and participation for deaf students in science learning opportunities. The lags of deaf students relative to their hearing peers tend to increase through the school years. By the time deaf students are 18 to 19 years of age, their measured reading ability is generally no better than the average 8- or 9-year-old, normally hearing student. Many deaf students experience complications in their development of knowledge and skills because of inadequate functional literacy levels for reading and writing (Marschark, Lang, & Albertini, 2002). Thus, science teachers must take reading comprehension into consideration in all aspects of instruction, especially in the use of textbooks and multimedia. Research has shown promise in the use of certain strategies such as adjunct questions with reading (Dowaliby & Lang, 1999).

Captions of science films or television shows may not be enough to provide meaningful access to information for deaf learners, even when the captions are edited. It is important that the reading level of captioned materials should be on a level commensurate with that of the students. In one study, two versions of a technical film, captioned at approximately 8th- and 11th-grade reading levels, were shown to 32 deaf college students (Hertzog, Stinson, & Keiffer, 1989). Fifteen of these students also received supplementary instruction from a teacher. Data from a comprehension test were analyzed to determine effects of instruction, level of captioning, test type (recall or recognition), and subject reading ability. Although both high and low reading groups benefited from instruction when students viewed 8th-grade-level modified captions, only the high reading group benefited from instruction when they viewed the 11th-grade-level original captions. The implications are that text should generally be "considerate" with regard to the students' ability to comprehend the material, thus accommodating the reading difficulties that deaf students demonstrate. The vocabulary load was reduced by using only those new terms that were necessary to the explanation. Vocabulary practice should be included before students begin the lesson. The language of science should not be "watered down" excessively, however. Ideally, a science teacher should provide progressively challenging language structures in all reading materials, so that both science literacy and English literacy are developed.

Careful Sequencing of Topics: Organization and Structure

Studies of learning styles indicate that deaf adolescents typically rely heavily on organization and structure in the instructional environment and may be classified as "dependent learners" (Lang et al., 1999). Similar findings have been reported by Grasha (1996) for hearing students. In these studies, "dependent learners" are defined as those who look to authority figures for guidelines on what to do. They find it difficult to develop skills for autonomy and self-direction. Such students may benefit from various forms of graphic organizers and other adjunct instructional aids to facilitate comprehension of text. These include, for example, concept maps, KWL forms (What I **K**now, What I **W**ant to Know, What I Have **L**earned), Venn diagrams, webbing, and main idea tables.

Bridging Research and Practice

Several controlled research studies have emphasized these features of cognitive engagement (addressing reading comprehension and the use of graphic organizers) and have shown promising results. In one multimedia research study with 144 deaf students, Dowaliby and Lang (1999) examined the influence of four types of adjunct instructional aids on immediate factual recall of science content in a series of 11 lessons about the human eye. Students were grouped by standardized test scores as low, middle, and high ability readers. They were also assigned to conditions which included (a) reading text plus viewing "content movies" (animation), (b) text plus sign language translations of the text, (c) text plus answering adjunct questions about the text, and (d) all conditions together (text, sign language translations, animations, and adjunct questions). As mentioned earlier, immediate factual recall for low-reading-ability students was significantly improved through the use of adjunct questions. The sign language translation movies and animations also resulted in increases in factual recall; however, the increases were not statistically significant. The improved recall was likely the result of the cognitively engaging nature of the adjunct questions.

Three research studies conducted by Steely at the Oregon Center for Applied Science have supported this notion of student engagement as compared to traditional lectures. Science learning by deaf middle school and high school students was greatly enhanced through the combined use of graphics, questions, text, and other features (Lang & Steely, 2003). The studies included non-web-based earth science and physical science and web-based chemistry, focusing on explicitly teaching underlying networks of concepts. Kameenui and Carnine (1998) have referred to these underlying conceptual networks as the "big ideas" for organizing facts and knowledge and simultaneously emphasizing higher-order thinking. The efficacy of this approach with hearing students has also been supported by numerous studies (e.g., Moore & Carnine, 1989; Woodward & Noell, 1991).

An example of a "big idea" in earth science is convection, which explains the movement of heat in the earth, in the oceans, and in the atmosphere. In physical science, a "big idea" is that energy can change between different forms (electrical, chemical, mechanical, heat, etc.) without being destroyed. By understanding the "big ideas," students are able to organize facts and concepts into a larger meaningful whole. The science teacher can use these "big ideas" to relate information that is found in the long lists of bench marks. Students should learn to use them to solve problems and integrate new knowledge. Both the National Science Education standards and the American Association for the Advancement of Science national standards encourage such use of underlying concepts. Science teachers should be thoroughly familiar with their school's standards, which most often are derived from the national projects.

Careful sequencing of materials so that concepts are partially developed in a lesson and reinforced in subsequent lessons was another important feature that was supported by these controlled research studies. Graphic organizers were used throughout each program as a means of helping students keep track of the important content they learn. Graphic organizers were schematics that included the core vocabulary, facts, and concepts of the lesson. They were designed to provide a clear diagram of how the knowledge is organized and related. Graphic organizers were also used as a concise way to review the important information.

It is important that the results of the empirical research study conducted at the National Technical Institute for the Deaf (Dowaliby & Lang, 1999) and the three conducted at the Oregon Center for Applied Science (Lang & Steely, 2003) indicate that the interactive approach yielded significantly greater knowledge gains for deaf students as compared to traditional classroom experiences.

Technology in the Classroom

Today, instructional technologies are popular in teaching science to deaf students. High-speed connections are changing the capability of carrying large amounts of text, voice, and video data over existing telephone and cable lines. Contemporary curriculum projects have shown great promise with deaf learners. An example of this type of project is the Classroom of the Sea, a grant project sponsored by the National Science Foundation. Its collaborators included a team from the National Undersea Research Center for the North Atlantic and Great Lakes, the University of Connecticut, the American School for the Deaf in Hartford, and the National Technical Institute for the Deaf at Rochester Institute of Technology. To develop a means for communicating in sign language with high quality transmissions over the Internet, a digital video camera was used with the deaf students on a boat, the *RV Connecticut*, on the Atlantic during a water-sampling activity. This signal was fed into the *RV Connecticut*'s network, and then transmitted from the vessel to the antenna on the Marine Sciences building on shore 5 miles from the ship at sea into the building's local area network

(LAN). From there the signal was sent to a server, which transcoded the signal to Windows Media. This process was the streaming format for viewing the web video by deaf students in various school programs around the country. The sign language over the Internet was of sufficient quality to continue planning for two-way transmissions on an ongoing basis. Experiments with classroom lectures, including the use of Power-Point slides, using this system were also successful. This procedure allowed the team of scientists and educators in four different locations to interact during various science learning excursions with deaf students (Lang et al., 2002).

Many forms of technology have potential for the instruction of deaf learners in science, including computers, calculators, captions, virtual dissection, virtual reality, assistive technologies, use of the World Wide Web, software for drill and practice, telecommunications, and visualizers. The general issues discussed in this chapter, however, apply to their use as much as they do to direct instruction by teachers. In particular, technologies that include "considerate" text and engage the students cognitively will be more effective than those that focus on passive viewing.

Self-Efficacy

Self-efficacy is the "belief in one's capabilities to organize and execute the sources of action required to manage prospective situations" (Bandura, 1986). According to Bandura, the strength of people's beliefs in their abilities to accomplish a task is one of the strongest influences upon the end result. A student with little confidence may very well not succeed because of a lack of belief, whereas one who is more confident has an increased chance of success. The amount of confidence a person has can be adversely affected by anxiety and tension.

Another factor that strongly influences people's confidence in their abilities is motivation. A person who is highly motivated to complete a task will be more likely to have a higher level of confidence in the end result. Motivation can also affect the amount of observational learning a person experiences. People tend to adapt strategies employed by others if they see that the end result is desirable. It is for this reason that Bandura suggests that rewards are not a consequence for behavior; instead, they are an antecedent. It is the expected reward at the end of a task that will influence a person's motivation.

Self-knowledge pertaining to appraisal of personal competence has been referred to as self-esteem (Stinson, 1994). Self-esteem is associated with academic success for both hearing and deaf students. Joiner, Erickson, and Crittenden (1966), for example, found that deaf students in a residential high school with relatively high self-esteem tended to have high grade-point averages. Koelle and Convey (1982), studying a similar population, found that self-esteem was positively related to performance on the Stanford Achievement Test for Hearing-Impaired Students.

Many ways exist to approach the development of positive self-esteem in the science classroom. Deaf students seldom have the chance to meet successful deaf scientists or even deaf science teachers. Although no research studies have been found with deaf role models, investigations with other culturally diverse students (African Americans,

Hispanics, Native Americans, etc.) have shown that culturally familiar role models, both in person and as role models in printed materials or textbooks, constitute an important variable that positively affects cognitive learning (Shade, 1982). Other reports have indicated that the presence of culturally familiar role models in textual materials increases students' self-esteem, concept acquisition, and motivation to pursue science careers (Healy, 1990).

The science teacher has numerous resources now that provide detailed information about the outstanding contributions of deaf women and men in various fields of science. These include, for example, *Silence of the Spheres: The Deaf Experience in the History of Science* (Lang, 1994) and *Deaf Persons in the Arts and Sciences: A Biographical Dictionary* (Lang & Meath-Lang, 1995). Strategies for infusing information about deaf scientists in the science classroom are highly recommended. In general, deaf students do not receive adequate career education in high school, in particular. This deficiency, along with inadequate academic preparation, are significant reasons why many deaf students do not complete their courses of study in college (Stinson & Walter, 1997).

Standards-Based Reform

The standards-based reform movement throughout the 1990s promoted the application of bench marks and standards to many of the important tasks that educators perform in their schools. Nelson (1997), Project 2061 director at the American Association for the Advancement of Science, writes that "although standards alone cannot bring all the necessary reforms, when used with effective implementation tools, they can make it possible to do some things better." For example, at the state and local levels, educators can use bench marks or standards to (a) define the territory; (b) promote K–12 coherence; (c) rationalize curriculum, instruction, and assessment; (d) provide a foundation for teacher preparation and continuing professional development programs; and (e) guide efforts to improve achievement for all students.

Another popular standards reform project is the National Science Education standards developed by the National Research Council. These standards are grouped into six areas: (a) science teaching; (b) professional development; (c) assessment; (d) science content; (e) science education programs; and (f) science education system standards. They write

> teachers need support from the rest of the educational system if they are to achieve the objectives embodied in the *Standards*. Schools, districts, local communities, and states need to provide teachers with the necessary resources—including time, appropriate numbers of students per teacher, materials, and schedules. For teachers to design and implement new ways of teaching and learning science, the practices, policies, and overall culture of most schools must change. (National Research Council, 1996, p. 4)

"Equity" is important to the leaders in science and education who developed the standards. The emphasis is on *all students* being capable of "full participation" and of making "meaningful contributions" in classes.

Science teachers should be well informed about the standards that are followed by their schools as well as the state and national standards from which they were derived.

Conclusion

Well-designed, efficacious science instructional programs for hearing students can be successfully adapted for use with deaf students by interspersing text and sign language explanations with content animation and graphic organizers, and by providing additional practice on vocabulary. Original materials can also be developed with these emphases. The materials can be effectively presented via the web or through more traditional classroom delivery, but in either approach the emphasis should be on cognitive engagement, self-efficacy, and language-considerate text.

Empirical research studies completed to date have revealed a possible synergistic effect whereby the use of a combination of various forms of adjunct instructional aids have a positive effect on learning, distinct from the contributions of the individual components (Dowaliby & Lang, 1999; Lang & Steely, 2003). Although further research may help us to understand the relative contributions of graphic organizers, adjunct questions, sign language explanations, and other forms of visual support to text comprehension, we have a growing body of knowledge that supports activity-based, student-centered instruction.

References

Bandura, A. (1986). *Social foundations of thought and action: A social cognitive theory.* Englewood Cliffs, NJ: Prentice Hall.

Boyd, E., & George, K. (1973). The effect of science inquiry on the abstract categorization behavior of deaf children. *Journal of Research in Science Teaching, 10*(1), 91–99.

Dowaliby, F. J., & Lang, H. G. (1999). Adjunct aids in instructional prose: A multimedia study with deaf college students. *Journal of Deaf Studies and Deaf Education, 4*(4), 270–282.

Foster, S., Long, G., & Snell, K. (1999). Inclusive instruction and learning for deaf students in postsecondary education. *Journal of Deaf Studies and Deaf Education, 4*(3), 225–235.

Grasha, A. F. (1996). *Teaching with style: A practical guide to enhancing learning by understanding teaching and learning styles.* Pittsburgh, PA: Alliance Publishers.

Healy, J. M. (1990). *Endangered minds: Why children don't think and what we can do about it.* New York: Simon & Schuster.

Hertzog, M., Stinson, M. S., & Keiffer, R. (1989). Effects of caption modification and instructor intervention on comprehension of a technical film. *Educational Technology Research and Development, 37*(2), 59–68.

Ingersoll, R. M. (1999). The problem of underqualified teachers in American secondary schools. *Educational Researcher, 28*(2), 26–37.

Joiner, L. M., Erickson, E. L., & Crittenden, J. B. (1969). Predicting the academic achievement of the acoustically impaired using intelligence and self-concept of academic ability. *Journal of Special Education, 3*(4), 425–431.

Kameenui, E., & Carnine, D. (Eds.). (1998). *Effective teaching strategies that accommodate diverse learners.* Upper Saddle River, NJ: Prentice-Hall.

Koelle, W. H., & Convey, J. J. (1982). The prediction of achievement of deaf adolescents from self-concept and locus of control measures. *American Annals of the Deaf, 127*(6), 769–779.

Lang, H. G. (1994). *Silence of the spheres: The deaf experience in the history of science.* Westport, CT: Bergin & Garvey.

Lang, H. G. (2002). Higher education for deaf students: Research priorities in the new millennium. *Journal of Deaf Studies and Deaf Education, 7*(4), 267–280.

Lang, H. G., Babb, I., Scheifele, P., Brown, S., LaPorta-Hupper, M., Monte, D., Johnson, P. R., & Zheng, D. (2002, Winter). Classroom of the sea. *NTID Research Bulletin 7*(1), 6–7.

Lang, H. G., & Meath-Lang, B. (1995). *Deaf persons in the arts and sciences: A biographical dictionary.* Westport, CT: Greenwood Press.

Lang, H. G., McKee, B. G., & Conner, K. N. (1993). Characteristics of effective teachers: A descriptive study of perceptions of faculty and deaf college students. *American Annals of the Deaf, 138*(3), 252–259.

Lang, H. G., Stinson, M. S., Kavanagh, F., Liu, Y., & Basile, M. (1999). Learning styles of deaf college students and instructors' teaching emphases. *Journal of Deaf Studies and Deaf Education, 4*(1), 16–27.

Lang, H. G., & Steely, D. (2003). Web-based science instruction for deaf students: What research says to the teacher. *Instructional Science, 31*(4–5), 277–298.

Mangrubang, F. (2004). Preparing elementary education majors to teach science using an inquiry-based approach: The full options science system. *American Annals of the Deaf, 149*(3), 42–55.

Marschark, M., Lang, H. G., & Albertini, J. A. (2002). *Educating deaf students: From research to practice.* New York: Oxford University Press.

Moore, L., & Carnine, D. (1989). Evaluating curriculum design in the context of active teaching. *Remedial and Special Education, 10*(4), 28–37.

Moores, D., Jatho, J., & Creech, B. (2001). Issues and trends in instruction and deafness. *American Annals of the Deaf, 146*(2), 72–76.

National Research Council. (1996). *National science education standards.* Washington, DC: National Academy Press.

National Science Teachers Association. (2000, May/June). Survey indicates high teacher turnover, job dissatisfaction. *NSTA Reports, 5,* 15.

Nelson, G. D. (1997). Benchmarks and standards as tools for science education reform. Retrieved November 3, 2004, from http://www.project 2061.org/publications/articles/nelson/nelson1.htm

Shade, B. J. (1982). Afro-American cognitive style: A variable in school success. *Review of Education Research, 52*(2), 219–244.

Stinson, M. S. (1994). Affective and social development. In R. C. Nowell & L. E. Marschark (Eds.), *Understanding deafness and the rehabilitation process*. Boston: Allyn and Bacon.

Stinson, M., & Walter, G. (1997). Improving retention for deaf and hard of hearing students: What the research tells us. *Journal of American Deafness and Rehabilitation Association, 30*(4), 14–23.

Woodward, J., & Noell, J. W. (1991). Science instruction at the secondary level: Implications for students with learning disabilities. *Journal of Learning Disabilities, 24*(5), 277–284.

DAVID S. MARTIN

The Social Studies Curriculum

W HAT WE KNOW TODAY AS SOCIAL STUDIES in American education had at one time a different label. Until well after World War II, some aspects of this current subject area were identified only as "history" and "geography," focusing on past events and on orienting oneself to the geographic world. The term "social studies" began to be used in earnest during the 1950s but was a term that still referred largely to the combination of history and geography.

In 1957 the Russian spacecraft *Sputnik* was launched, however, which resulted in a shock to America and in particular to America's educators, who were asked, "Why are we behind? It must be the curriculum." The subsequent curriculum revolution permanently changed the face of American education.

As a result of that shock, innovations soon developed in the science curriculum and subsequently in the mathematics curriculum. Not far behind, even though not related directly to the concerns that followed *Sputnik*, were the social studies. The term began to be broadened to include all of the social sciences—not only geography, but also economics, political science, sociology, and anthropology, with some elements of psychology and philosophy (although philosophy is not a social science). History, technically defined, is not a social *science*, but was included in social *studies*. Thus, the school subject of social studies became interdisciplinary.

Significant Changes in Teaching Methods

The important changes resulting from the specially funded curriculum projects of the 1960s in social studies involved a number of characteristics. These innovations were made possible by a first-time-ever combination of collaborators in the curriculum projects—a coalition of educational psychologists, teachers, and university scholars working together to produce intellectually strong curricula that represented a number of significant changes from social studies prior to the 1960s. This chapter includes a review of those changes and suggests that these criteria are still very relevant for teachers who are intent on making intelligent choices in social studies curriculum and methodology. Strong social studies curricula feature these characteristics:

1. An in-depth approach to the study of periods in the past, as opposed to superficial survey "coverage" of the past.

2. A conceptually based rather than a factually based approach to knowledge in social studies.

3. An interdisciplinary approach to the study of social phenomena rather than a single-discipline approach, one looks at social phenomena from a cultural, sociological, economic, geographic, and political point of view instead of through only one of these disciplines.

4. Use of facsimiles of primary documents wherever possible, to supplement secondary documents—for example, they may include, in addition to what a historian has written about John Adams, some of Adams' letters to his wife, Abigail, and her replies. This allows students to form their own opinion of what really transpired.

5. Use of visual media, such as PowerPoint, overhead transparencies, videotapes, and so forth to bring a visual reality to social studies; this dimension, of course, is particularly relevant to deaf learners who depend on the visual not only for excitement about the topic but also for primary sensory input.

6. Use of cultural artifacts wherever possible, or reproductions of such artifacts— for example, in a study of a culture that is different from the students', curricula may include examination of kits of materials such as tools and works of art from that culture, as well as reading material.

7. Classroom debates on critical issues related to the topic of study, so that students have to take and defend their own positions on issues related directly to the topic.

8. Use of field experiences to make the topic come alive—for example, a structured visit to a local museum that has displays related to a culture being studied.

9. Community resource people who visit the classroom to make presentations on some aspect of the topic on which they have particular expertise—for example, when studying the history of seafaring in New England, an invitation to a retired sea captain to share anecdotes with students about life at sea.

10. Role play activities and simulation games that give students the experience of being an active part of some social studies phenomena; for example, different students may play the role of judge, jury, defendant, and prosecutor when re-enacting scenes from the famous Scopes Trial, in which evolution was debated early in the 20th century.

One could easily add more dimensions to make social studies come alive.

Pace-Setting Curriculum Model

During the mid-1960s an outstanding social studies curriculum was developed through a collaboration of teachers, scholars, and psychologists, supported by funds from the National Science Foundation. Called *Man: A Course of Study* (Curriculum Development Associates, 1970), the curriculum was designed as a model upon which later social studies curriculum could be modeled. The curriculum was the brainchild of Jerome Bruner, the Harvard psychologist. Nearly all of the previous 10 elements of strong social studies teaching were involved; the subject matter included a comparison of human beings with other animals to determine how humans are unique, followed by an in-depth study of one particular Canadian Inuit culture using authentic videotaped anthropological scenes showing that culture in action. (The author had the good fortune to be a member of that curriculum development team in Cambridge, Massachusetts.)

Although that curriculum was eventually published and disseminated together with a required teacher-training workshop series, and although it had some indirect influence on other published curricula later, it was also the target of a conservative political backlash that for a time threatened its future by taking some elements of the curriculum out of context and focusing public attention on them. The controversy is the subject of a fascinating book by Peter Dow (1991), which shows how social studies can become a focus of politics. In any case, the legacy of that curriculum—which is still in use in some schools—was to give life to these innovations as part of social studies in schools.

Developmental Perspective

Good teachers always consider the developmental stages of their students when making decisions about any aspect of curriculum. Social studies is no exception. However, it is important to bear in mind a principle of Jerome Bruner—that it is possible at *any* age for a child to learn something "honest" about any subject (1960). Thus, if the study of different cultures is one thread in a school's social studies program, then in the first grade the children could study the family life in another culture, whereas in a later grade they could study the community life in the same or a different culture, and in a still later grade they could study the political and economic dimensions of the same or a different culture. In this way, culture study becomes a "spiral" theme (Bruner, 1966), with an ever-increasing sophistication in concepts; yet, the idea of studying another culture can be introduced early on nonetheless In other words, the old idea of the expanding-horizons approach (study *our* family first, then *our* community, then *our* state, etc.) is not needed; it is perfectly possible for young children to learn something interesting and honest about another culture right away.

Teachers, of course, would adapt the kinds of activities to the age level of the students—more concrete activities in early years, followed by more representational activities in the middle years, followed by more symbolic and abstract activities in the later years. However, history and the social sciences can become the foundation for social studies from the earliest grade levels onward.

Problem-Centered Approach

One of the most effective and motivating approaches in the social studies classroom is the problem-centered focus. In this approach, a series of challenging problems is presented to the students, who then work in pairs or small groups during a period of time to collect data on the problem and discuss possible solutions. They then present their findings to the large group.

An example of such an approach, using the field of geography, is to explain how we know that the earth is round (without resorting to space travel or the use of earth-circling satellites). This problem is intriguing, and readers are invited to think about this problem; in actuality there are four different ways to prove that the earth is round. (Hint: one way is to notice the shadow of the earth against the moon during a partial or full lunar eclipse; can you identify the other three ways?)

Other more long-term problems would be questions about the behaviors and beliefs of a particular culture, which would require investigation involving Internet research, library research, videotapes, and a visit to an anthropological museum.

National Standards

The national professional organization in social studies is the National Council for the Social Studies (NCSS), and their website is http://ncss.org, which serves as a useful resource for teachers. As part of their national efforts during the 1990s, they (together with other subject-area professional organizations) developed a voluntary set of curriculum standards for social studies, built around 10 key goals that could organize all social studies programs at all age levels in schools (NCSS, 1994). These standards later became the foundation for determining whether a teacher education program in social studies was meeting the subject matter requirements for that discipline, and these standards are currently used for the formal evaluation of the quality of teacher education programs in social studies.

The standards later became the foundation for some of the development of state-wide curriculum standards in social studies, and in that sense, they stopped being voluntary and became required (even though the intention of NCSS was originally to recommend rather than mandate). In connection with the No Child Left Behind Act of 2001, it is now expected that the states will gradually implement testing programs in social studies to accompany the already mandated tests in the subject areas of mathematics and language. When that development is fully implemented, it will become even more important for teachers of social studies to view those curriculum mandates only as a framework for skills and concepts, within which they will still have the latitude to adopt or adapt a particular social studies content that they believe fits their community and interests.

In the climate of the early years of the 21st century, we see a return to more exclusive attention to history and geography and a setting aside of some of the other social sciences. We urge teachers, however, to reemphasize the importance and place of the other social sciences in providing a balanced social studies curriculum for students. Social studies, perhaps more than some other curriculum disciplines, is subject to political trends; in politically conservative times, a return to fact-based study of history and geography alone, with emphasis on American and Western history, is typical of the emphasis during a conservative movement.

Curriculum Content

What, then, could be the content of the modern social studies curriculum for students who are deaf or hard of hearing, as well as for other students? As noted previously, the "old" approach in the social studies focused on what was termed the "expanding horizons" approach—the first grade was a study of the students' families, the second grade was a study of the students' school, the third grade was the local community, the fourth grade was the state, the fifth grade was the nation, and so forth. This model was based on the developmental hypothesis that children needed to study what was close to their experience before studying other areas that were more external to them.

As we have seen, that approach has, happily, been proven unnecessary; we know now that young children are perfectly capable of studying phenomena that are not in their experience as long as the methodology is based on their learning capabilities—that is, it uses concrete materials for the younger children, and so forth, based on Piagetian principles.

That liberating viewpoint opens up a rich host of curriculum possibilities, and no one prescribed sequence of content is necessarily better than any other. However, the structure of whatever content is selected is best built around key concepts; the concepts of the NCSS are well thought out and can form as good an organizing scheme as any other. The list of those 10 concepts is as follows:

1. culture;
2. time, continuity, and change;
3. people, places, and environments;
4. individual development and identity;
5. individuals, groups, and institutions;
6. power, authority, and governance;
7. production, distribution, and consumption;
8. science, technology, and society;
9. global connections; and
10. civic ideals and practices.

This list is not intended to be sequential across age or grade levels; rather, it is intended that several, if not all, of these would be treated within some social studies content at multiple grade levels. For example, the seventh concept—production, distribution, and consumption—at first sight appears to be high-level economics. Not so—even first graders can learn about basic principles of production and distribution through a study of the products made at a local factory; those same ideas would be studied in more abstract form in high school. Thus, the spiral curriculum concept is alive and well.

We would leave it to teachers to select published curricula that incorporate these 10 concepts in a spiral fashion, using attractive and engaging materials; we urge that teachers apply the criteria from the chapter in this book by Martin, Moores, and Luft in the selection of such published curricula. If these criteria are applied faithfully, the particular content will follow logically, and materials and media will be available through the published form. However, if a prospective published curriculum does not address in some way most or all of these 10 concepts, then it should not be recommended because it will not provide the all-important balance that the curriculum should have.

Good teachers of social studies are also constantly on the lookout for interesting materials to supplement whatever published content is in use. The sources for those could be current events from news magazines and newspapers; news broadcasts of breaking worldwide or national news items; local, regional, or national elections that allow an in-depth focus on candidates' positions; and such sources as the monthly journal of the NCSS (*Social Education*) for other topics and methods.

On the latter topic, an example will illustrate the point: the October 2003 issue of this journal, which is available to members of the NCSS, included features on the deep background of the Marshall Plan for post–World War II Europe, First Amendment issues for the Constitution, two sides of the debate on whether the pledge of allegiance should be voluntary or required in schools, human rights trends in a variety of countries, the affidavit used in the lawsuit by the Wright brothers against Glenn Curtis about who achieved the first real airplane flight, and several classroom activities on the latest rulings from the Supreme Court (*Social Education,* 2003). It is easy to see how these articles could supplement any social studies curriculum.

Additional Dimensions

In spite of current (re)emphases on history and geography, several new dimensions of social studies make it possible to keep the subject lively for students. One of those is a renewed interest in moral or character education, not for the purpose of didactically inculcating one narrow set of values but rather for the purpose of having students mentally wrestle with important moral issues. Moral education is definitely not new per se; it got its strong beginning in the 1970s with the work of Lawrence Kohlberg, a professor at Harvard. However, with the apparent breakdown of some family cohesion and the apparent lack of a unified set of community values because of our multicultural environment, some schools are seeing the need to reemphasize this direction. One of the still effective techniques in this domain is the use of dilemma stories in which students must debate the appropriate action to the open-ended narrative that deliberately raises moral decision issues.

Another relatively new dimension is community service. Although required community service in secondary schools has been with us since the 1990s, it is also another way of directly relating social studies learning to community experiences. Teachers can build upon the varied experiences of their students when they ask students to share significant learning from their community service experiences; they can also structure community service experiences to yield important social learning. For example, if a group of high school students is satisfying their community service requirement by volunteering to serve food in a shelter for homeless people, the social studies teacher can capitalize on their experiences by a classroom project that examines the sociology and economics of homelessness—how such people become homeless, what their alternatives are, and how to possibly reduce the number of homeless people in that community.

Still another newer dimension is the study of one's own family history. Several publishers now have units available for genealogical study, which brings students' sense of the past alive when they are able to connect their personal family history with significant world events that were contemporary with some of their ancestors. Of course this area must be handled sensitively when some students may either know little or nothing about their family's history or have been adopted. However, teachers have found techniques to deal appropriately with both of these situations, allowing students to work with hypothetical families whose information the teacher provides to these particular students.

Call to Action

If social studies can be summarized as the study of citizens in a society—past, present, and future—in order to make personal and policy decisions (Bragaw & Hartoonian, 1988), then the agenda is clear for teachers of social studies who work with deaf students. Deaf students have a particularly rich source of data on which to draw as part of their social studies—Deaf culture and the traditions that accompany it. As is indicated elsewhere in this book, Deaf culture has a clear place within the curriculum; teachers of deaf students in social studies can then build upon and take advantage of this dimension of the curriculum to help students learn important points about the traditions, myths, legends, belief systems, and the norms of social interaction in other cultures in addition to Deaf culture.

For social studies teachers, it is essential to move beyond any short-term educational fads or politically motivated mandates and steadily bear in mind the fundamental values of strong social studies teaching—the listed characteristics of social studies provided at the beginning of this chapter. After all, social studies is about *life* and has the constant potential to be exciting, real, and very relevant not only to the lives of others living elsewhere and in the past but also to students' own lives right now and their personal futures.

References

Bragaw, D., & Hartoonian, H. (1988). Social studies: The study of people in society. In R. Brandt (Ed.), *Content of the curriculum*. Alexandria, VA: Association for Supervision and Curriculum Development.

Bruner, J. (1960). *The process of education*. Cambridge, MA: Harvard University Press.

Bruner, J. (1966). *Toward a theory of instruction*. Cambridge, MA: Harvard University Press.

Curriculum Development Associates. (1970). *Man: A course of study*. Washington, DC: Author.

Dow, P. (1991). *Schoolhouse politics: Lessons from the Sputnik era.* Cambridge, MA: Harvard University Press.

National Council for the Social Studies. (1994). *Expectations of excellence: Curriculum standards for social studies.* Washington, DC: Author.

Social Education. (2003). *67*(6).

D A V I D A . S T E W A R T

M . K A T H L E E N E L L I S

Revisiting the Role of Physical Education for Deaf Children

PERHAPS IT SHOULDN'T COME AS A SURPRISE that for the past 20 years or so, physical education (PE) has been derided as the ugly duckling of the curriculum. This is true in many public schools where elementary age children take PE in their street clothes and, after doing a few minutes of stretching and running, play kickball, dodge ball, and other simple games (Sammann, 1998). Deaf children fare worse than their hearing peers. In public schools, PE is often used as the subject from which they are pulled for support services provided by audiologists and speech therapists (Stewart & Kluwin, 2001). Even in schools for deaf children where PE is usually seen as an important part of the curriculum, there is evidence of children's fitness getting shortchanged. One school for the deaf we contacted has had a different PE teacher in each of the past 5 years, none of whom were certified to teach PE. Moreover, in this same school, classroom teachers hold back their students from attending their PE class if they have not completed their school work or as a form of punishment.

All of this is occurring at a time when the media and medical professions are calling America a nation of overweight children and adults. In fact, today's generation of children are slated to be the first generation not to outlive their parents because of reduced life expectancy related to diseases associated with overweight bodies and inactive lifestyles. This is in sharp contrast to the growing availability of exercise equipment, TV fitness programs, community sports opportunities, and recreation facilities. Plus, there are constant reminders for people to eat better, and wherever there is food you can find reams of nutritional information. Schools, too, are taking steps to create healthier lunch programs and reduce or eliminate the proliferation of candy and soft drink vending machines. However, schools must go farther and investigate why many of their PE programs now favor activities that are not physically challenging and ultimately do little to increase fitness levels of students.

In this chapter, we review the status of physical fitness in light of today's world—a world where computers and the entertainment industry are conspiring to entrench us into an increasingly sedentary lifestyle—and review what we know about the fitness levels and motor performance skills of deaf children. Following this we describe changes that are occurring in PE curriculum and how teachers and schools can make the curriculum more amenable to the physical needs of deaf children from elementary through high school grades.

What Teachers Should Know About Physical Fitness

Physical fitness is a measure of the ability of the body to effectively function physiologically and is categorized as being either skill-related or health-related (Hastad & Lacy, 1998). Skill-related physical fitness involves components related to sports and athletic performance, such as balance, agility, coordination, and power. Health-related physical fitness refers to components of everyday functional fitness, such as cardiorespiratory endurance, muscular strength and endurance, body composition, and flexibility. Although both types of fitness are important, medical professions have emphasized health-related physical fitness the most because of its connection to various diseases and disabilities (Public Health Service, 1990).

In general terms, health-related physical fitness is defined as the physiological functions that offer protection from diseases and disabilities associated with inactive habits (Wilmore & Costill, 1994). To experience such protection from disease and disability, minimally appropriate fitness levels are required, which are defined as performing at or above the 20th percentile on individual measures of health-related physical fitness (Cooper Institute of Aerobic Research, 1999). Research has indicated that being above the 20th percentile, especially with respect to cardiorespiratory endurance and body composition, provides the greatest overall benefits to achieving and maintaining appropriate health-related physical fitness levels. Although it is desirable to have at least moderate levels of physical fitness, the gains in fitness that push the individual past the 20th percentile may have effects that are just as positive as those that would occur with performance at a higher level of fitness. This level of fitness is an important concept for encouraging and motivating children and adults alike to improve fitness levels even a minimal amount.

All teachers, including teachers of deaf students, need to be aware of four categories of health-related physical fitness that play a role in the overall health and well-being of an individual:

1. *Cardiorespiratory endurance* is the ability of the body to move over a period of time without undue stress or fatigue (Wilmore & Costill, 1994). It is the ability of the heart and lung systems to provide the body with oxygen during continuous movement. An individual with appropriate cardiorespiratory endurance is able to participate in exercise longer before fatiguing than someone with lower cardiorespiratory endurance.
2. *Body composition* is the relative amounts of bone, fat, muscle, and other vital tissues and parts within the body (Wilmore & Costill, 1994). Body composition is generally evaluated in terms of percent body fat and is the only health-related physical fitness component that is not a performance measure.

The ratio between lean body mass and fat mass is important in an individual's ability to perform functional movements, because body fat has been connected with performance on many weight-bearing activities (Rowland, 1999). A high percentage of body fat will cause an individual to have difficulty moving their body efficiently. This is one of the reasons why many children and adults drop out of physical activity: it becomes difficult and cumbersome to move the additional fat mass.

To be considered physically fit, individuals must demonstrate appropriate age- and gender-specific levels for at least four components of health-related physical fitness, two of which must be the previously discussed cardiorespiratory endurance and percent body fat—the two most important components of health-related physical fitness because of their direct connection with hypokinetic diseases and disabilities (Rowland & Freedson, 1994).

3. *Muscular strength and endurance* allow an individual to exert enough force to perform functional everyday activities with ease, such as climbing stairs, carrying books, or completing tasks around the house. Muscular strength and endurance refer to the ability of the upper and lower body to exert muscular force initially and continually over a prolonged period (Cooper Institute of Aerobic Research, 1999). As with a high percentage of body fat, low muscular strength and endurance cause many movements to become arduous and may possibly lead to the same outcome of sedentary lifestyle habits.

4. *Flexibility* is the movement of body joints through their functional range of motion. This relates to the elasticity of muscles, ligaments, and tendons (Rowland, 1999). Flexibility is important during physical activity participation because appropriate levels help to decrease injuries associated with body joints and thus decrease the chance of physical inactivity caused by such injuries.

Stewart and Kluwin (2001) challenged teachers of deaf students to recognize the importance of fitness goals in drawing up individualized education plans (IEPs): "Simply stated, physical fitness is too important to leave to chance alone. Teachers of the deaf need to be aware of this and insist that educational programming include full participation in a physical education program as well as assessment" (p. 159). They also called for teachers to use the IEP to take advantage of the educational and sociocultural benefits of PE and involvement in extracurricular activities such as sports and clubs. Although this may seem to be a radical notion, attending to the physical, educational, and sociocultural benefits of PE in a deaf child's IEP is not outside the range of responsibilities for teachers of deaf students. At the very least, fitness goals appropriate to an individual child should become a staple in IEPs.

Physical Fitness and the Deaf Child

Fitness is important to all children and for that matter all people. The social aspects of participating in activities that lead to greater fitness levels are also critical, especially for deaf children who often experience a narrow range of social experiences in their day-to-day lives when compared with their hearing peers. Still, the main reason for having PE classes is physical fitness, and when you look at how physical fitness affects people's lives, an argument for making fitness an integral part of an educational plan for all children is hard to dispute.

Why Physical Fitness Is Important for All Children

Health-related physical fitness plays an important role in the daily life of an individual, regardless of hearing status. The ability to perform everyday activities easily and without undue stress and fatigue, which thus promotes overall quality and enjoyment of life, is a major reason for the importance of physical fitness (Kohl & Hobbs, 1998; Pate, Baranowski, Dowda, & Trost, 1996; Wilmore & Costill, 1994). Participation in leisure activities within the exercise and recreational arena, such as walking, bicycling, and swimming, can be enjoyable for individuals who have attained appropriate fitness levels (Heyward, 1990).

Interaction and socialization with others in a physical activity and recreational setting is another benefit. Individuals who have appropriate fitness levels and are involved in sport and recreational activities participate in a setting where interaction with others is an important objective (Stucky-Ropp & DiLorenzo, 1993). Participation in physical activity promotes socialization and cooperation among participants, an experience that is very important for children (Ramsey & Rank, 1997). Successful interaction and socialization with others encourages participation in physical activity, increases self-worth, promotes socialization and teamwork skills, and generates friendships among participants (Stucky-Ropp & DiLorenzo, 1993).

Maintaining appropriate fitness levels increases one's overall quality of life, both physically and psychologically (Ford, Puckett, Blessing, & Tucker, 1989; Leith & Taylor, 1991). Children feel better about themselves and their abilities when they are more capable of performing even the most basic tasks without great effort (Fox, 1992; Martinsen & Stephens, 1994). Enhanced self-concept in children and an increased ability to cope with everyday stress and anxiety are also positive outcomes of physical fitness and activity participation (Faigenbaum, Zaichkowsky, Westcott, & Long, 1997; Harris, 1996; Salokum, 1994).

Finally, appropriate health-related physical fitness has the potential to decrease the risk of hypokinetic diseases and disabilities, a critical long-term benefit. Maintaining appropriate fitness levels and participating in regular physical activities reduces the risk and onset of diseases such as cardiovascular disease, diabetes, and bone and joint problems. This in itself is an important reason for all children to be introduced from a young age to participation in regular physical activities that lead to attainment and maintenance of appropriate physical fitness levels.

Why Physical Fitness Is Important for Deaf Children

Although physical fitness is important for deaf children for the same reasons as hearing children, there are some reasons specific to deafness as well. One of the most important mainstays of Deaf culture is Deaf sport (Stewart, 1991). Readiness for Deaf sport not only entails participation in sports and physical activities, but also being physically capable of participation by demonstrating appropriate physical fitness and motor performance levels. An individual who is not physically fit may be less likely to become involved in any form of physical activity (Francis, 1999), which reduces the chance of the deaf individual participating in Deaf sporting events.

Participation in Deaf sport can lead to enhanced pride and self-concept because of interactions that occur with others who share similar language and forms of communication and cultural experiences (Stewart, 1991). Deaf children need to learn about opportunities that they will have as adults for participation as athletes, coaches, officials, volunteers, and spectators in local through international levels of competition in Deaf sport events. This participation covers a variety of sports as well as types of involvement and is suitable for people of all ages. The authors, for example, have engaged in Deaf sport activities as athletes, coaches, sport directors, event organizers, story writers, researchers, and fans. Beyond the actual sporting event there is also a host of associated activities that may be formal, such as sports banquets and ceremonies, or they may be informal, such as when athletes and others get together to socialize after a practice or a game. Therefore, a deaf student who is not taught the benefits of participation in physical activities and subsequently the chances for participation in Deaf sport activities may miss out on critical socialization and interaction opportunities during their adult years.

Social status among peers is a great source of pride and self-worth (Williams & White, 1983). Increased pride and self-worth lead to positive feelings toward oneself and to one's belief that he or she can successfully attempt and accomplish things that that person may otherwise have avoided (Coakley, 1990; Williams & White, 1983). Participation in sporting events and attainment of physical fitness can lead to popularity among peers and improved personal appearance, both of which are important to school-age children (Chase & Dummer, 1992). For many individuals, acceptance and social status among peers extends into other settings, such as academics and other school-related activities, and involvement in physical fitness and activities tends to increase this acceptance among peers, both active and inactive (Coakley, 1990; Stewart, 2001).

Socialization and social status among peers are critical factors for deaf children, especially because of the barriers to communication that are present for deaf children in many settings. Barriers to communication can and do prevent deaf children from complete participation in many activities, mainly in school settings, and affect success in both learning and socialization (Stewart, 1991, 2001). Physical activity is a setting that typically offers a level playing field for deaf and hard of hearing individuals, where deaf children should not be at a disadvantage (Stewart, 1991).

Deaf children who are physically fit and active are likely to experience the same benefits as hearing children, including increased social status among their peers and feelings of pride and self-worth (Coakley, 1990; Stewart, 2001). Individuals with poor fitness, regardless of hearing status, are more susceptible to isolation from their peers. This leads to decreased socialization opportunities, a situation that could have a devastating effect on deaf children who already may have decreased socialization opportunities because of communication barriers (Coakley, 1990; Greenberg & Kusche, 1989).

From a sociological standpoint, it is important for deaf children to demonstrate an acceptable level of physical fitness and active habits so that they may reap the benefits of socialization and social status among their peers.

Physical Fitness Levels of Deaf Children

An important question that teachers of deaf students must consider with respect to PE is whether deaf children as a group are physically fit. An understanding of the fitness levels of deaf children will help teachers of deaf students accept the idea that PE is a critical part of a school's curriculum. Unfortunately, only a limited number of studies have investigated physical fitness and motor skill development of deaf children. Many earlier studies evaluating the physical fitness of deaf children focused on skill-related physical fitness rather than the more everyday health-related physical fitness components. Hence, few studies actually exist that focus on health-related physical fitness of deaf children.

Goodman and Hopper (1992) completed a review of studies evaluating the health-related physical fitness of deaf children. Of all the studies reviewed, only five evaluated health-related physical fitness, and the findings of these studies are discussed in this section. According to Goodman and Hopper, the results of these studies generally indicated that deaf children demonstrate lower physical fitness levels than their hearing peers.

This conclusion was evident in several studies. Pender and Patterson (1982) evaluated the fitness of 60 deaf and 60 hearing children aged 6–11 years. Hearing participants demonstrated significantly higher performance for measures of upper body strength and endurance, whereas deaf participants showed superior performance in the step test. The authors did mention, however, that although the deaf participants' performance was higher than the hearing participants, they had greater difficulties maintaining pace on the step test. It is impossible to determine if the performance by deaf children was a demonstration of their fitness or if other factors accounted for the differences, such as age (all older deaf students versus younger hearing students) or gender (males versus females).

Wiegersman and Van Der Velde (1983) evaluated the physical fitness levels of 25 hearing and 32 deaf children aged 6–8 years. The conclusions of this study indicated deficiencies in fitness by deaf children across all ages, except for flexibility, where negligible differences were found for the 8-year-old group. The authors postulated that the smaller gap in fitness seen with the 8-year-old group may have resulted from a greater number of activities offered through the residential school setting as compared to the nonresidential or public school setting.

Winnick and Short (1986) completed a large-scale study evaluating the physical fitness of deaf and hearing children with a sample of 686 hearing, 153 hard of hearing, and 892 deaf children aged 10–17 years. Individuals with hearing losses in the 27-dB to 90-dB range were classified as hard of hearing, and those with hearing losses exceeding 90 dB were classified as deaf. The results indicated that hearing children performed at higher levels on all fitness measures than the hard of hearing and deaf children. The difference between the hearing and nonhearing children in abdominal strength and endurance and flexibility was statistically significant. The deaf participants had a significantly higher percentage of body fat than both the hard of hearing and hearing participants.

Ellis (2001) completed a comprehensive fitness analysis of 73 deaf children aged 6–16 years and compared the results to the AAHPERD national standard norms (AAHPERD, 1984; Hastad & Lacy, 1998). Directions for the test were presented to the children using a combination of sign language and vocal communication. The results of this study indicated that this group of deaf children demonstrated physical fitness performances below the 40th percentile on national standard norms for all tests with the exception of flexibility. A number of results fell below the critical 20th percentile level, particularly cardiorespiratory endurance (M = 19th percentile) and percentage of body fat (M = 20th percentile), the two most important measures of health-related physical fitness. Performances on the abdominal strength and endurance (M = 33rd percentile) and upper body strength and endurance (M = 23rd percentile) were well below the 40th percentile. The results of this study would indicate that deaf children performed below the median on standard national norms for health-related physical fitness measures, with the exception of flexibility (M = 58th percentile). This information agrees with the literature that deaf children demonstrate below-average fitness levels when compared to norms formulated for hearing children.

Taking into account those studies that evaluated health-related physical fitness variables, the general consensus remains that deaf children, as a group, demonstrate lower fitness levels than their hearing peers.

Concerns in Measuring Deaf Children's Fitness

The majority of studies investigating physical fitness of deaf children have relative flaws in their research design. For example, many of the studies did not match hearing and deaf students by age, gender, height, or weight. Including these characteristics in an analysis would increase confidence in the results of the study. Most studies did not indicate how tests were administered or the communication modalities used when giving directions to the deaf participants, a critical aspect of ensuring understanding and accurate performance by the participants (Stewart, Dummer, & Haubenstricker, 1990). In addition, some critical demographic information such as school placement, age at onset of hearing loss, and classification method used for deafness were not included in several studies.

None of these studies can be compared across the years to updated studies because of differences in test administration, lack of replication information, and inadequate descriptions of the participant base. Moreover, the majority of these studies compared deaf children to hearing children and made the determination of physical fitness levels based on that comparison rather than investigating fitness relative to national fitness norms. Finally, only two of the five studies used tests that were validated for the subject group being evaluated. For example, Pender and Patterson (1982) used the Harvard Step Test on 120 children aged 6–11 years; however, this test has only been validated for use with college-age males. Finally, only Ellis (2001) evaluated all of the components of health-related physical fitness and compared the results to national fitness norms. It is difficult to gain a true picture of deaf children's physical fitness level based on one comprehensive study and several studies that used various testing instruments for the same fitness component and that did not compare results with standardized fitness norms. However, even considering the variability in fitness measures used in the studies, the outcome of each remained consistent: deaf children were found to perform lower on many of the physical fitness tests than their hearing peers.

These concerns regarding the assessment of deaf children's fitness make it imperative that teachers of deaf students attend to the following two guidelines when monitoring their deaf students' participation in a PE program:

- Request that their deaf students are assessed using national-based norms for physical fitness.
- Ensure that accommodations for assessment are available where necessary. Such accommodations include the use of a qualified interpreter and the provision of test administration procedures in a manner that will be comprehended by the student.

Physical Education Curriculum for Lifelong Health

Three major goals associated with PE and deaf children are the following:

1. Achieving physical fitness levels that are adequate for a healthy lifestyle.
2. Engaging in physical activities that will maintain or improve upon this level of fitness throughout their lives.
3. Acquiring knowledge for participating in physical activities within the Deaf community and, more generally, within society.

Despite the validity of these goals (Stewart & Kluwin, 2001), far too many individuals are stuck on the notion that PE is still "gym" and a period of time during the school day where students are playing and not learning. Implementing an exemplary curriculum requires the full support of school personnel and parents in making PE a valued academic discipline. It is difficult to tell parents of deaf children that three days a week of PE is as valuable as three extra hours of language development. Parents are more likely to lean toward educational planning that aims to narrow the gap in their deaf children's academic delay than to give PE programming equal footing with language, science, mathematics, and social studies in IEPs. Obviously if PE is to be valued then the attitude of school personnel and parents must reflect an appreciation of how participation in PE will improve the education and overall well-being of students. In conjunction with a change in attitude, a curriculum is needed that will ensure that a PE program is designed to achieve the aforementioned goals.

In general, exemplary PE programs will have three things in common:

- qualified PE specialists,
- curricula that aim to meet standards associated with helping students become physically educated individuals, and
- administration support.

When planning any curriculum, no matter the discipline, a thorough needs assessment must first be completed, followed by the organization of a PE program containing content that will meet the needs of all students.

The Needs Assessment

When forming a PE curriculum for any group of students, it is imperative to assess the physical needs of each individual prior to implementing programs. Students should be evaluated on measures of health-related and skill-related physical fitness. Health-related physical fitness is important for both everyday living activities and prolonged physical activity participation. Skill-related physical fitness is directly associated with patterns related to efficient and skilled movement and ultimately to an individual's willingness and ability to participate in sports and physical games. Individuals who are proficient in both types of fitness will be more physically active throughout their lives.

As described earlier, health-related physical fitness consists of cardiorespiratory endurance, body composition, muscular strength and endurance, and flexibility. There are a variety of test batteries available to evaluate health-related physical fitness of school-age children. However, one specific test battery, the FITNESSGRAM, has been modified and validated for use with deaf children (Dummer & Ellis, 2004). The FITNESSGRAM consists of the following tests, all of which can easily be conducted by a teacher of deaf students or any other teacher (Cooper Institute of Aerobic Research, 1999; Ellis, 2001):

- the PACER test—a 20-meter shuttle run of increasing pace, which measures cardiorespiratory endurance;
- skinfold measures—sum of skinfolds from 2 or 3 regions, usually tricep and calf locations, as a measure of body fat (component of body composition);
- curl-ups—"abdominal crunches" completed to a 3-second count as a measure of abdominal strength and endurance;
- push-ups—regulation push-ups completed to a 3-second count as a measure of upper body strength and endurance;
- trunk lift—measure of lower back flexibility; and
- sit-and-reach—measure of abdominal, thigh, and hip flexibility.

Three of the foregoing tests were modified for use with deaf children because of the test's original requirement of an auditory cue for initiating movement. The PACER consists of participants running a 20-meter shuttle course from one line to the other and leaving a line only after they have heard an auditory beep indicating for them to run. For deaf children, this test can be modified with a string of cable lights placed on the floor at each end of the 20-meter running area (Ellis, 2001). Lights can activate in accordance with the test's auditory cues, which would then cue the deaf participants when they should run. In the FITNESSGRAM test administration manual, curl-ups and push-ups are performed to a 3-second auditory count. Rather than using the auditory count, the tester could substitute hand signals to indicate up and down motions for both tests. None of the other tests required any modifications and can be administered as designed.

Skill-related physical fitness consists of those movements related to participation in various forms of games and activities. One aspect of skill-related physical fitness involves psychomotor skills from within the hierarchy of motor development, beginning with the most basic skills and moving to the most complex. The following demonstrates this hierarchy:

- Basic body management competence—Being able to move the body in simple motion while stationary. Bending and stretching are examples of this type of competence.
- Development of fundamental motor skills:
  o locomotor skills—running, hopping, skipping, jumping, leaping, sliding, walking, and galloping;
  o nonlocomotor skills—bouncing, swaying, bending, twisting, and shaking; and
  o manipulative skills—handling some kind of object with one or more body parts using hand-eye and foot-eye coordination.
- Acquisition of specialized motor skills—Learning skills that are more directly associated with participation in specific games and activities such as kicking a soccer ball while running, changing hands while dribbling a basketball, and moving to get into position and completing a backhand strike in tennis.
- Attainment of higher skill levels—Development of mature movement patterns and focus on specific sports or activities for lifetime participation.

PE classes are supposed to provide deaf students with opportunities to learn and practice these movements. They also provide specialized instruction and movement activities designed to help students learn movement patterns associated with many games and activities.

With information on a deaf student's health-related and skill-related physical fitness, the PE teacher can then design a program to meet the needs of this student. As we discuss later, the national PE standards provide guidance for designing such a program.

The Structure of a Physical Education Curriculum

Stewart and Ellis (1999) designed and implemented a PE curriculum at a school for the deaf that was based on the following standards:

Content standards were derived from the Michigan Exemplary Physical Education Curriculum (MI-EPEC), which defines a PE program on the basis of development in the following areas: body management skills; fundamental motor skills; physical fitness; games, sports, and dance skills; activity-related cognitive skills; and activity-related social skills. Instructional objectives for each content area were progressive and addressed not only individual performance levels but also their interests in participating in certain types of physical activities.

Performance standards were drawn up for each of the content areas and included "students' overall level of participation, following of gym rules, overall attitude and conduct, and to a lesser extent, their ability to perform certain activities" (Stewart & Ellis, 1999, p. 317). In addition, fitness levels and motor performance skills were measured at the beginning, middle, and end of the school year.

Opportunity-to-learn standards reflected the commitment of resources so that all students could participate in the PE program. These resources included the facilities and a variety of equipment associated with games, sports, fitness, and motor skill development as well as a commitment that PE be seen as a valued part of deaf students' overall educational plan.

It is interesting to note that the PE curriculum described by Stewart and Ellis (1999) succeeded for just a single year in a school for the deaf, during which time Ellis was the school's PE teacher. Her endorsement in PE and adapted PE enabled her to understand the PE curriculum requirements, select activities appropriate to the content standards, and monitor students' progress during the year. When Ellis left her teaching position, the teacher who replaced her did not have an endorsement in PE. Consequently, the PE curriculum that was designed for deaf children in this school was eventually disregarded and the school's PE program became unstructured with no attempt to assess fitness levels or motor skill performance. This development mirrors concerns in other subject matter areas where there is a call for teachers to teach only those subject areas in which they have content and pedagogical expertise.

The need for content area expertise in PE teachers becomes more apparent when one examines the requirements of national PE standards that are presently being espoused by national organizations such as the National Association for Sport and Physical Education (NASPE) and the National Council for Accreditation of Teacher Education (NCATE). These national standards focus on interpersonal skills, movement skills, and lifetime fitness through physical activity. The national standards aim for all students to accomplish the following goals:

1. demonstrate competency in various movement patterns and proficiency in a few movement patterns,
2. understand and apply movement principles and concepts to motor skill learning and development,
3. demonstrate a physically active lifestyle,
4. achieve and maintain an appropriate level of health-related physical fitness,
5. acknowledge and respect individual differences in the physical activity setting,

6. demonstrate understanding of and behaviors associated with responsible personal and social skills in the physical activity setting, and

7. understand that physical activity participation allows for opportunities for self-expression, platforms for social interaction, and enjoyment in a health-enhancing environment.

A qualified teacher with a certification in PE is needed to ensure that these goals are met. However, teachers of deaf students can use the IEP as a vehicle for insuring that their students receive the program necessary to help them accomplish each of the national goals.

The New PE

As this chapter draws to an end, it is noteworthy that the U.S. surgeon general has recommended that children participate in quality, daily PE programs in grades K–12 (NASPE, 1997; Schnirring, 1999). For the first time in many decades, the surgeon general and president of the United States have emphasized the importance of PE in educating children about healthy lifestyle habits. This new emphasis may be the result of a growing body of research that has found the following causes for alarm among the health and fitness levels of today's school children:

- More than 25% of school-age children are at risk for being overweight or obese, a number that has more than doubled during the past 30 years (NCHS, 2005).
- Close to 65% of children and teenagers have at least one risk factor for heart disease (CDC, 2004).
- For children aged 6–12 years, 40% of males and 70% of females could only do one pull-up, and 25% of males and 55% of females could not do any at all (Reiff et al., 1986).
- Inactive children tend to become inactive adults, which bodes poorly for the future health of the nation, given that more than 65% of adults are overweight or obese and only one in three exercise regularly (U.S. Department of Health and Human Services, 2004).
- Only one state requires daily physical education in grades K–12 (Burgeson, 2000; Simons-Muton, Eitel, & Small, 1999).

More and more PE professionals are turning to what is called the "New PE," a program designed to meet the NASPE standards of a physically educated person in a fun and educative way. The NASPE program relies on involvement in physical activities and direct instructions on the benefits of such involvement to encourage children to become physically active throughout their lives.

So, what is different about the New PE curriculum? First of all, it avoids repeating the unproductive and oftentimes self-esteem-deflating practices of traditional PE programs. Examples of some of the practices that are no longer acceptable are letting students opt out of PE for frivolous health claims; allowing students to select their own teams, which inevitably results in the same children being selected last again and again; using games that favor the highly skilled athlete; and eliminating playground-oriented games such as tag and duck, duck, goose that serve mainly to fill in time. Moreover, teachers are discouraged from announcing physical fitness test results in a manner that allows students to know their rank among their classmates. Although sports are still played in the New PE that are physically challenging and require certain skills to be developed, there is a greater focus on games and physical activities that can benefit all students across their life spans. Such activities include walking, wall/rock climbing, ultimate Frisbee, rollerblading, biking, karate, and dance, all of which are outside the realm of historically more traditional PE games and sports.

The New PE curriculum looks more like something out of an edition of *Outdoor Magazine* than *Sports Illustrated*. Activities selected aim to give every student a chance to find something of interest. Students must participate in one or more activities that will help increase and maintain their heart rates for a period of time. Examples of these types of activities range from jumping rope to mountain biking; vertical wall climbing to inline skating; dancing to white-water rafting. The goal is to introduce children to activities that they find enjoyable and can participate in through the years. Thus, the New PE emphasizes activities that are useful after the completion of formal schooling and ones in which all children experience success.

Modifying the New PE Curriculum for Deaf Children

Deaf children can participate in all of the same activities introduced within the New PE curriculum as their hearing peers. Giving directions or instructions for participation before beginning the activity may be the only modification needed. One of the advantages of the New PE curriculum is that it can incorporate any activity—there are no restrictions as long as the activity itself raises and maintains heart rates. Thus, PE instructors can take advantage of many Deaf sport events and those that are strong within the Deaf community, including intellectually stimulating activities, such as orienteering with its emphasis on teamwork and fast-paced fun. Moreover, many of the activities used in the New PE curriculum can overlap into other academic areas as seen with the following examples:

- Heart-rate monitors are used to ensure increased rate during an appropriate period of time—this concept involves the use of mathematics.
- Lessons on body composition involve understanding nutrition and scientific concepts of calorie usage.
- Understanding healthy hearts puts to work concepts associated with anatomy and physiology.
- Weight management involves not only understanding workload versus calorie use, but also nutritional and scientific concepts associated with burning fuel and the exercise time required to burn a certain number of calories.
- Fundamentals of games, especially those from foreign countries, such as orienteering, can be combined with historical information about game formation, culture, and countries where they originated.

An astute teacher of deaf students will recognize the opportunities to use the authentic experiences occurring in a PE class as a platform to teach skills relating to mathematics, literacy, social studies, and science. In fact, cross-subject matter teaching is a key component of an instructional approach designed to make learning more meaningful and accessible to deaf children (Stewart & Kluwin, 2001). For example, calculating how many calories you are consuming a day and how many calories are burned by your day's activities has a greater appeal to students learning mathematics than fictional word problems to which few students relate.

The New PE curriculum is designed to offer real-world opportunities to the students of all ages, opportunities that guide students to the type of future physical activities they can participate in long after completing their education. By giving deaf children the skills to make educated choices related to productive and healthy lifestyle habits, we are helping them become better able to enjoy such lifestyles. This is precisely what we want a PE curriculum to do: Engage deaf students in physical activities that lead to enjoyment of life and the maintenance of lifelong wellness. That is the goal that all teachers of deaf students must keep in mind when developing an education plan for their students.

Conclusion

There is no question about the importance of being physically fit and practicing a physically active and healthy lifestyle. Even with the U.S. surgeon general and numerous daily reminders through news programs, food nutritional information, and physicians battling the obesity epidemic reinforcing this importance, the numbers of overweight people as well as those battling hypokinetic diseases are increasing drastically with each passing year. This is occurring despite the fact that there are numerous opportunities for students of all ages to be active in the community.

PE offers a setting where students can be physically active during the day as well as a place where they can learn about healthy ways of living. Too often unhealthy lifestyles are not due to lack of opportunities to remain fit and healthy, but rather to a lack of knowledge and understanding of how to become and remain healthy. The New PE curriculum focuses on offering physical activity programs that are fun, develop positive attitudes, and promote health benefits. For deaf students, a PE program may also serve as a bridge to Deaf sport, leading to lifelong activity opportunities within the Deaf community. The role for teachers of deaf students is to use the IEP as a means for ensuring that the PE program is accountable for facilitating deaf students' fitness, motor skill development, and knowledge of lifelong opportunities for maintaining healthy and active lifestyles.

References

American Alliance of Health, Physical Education, Recreation, and Dance. (1984). *Technical manual: Health related physical fitness*. Reston, VA: Author.

Burgeson, C. R., Wechsler, H., Brener, N. D., Young, J. C., & Spain, C. G. (2001). Physical education and activity: Results from the School Health Policies and Programs Study 2000. *Journal of School Health*, 71(7), 279–293.

Centers for Disease Control. (2004). Prevalence of overweight among children and adolescents ages 6–19 years. National Center for Health Statistics. Retrieved March 4, 2004, from http://www.cdc.gov/nchs

Chase, M. A., & Dummer, G. M. (1992). The role of sports as a social status determinant for children. *Research Quarterly for Exercise and Sport*, 63(4), 418–424.

Coakley, J. J. (1990). *Sports in society: Issues and controversies.* St. Louis, MO: Mosby/Times Mirror.

Cooper Institute of Aerobic Research. (1999). *FITNESSGRAM test administration manual.* Champaign, IL: Human Kinetics.

Dummer, G. M., & Ellis, M. K. (2004). *Validation of the FITNESSGRAM for use with deaf children.* Manuscript submitted for publication.

Ellis, M. K. (2001). The influence of parents' hearing level and residential status on health-related physical fitness and community sports involvement of deaf children. *Palaestra*, 17(1), 44–49.

Faigenbaum, A., Zaichkowsky, L. D., Westcott, W. L., & Long, C. L. (1997). Psychological effects of strength training on children. *Journal of Sport Behavior*, 20(2), 164–175.

Ford, H. T., Puckett, J. R., Blessing, D. L., & Tucker, L. A. (1989). Effects of selected physical activities on health-related fitness and psychological well-being. *Psychological Reports*, 64(1), 203.

Fox, K. (1992). Physical education and development of self-esteem in children. In N. Armstrong (Ed.), *New directions in physical education II: Toward a national curriculum* (p. 3344). Champaign, IL: Human Kinetics.

Francis, K. T. (1999). Status of the year 2000 health goals for physical activity and fitness. *Physical Therapy*, 79(4), 405.

Goodman, J., & Hopper, C. (1992). Hearing impaired children and youth: A review of psychomotor behavior. *Adapted Physical Activity Quarterly*, 9, 214–236.

Greenberg, M., & Kusche. C. (1989). Cognitive, personal, and social development of deaf children and adolescents. In M. C. Wang, M. C. Reynolds, & H. J. Walberg (Eds.), *Handbook of special education: Research and practice* (pp. 95–129). Oxford, U.K.: Pergamon.

Harris, D. R. (Ed.). (1996). *Fitness and exercise sourcebook.* Detroit, MI: Omnigraphics.

Hastad, D. N., & Lacy, A. C. (1998). *Measurement and evaluation in physical education and exercise science.* Boston: Allyn and Bacon.

Heyward, V. J. (1990). *Advanced fitness assessment and exercise prescription.* Champaign, IL: Human Kinetics.

Kohl, H. W., & Hobbs, K. E. (1998). Development of physical activity behaviors among children and adolescents. *Pediatrics*, 101, 549–554.

Leith, M. L., & Taylor, A. H. (1991). Behavior modification and exercise adherence: A literature review. *Journal of Sport Behavior*, 15, 60–74.

Martinsen, E. W., & Stephens, T. (1994). Exercise and mental health in clinical and free-living populations. In R. K. Dishman (Ed.), *Advances in exercise adherence* (pp. 55–71). Champaign, IL: Human Kinetics.

National Association for Sport and Physical Education. (1997). *National Association for Sport and Physical Education: Shape of the nation*. Reston, VA: Author.

National Center for Health Statistics (2005). America's children. Key national indicators of well-being 2005. Retrieved July 20, 2005 from http://www.childstats.gov/pubs.asp

Pate, R. R., Baranowski, T., Dowda, M., & Trost, S. G. (1996). Tracking of physical activity in young children. *Medicine and Science in Sports and Exercise, 28*(1), 92–96.

Pender, R. H., & Patterson, P. E. (1982). A comparison of selected motor fitness items between congenitally deaf and hearing children. *The Journal for Special Educators, 18*(4), 71–75.

Public Health Service. (1990). *Healthy people 2000: National health promotion and disease prevention objectives* (DHHS Publication No. PHS 91-50212).Washington, DC: U.S. Department of Health and Human Services.

Ramsey, G., & Rank, B. (1997). Rethinking youth sport. *Parks and Recreation, 32*(12), 30–36.

Reiff, G. G., Dixon, W. R., Jacoby, D., Ye, G. X., Spain, C. G., & Hunsicker, P. A. (1986). The President's Council on Physical Fitness and Sports, 1985 national school population fitness survey (HHS, Office of the Assistant Secretary of Health, Research Project No. 282-84-0086). Ann Arbor: University of Michigan.

Rowland, T. W. (1999). One-mile run performance and cardiovascular fitness in children. *Archives in Pediatric and Adolescent Medicine, 153*(8), 845–849.

Rowland, T. W., & Freedson, P. S. (1994). Physical activity, fitness, and health in children: A close look. *Pediatrics, 93*, 669–672.

Sammann, P. (1998). *Active youth: Ideas for implementing CDC physical activity promotion guidelines.* Champaign, IL: Human Kinetics.

Salokum, S. O. (1994). Positive change in self-concept as a function of improved performance in sports. *Perceptual and Motor Skills, 78*(3), 752.

Schnirring, L. (1999). Can school PE make fitter kids? *The Physician and Sportsmedicine, 27*(13). Retrieved March 4, 2004, from http://www.physsortsmed.com/issues/1999/12_99/news.htm

Simons-Morton, B., Eitel, P., & Small, M. L. (1999). School physical education: Secondary analyses of the School Health Policies and Programs Study. *Journal of Health Education*, 30(5), 558–564.

Stewart, D. A. (1991). *Deaf sport: The impact of sports within the Deaf community.* Washington, DC: Gallaudet University Press.

Stewart, D. (2001, fall). The power of IDEA: Kling vs. Mentor School District. *Palaestra, 17*(4), 28–30, 32.

Stewart, D. A., Dummer, G. M., & Haubenstricker, J. L. (1990). Review of administration procedures used to assess the motor skills of deaf children and youth. *Adapted Physical Activity Quarterly, 7*(3), 231–239.

Stewart, D., & Ellis, K. (1999). Physical education for deaf students. *American Annals of the Deaf, 144*(4), 315–319.

Stewart, D., & Kluwin, T. (2001). *Teaching deaf and hard of hearing students: Content, strategies, and curriculum.* Boston: Allyn & Bacon.

Stucky-Ropp, R. C., & DiLorenzo, T. M. (1993). Determinants of exercise in children. *Preventive Medicine, 22*, 880–889.

U.S. Department of Health and Human Services. (2004). Health, U.S., 2004. Retrieved July 20, 2005, from http://www.cdc.gov/nchs/data/hus.htm

Wiegersman, P. H., & Van Der Velde, A. (1983). Motor development of deaf children. *Journal of Child Psychology, Psychiatry, and Allied Disciplines, 24*, 103–111.

Williams, J. M., & White, K. A. (1983). Adolescent status systems for males and females at three age levels. *Adolescence, 18*, 381–389.

Wilmore, J. H., & Costill, D. L. (1994). *Physiology of sport and exercise.* Champaign, IL: Human Kinetics.

Winnick, J. P., & Short, F. X. (1986). A comparison of the physical fitness of segregated and integrated hearing impaired adolescents. *Clinical Kinesiology, 42*(4), 104–109.

J O H N   L U C K N E R

Providing Itinerant Services

"For the times they are a-changin'"

—Bob Dylan

NOT LONG AGO, the majority of students who were deaf or hard of hearing were educated in specialized residential or day schools. Then, in 1975 the Education for All Handicapped Children Act was passed and a variety of educational options for children with hearing losses became available. Since then, the law has been reauthorized several times and renamed the Individuals With Disabilities Education Act (IDEA, 2004), and students who are deaf or hard of hearing have increasingly been educated alongside their chronological-age hearing peers.

The U.S. Department of Education (2002) estimates that on a national level, approximately 84% of students who are deaf or hard of hearing are served at least on a part-time basis in general education classrooms. Consequently, the majority of students who are deaf or hard of hearing currently receive special education services in their home school provided by an itinerant teacher who comes to the school for a designated period of time on a weekly basis (Moores, 2001). This trend is likely to stay consistent in the near future or increase for four specific reasons:

1. the implementation of universal newborn hearing screening programs, early intervention, and the related positive effects on the development of language skills (Yoshinaga-Itano, 2003),
2. the decrease in severe to profound deafness (Holden-Pitt & Diaz, 1998),
3. the continuing improvement in hearing aid technology (Johnson, Benson, & Seaton, 1997), and
4. the increase in the number of deaf children who receive cochlear implants (Easterbrooks, 2002).

Given the trends noted, it is anticipated that increasing numbers of preservice teachers of students who are deaf or hard of hearing will graduate from their teacher preparation program and be offered jobs as itinerant teachers. Accordingly, it is essential that they have

1. an awareness of how itinerant teaching differs from self-contained classrooms and the resource-room model of service delivery;

2. an understanding of the roles and responsibilities of itinerant teachers;
3. knowledge of specific actions they can take to work effectively with students, families, and educators; and
4. information about practical suggestions for effectively working as an itinerant teacher of students who are deaf or hard of hearing.

What Is Itinerant Teaching?

An itinerant teacher has been defined as a professional who provides instruction and consultation for students who are deaf or hard of hearing and most generally travels from school to school. However, professionals who have experience working as an itinerant teacher may better identify with one of the following definitions. An itinerant is a teacher who

1. has stains all over his or her clothes from driving with one hand and eating with the other and
2. knows the first names of more secretaries and custodians than the personnel director of the school district (Luckner & Miller, 1993).

Roles and Responsibilities of Itinerant Teachers

The itinerant model of service delivery differs from teaching in self-contained classrooms, resource rooms, or co-taught classrooms in a variety of ways. First, as previously noted, itinerant teachers travel from school to school to provide instruction to students who are deaf or hard of hearing as well as consultation with families and school personnel. As a consequence, itinerant teachers do not have their own classrooms to work in and therefore work with students in a variety of locations, such as the back of classrooms, speech therapy rooms, hallways, gymnasiums, libraries, closets, and lunchrooms. Also, the lack of classroom space causes itinerant teachers to use their cars as mobile offices, where the trunks and back seats are full of amplification equipment, teaching materials, and office supplies, which they carry in and out of schools. Second, itinerant teachers often spend equal amounts of time working with children and with adults. They provide direct instruction to students and spend almost equal blocks of time consulting and collaborating with educators and family members (Luckner & Howell, 2002). Third, in the course of a week, itinerant teachers often work with students ranging in ages from preschool to high school. Fourth, the caseload of itinerant teachers frequently includes students who use a variety of different communication modes (i.e., spoken English, American Sign Language, Signing Exact English, Cued Speech). Fifth, although itinerant teachers spend part of their time working with students on their individual education program (IEP) objectives, they also commonly spend time preteaching and reviewing content from the general education curriculum or working on lessons suggested by the general education teacher (Smith, 1997). Sixth, the very nature of itinerant teaching, that is, traveling between schools to provide services, creates a work schedule that provides a great deal of independence, minimal supervision, and limited opportunities to interact with other teachers of students who are deaf or hard of hearing (Yarger & Luckner, 1999).

Essential Knowledge and Skills for Itinerant Teachers

Recently, a group of veteran itinerant teachers were asked how they allocate their time while at work. They reported that 42% of their time was used for providing direct instruction to students who are deaf or hard of hearing, 18% was driving, 16% was consulting with educational personnel and families, 10% was used for planning, 4% was used for testing, 3% for staff development, and 1% was other activities (Luckner & Howell, 2002). As part of the same study, the teachers were asked what they thought was the most important aspect of their job. They reported that it was consulting with educational personnel and families. They explained that family members, general education teachers, and support staff (i.e., interpreters, note takers, paraprofessionals) spend significantly larger blocks of time interacting and working with the student with a hearing loss than they did. Because most general education teachers have limited training or experience in working with students who have a hearing loss, they rely on teachers of students who are deaf or hard of hearing to help them identify and implement ways to make curriculum and social interactions accessible, and assure assessment and grading are valid and reliable. Similar collaboration and consultation skills are necessary for deaf educators who work with families and young children who are deaf or hard of hearing (Calderon & Naidu, 2000; Pipp-Siegel & Biringen, 2000). Table 1 provides a list of the suggested coursework and experiences that veteran itinerant teachers reported as being essential for future itinerant teachers (Luckner & Howell, 2002).

Collaboration and Consultation With General Education Teachers, Interpreters, and Families

As previously stated, collaboration and consultation skills are essential for itinerant teachers. This is true for four reasons. First, approximately 90% of children who are deaf or hard of hearing have hearing parents (Moores, 2001). Because hearing loss is a low-incidence disability, most of these adults have never come in contact with a person who is deaf or hard of hearing. As a consequence, they have a limited understanding of what it is like to have a hearing loss or how to parent a child with a hearing loss. As such, they often rely on the teacher of students who are deaf or hard of hearing for support, to help them identify resources, and to help make decisions (Meadow-Orlans, Mertens, & Sass-Lehrer, 2003).

Second, for students who are deaf or hard of hearing to succeed in general education settings, specific adaptations in instruction, assessment, and social interactions that meet individual needs must be made (Luckner & Denzin, 1998; Nowell & Innes,

TABLE 1	
Suggested Areas of Coursework and Experiences Needed to Prepare Future Itinerant Teachers	
1.	Interpersonal skills.
2.	Student teaching experience as an itinerant.
3.	How to work with students who are deaf and have additional disabilities.
4.	Troubleshooting hearing aids and FM systems.
5.	Consultation models and methods.
6.	Organizational skills including scheduling and time management.
7.	Reading and language instruction.
8.	The general educational curriculum and educational standards.
9.	Working with students who are hard of hearing.
10.	Promoting social-emotional development.
11.	Working with non-English-speaking students and families.
12.	The law and the IEP process.
13.	Cochlear implants.
14.	Helping students understand their hearing loss and develop self-advocacy skills.

1997). Because most general education teachers have limited experience and knowledge about how to work with students who are deaf or hard of hearing, they rely on the teacher of students who are deaf or hard of hearing to help them make appropriate adaptations and modifications.

Third, general education teachers, interpreters, note takers, and family members spend significantly more time interacting with the student who is deaf or hard of hearing than the itinerant teacher does. For example, if an itinerant teacher works with a student for 2 hours a week, he or she will provide approximately 72 hours of direct service to the student during the course of a school year. Contrast this with the same student who is likely to spend approximately 900 hours with a general education teacher during the school year and 1,852 hours with a parent during the course of the year. Simple math suggests that the time spent collaborating and consulting with other adults may pay larger dividends over time than working in isolation with the student.

Fourth, the Individual With Disabilities Education Act mandates team decision making for assessment, placement, and transition planning processes.

Collaborative consultation involves a cooperative problem-solving relationship between two individuals who have somewhat different bodies of expertise. This approach values collegiality and seeks to build a network of mutual support while simultaneously opposing the perspective that one person is the expert. Collaboration and consultation offers a need-based, student-centered approach to support the development of students who are deaf or hard of hearing. The support can be focused on challenges that occur at home, in school, or in the community. The shared responsibility, expertise, and open communication among professionals and family members encourage everyone to work together for the benefit of the student. By fostering cooperative relationships, each team member functions as an equal and brings unique knowledge, skills, and perspectives to the problem at hand.

In view of the fact that few general education teachers understand the true effects of a hearing loss, one of the itinerant teacher's primary goals is trying to positively affect the attitude, knowledge, and skills of general education teachers about working with students who are deaf or hard of hearing. Figure 1 provides a six-step sequence that is often used during the process of collaboration and consultation. Of primary importance in this process is taking time to develop appropriate working relationships and to involve all team members in the identification of problems and generation of potential solutions. One way to help establish a relationship is to function actively as a resource person. In addition to providing information, materials, and equipment, itinerant teachers can (a) offer to team teach a unit, (b) ask the general education teacher if there are hearing students in the class who also would benefit from the additional review of content that is going to be provided for the student who is deaf or hard of hearing, (c) present a unit on the acoustics of sound or demonstrate how a hearing aid, frequency modulation (FM) system, or cochlear implant work, and (d) teach hearing students some functional sign language for a brief block of time weekly.

Figure 1
COLLABORATION AND CONSULTATION PROCESS

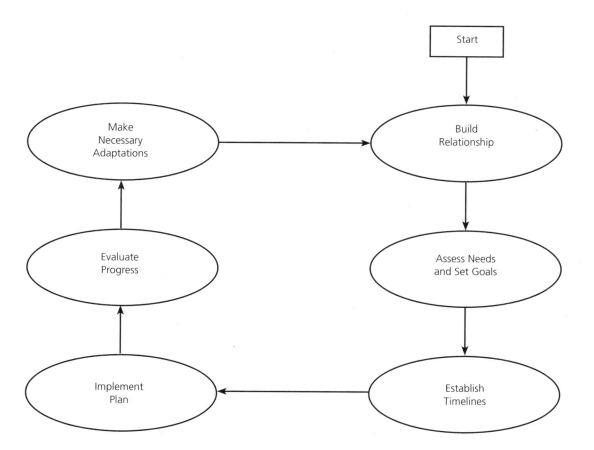

Table 2 contains a list of the 15 most important consultation and collaboration skills that teachers of deaf or hard of hearing students who work with general education teachers should possess. The list is presented in rank order of importance and reflects the opinions of a group of 631consulting teachers of students who are deaf or hard of hearing (Luckner, 1991). Examination of the list of competencies suggests that an important component of successful collaboration and consultation is communication between general education teachers, teachers of students who are deaf or hard of hearing, interpreters, and note takers. Ongoing interaction allows the teacher of deaf or hard of hearing students to form partnerships with the interpreters and note takers, to identify problems, and to provide assistance in planning and implementing adaptations that promote student success in the general education setting. Examples of assistance that may be provided are the demonstration of instructional techniques including visual teaching strategies; the discussion of specific academic, social, or behavior problems; assessment of the student's abilities and progress; the pre-teaching of specific vocabulary and concepts for upcoming lessons; and reviewing previously discussed material.

Given the demanding schedules of all teachers, it is beneficial to develop a communication system that allows professionals to exchange information about students on a regular basis. Checklists and short-answer progress forms can be used to augment the communication process among team members. The purpose of these forms is not to replace personal conferences among professionals but rather to speed up and enhance

Table 2	
Important Consultation Behaviors for Teachers of Students Who Are Deaf or Hard of Hearing	
1.	Remaining available throughout the academic year for support, modeling, and/or assistance in modifying the educational program for students who are deaf or hard of hearing.
2.	Possessing effective communication skills.
3.	Giving credit to general educational teachers for their ideas and accomplishments.
4.	Exhibiting an ability to be caring, respectful, empathic, and open in consultation interactions.
5.	Establishing a mutual trust with other individuals.
6.	Demonstrating a willingness to learn from others throughout the consultation process.
7.	Establishing and maintaining rapport with all people involved in the consultation process, in both formal and informal interactions.
8.	Functioning as a "resource link" between general educational teachers and other individuals and agencies.
9.	Facilitating progress in consultation situations by managing personal stress, maintaining calm in times of crisis, and remaining flexible and resilient.
10.	Resolving conflicts with others in a constructive manner.
11.	Meeting informally with general educational teachers to discuss deaf or hard of hearing students' progress.
12.	Providing information on the academic, social, and emotional characteristics of students who are deaf or hard of hearing.
13.	Helping general educational teachers work with interpreters and/or note takers.
14.	Entering into equal working relationships with other individuals in the planning and development of programs for students who are deaf or hard of hearing.
15.	Demonstrating the use of materials and equipment used with students who are deaf or hard of hearing.

the communication process. Regular use of the form provides the teacher of students who are deaf or hard of hearing with an ongoing record of the student's progress in each general education classroom. In addition, it enables general education teachers and other staff members to inform the teacher of students who are deaf or hard of hearing when things are going well, when concerns or problems arise, and when specific topics need additional attention. Figure 2 is an example of a form that can be used to facilitate the communication process.

Itinerant teachers of students who are deaf or hard of hearing also should make time to observe students in the general education setting. Spending time in the general education classroom will help the teacher of students who are deaf or hard of hearing assess the student's ability to function in the environment as well as to collect data that can be used for providing positive feedback for all the teaching/learning/management procedures that are effective as well as for identifying elements that can be improved.

Figure 2
SAMPLE COMMUNICATION FORM

Teacher _____

Student _____

Date _____

Student Progress	Excellent	Good	Fair	Poor
Academic subjects				
Behavior				
Social skills				
Organization/study skills				
Independent work				
Homework				

Any Problems with:

Personal hearing aids/fm equipment/ cochlear implant?	yes	no
Interpreter services?	yes	no
Note-taker services?	yes	no

Upcoming Assignments and Topics of Study

Reading: book title/pages _____

Math: pages and/or important concepts _____

Science: pages and/or important concepts _____

Social studies: pages and/or important concepts _____

Language arts: pages and/or important concepts _____

Spelling words: pages or attach list _____

Are there future tests, quizzes, reports, or projects that the student will need additional help with? If yes, what and when?

Would you like to set up a face-to-face conference?	yes	no
Would you like to set up a phone conference?	yes	no

There are a variety of elements within the classroom environment that affect the degree of academic and social success attained by students who are deaf or hard of hearing. Factors within the classroom environment that potentially increase or hinder learning that should be examined along with specific questions to help guide the evaluation process are presented in Table 3.

Table 3	
QUESTIONS TO GUIDE OBSERVATION OF STUDENTS WHO ARE DEAF OR HARD OF HEARING IN GENERAL EDUCATIONAL SETTINGS	
A. Student Behavior and Participation	
1.	Does the student attend to classroom instruction?
2.	What percentage of time is the student on-task?
3.	Is the student able to understand and follow directions?
4.	Does the student ask questions when he or she does not understand?
5.	Does the student seek assistance appropriately?
6.	Is the student able to follow the speaker(s) during classroom discussions?
7.	Does the student raise his or her hand to answer questions, volunteer additional information, or volunteer for classroom activities and responsibilities?
8.	Can the student work independently?
9.	Does the student know how to use an educational interpreter?
10.	Would/does the student benefit from the services of a note taker?
B. The Teacher's Classroom Style	
1.	Is the student encouraged to participate in discussions or answer questions?
2.	Does the teacher periodically check for student comprehension?
3.	Does the teacher use visual teaching strategies and visual aids?
4.	Does the teacher modify his or her teaching to help students comprehend important concepts and vocabulary?
5.	Are the questions and responses of other students being repeating by the teacher or interpreter?
6.	Do the classroom teacher and educational interpreter work well together?
7.	Does the teacher provide appropriate wait time for student responses?
C. Student and Teacher Interactions	
1.	Is the student treated like he or she is a member of the class?
2.	Are there interactions between the student and the teacher?
3.	Are the expectations of the teacher appropriate?
4.	Is the teacher patient?
D. Student and Peer Interactions	
1.	How does the student and his or her peers communicate with each other?
2.	Does the student have friends?
3.	Are efforts made to help the student follow social conversations?
4.	Is there an effort on the part of the teacher to help the student become accepted by his or her peers?

E. Level, Location, and Source of Speech and Noise Sources	
1.	What are the major noise sources in the room? Can some of them be eliminated?
2.	Is the student sitting next to a fan, air conditioner, overhead projector, film projector, heater, or an open window or the door (hallway noise) that could cause distractions?
3.	What type of acoustics does the classroom have? Do they reflect or absorb sound?
F. The Use of an FM Auditory Trainer	
1.	Does the student benefit from an FM auditory trainer?
2.	Do the teacher and the student know how to use the unit properly?
3.	Does the student inform the teacher when something is wrong or if the teacher is using the unit incorrectly?
4.	Is the unit being checked daily to make sure that it is in working order?

Providing Direct Service

Many students who are deaf or hard of hearing have the ability to make academic progress in content areas of the curriculum, but they require additional support to complete the learning tasks successfully. That support can come in a variety of forms. One practical approach for working with students who are deaf or hard of hearing is the use of a pre- and post-teaching sequence to supplement daily lessons and help make the content accessible (Luckner & Muir, 2001). Pre-teaching essential vocabulary and concepts assists students in establishing the knowledge base needed to understand new information. Post-teaching can be used to review key concepts, clarify misconceptions, organize information, and expand the students' knowledge of content or skills emphasized during the lesson (Conway, 1990). As noted earlier, for pre- and post-teaching to be effective, there needs to be ongoing communication between the general education teacher and the itinerant teacher.

In addition to supporting the learning of content from the general education classroom, itinerant teachers are often responsible for addressing additional IEP goals such as increasing expressive language skills, improving reading and writing skills, developing social skills, improving mathematical problem-solving abilities, and fostering career exploration and transition planning. When working directly with students there are several factors to keep in mind (Mastropieri & Scruggs, 2000; Rosenshine, 1986). They include

Structure—Teachers should (a) secure students' attention, (b) briefly review previous learning, (c) communicate to students the overall organization and purpose of the lesson, (d) introduce new material in small steps, (e) emphasize the critical points of the lesson by providing examples and non-examples, (f) provide opportunities for practice, and (g) summarize what has been learned near the end of a lesson.

Enthusiasm—Students learn more and appreciate the content more when teachers are enthusiastic.

Engagement—Teachers can keep students involved by selecting materials that are motivating, interesting, and at the correct level of difficulty for students and by careful implementation of questioning, guided practice, and independent practice.

Accommodations and Modifications

As previously noted, a major obstacle to the provision of appropriate services for students who are deaf or hard of hearing in general education classrooms is the simple fact that most general education teachers do not feel that they are adequately prepared to educate students who are deaf or hard of hearing (Chorost, 1988; Martin, Bernstein, Daly & Cody, 1988). Research consistently indicates that education of students with any type of disability in the general education classroom is most effective when the general education teacher is able to make accommodations in instruction and assessment to meet students' individual needs (Algozzine & Maheady, 1986). A variety of reasonable accommodations for instruction and assessment currently exist. The choice of accommodations will depend on the needs of the individual student as well as the instructional style of the teacher. Usually, teachers will want to choose accommodations based on three guidelines: (a) those that are most likely to positively affect the student, (b) those that require the least time and effort on the part of the teacher, and (c) those that the general education teacher feels comfortable with. In regard to the second point, in spite of the fact that making adaptations often requires some additional work for teachers, they should not demand so much time and effort that they interfere with teaching other students. A more involved adaptation should be tried only if needed. In regard to the third point, each of us is more likely to implement an approach successfully if we believe in it. A list of potential adaptations for students who are deaf or hard of hearing in general education settings is provided in Table 4.

Promoting Self-Determination and Teaching Students Self-Advocacy Skills

To succeed in school, employment, and community life, individuals need to develop the ability to define goals for themselves as well as to take the initiative to achieve the goals. This set of knowledge and skills is generally referred to as self-determination (Ward, 1988). Individuals who are self-determined play an active role in creating their lives and assume responsibility for initiating action to achieve what they desire and for responding to events in a manner that is consistent with their goals (Field & Hoffman, 1996). Thus, for individuals to be self-determined, they must know what they want, understand their strengths and limitations, and view themselves as being able to take control of their lives so that they can assume adult roles.

Acquiring the attitudes and abilities associated with self-determination is a developmental process that begins in early childhood and continues throughout adult life. Students who have not been provided opportunities to make choices, experience the consequences of their behavior, or instruction in the area of self-determination in the

Table 4

MENU OF POSSIBLE ADAPTATIONS FOR STUDENTS WHO ARE DEAF OR HARD OF HEARING

Environmental

Seat student in best place to permit attendance and participation.

Use a swivel chair on casters.

Set up a semicircular seating arrangement.

Reduce noise and reverberation by carpeting, draperies, acoustic ceiling tile, and acoustical wall treatments.

Input

Use a frequency modulated (FM) system, an induction loop system, an infrared system, or a sound-field system.

Stand where the student can speechread.

Face the student when talking.

Use an overhead projector.

Employ an educational interpreter.

Team teach with a teacher of students who are deaf or hard of hearing.

Pre-teach important vocabulary and concepts.

Provide a study guide of the key concepts, questions, and course requirements when introducing new material.

Provide a copy of the teacher's notes.

Provide an outline of the key concepts when introducing new material.

Highlight key words or concepts in printed material.

Provide a list of key vocabulary or concepts for new material.

Supplement lesson with visual materials (i.e., real objects, pictures, photographs, charts, videos).

Use graphic organizers to present material.

Provide manipulatives for multisensory, hands-on instruction or activities.

Use peer tutoring.

Use a note taker.

Use cooperative learning experiences.

Develop learning centers.

Use games for drill and practice.

Use concise statements or simplified vocabulary.

Use a "buddy system" whereby another student restates the directions or helps the student who is deaf or hard of hearing stay on task.

Cue student visually to indicate that someone is talking during class discussions or during intercom messages.

Repeat information that has been expressed by a person out of view or delivered over the intercom.

Write short summaries of the lesson or of the chapters of the textbook.

Use a peer tutor, paraprofessional, or volunteer to review work, important concepts, vocabulary, and facts with student.

Use commercial software to provide practice and review material.

Use captioned movies and television programs.

Divide and organize lengthy directions into multiple steps.

Demonstrate directions to clarify what needs to be undertaken.

Break long-range projects into short-term assignments.

Input (continued)

Post the date on the board when assignments and projects are due. Remind frequently.

Increase the number of practice examples of a rule, concept, or strategy prior to assigning seatwork or homework.

Shorten length of assignments.

Teach organizational skills and assist student to generalize these skills.

Teach student reading comprehension strategies (i.e., PARS, RAP).

Provide duplicate sets of materials for family use and review.

Have student summarize at the end of the lesson.

Use thematic instruction to unify curriculum.

Output

Allow more time to complete assignments.

Allow students to make models, role play, develop skits, and create art projects to demonstrate their understanding of the information.

Allow written or drawn responses to serve as an alternative to oral presentations.

Allow student to use computers or word processors.

Use cooperative learning experiences to develop cooperative small group projects.

Provide some self-pacing activities (i.e., matching cards for math facts).

Use peer tutor, paraprofessional, or volunteer to work with student on task.

Social

Teach hearing students to sign.

Make books about hearing loss and deafness available.

Invite Deaf adults to come to school and share stories.

Implement a circle of friends program.

Structure activities and experiences for deaf and hearing students to work together.

Teach a unit on specific topics (i.e., friendship, avoiding fights, emotions, stealing, dating, dealing with divorce).

Provide direct instruction on specific social skills (i.e., starting conversations, giving compliments, responding to criticism).

Behavioral

Provide consistent expectations and consequences with regard to classroom routines and rules.

Use interest inventories to identify positive and negative reinforcements for each individual.

Use assignment books and/or folders to increase organizational and memory skills.

Provide regular feedback and check progress often.

Home-school contracts: develop a contract with student's family whereby when specific behaviors are demonstrated in school, the student receives a specified reinforcement at home.

Send a daily report card home.

Use corrective feedback. ("I would like you to take out a book and read when you finish your work, rather than bothering the person sitting next to you.")

Increase frequency of descriptive praise. ("You really paid attention and stayed in your seat for the past 15 minutes.")

Use behavioral contract (written agreement between teacher and student regarding student behavior and agreed-upon consequences).

Behavioral (continued)
Use response cost procedures (taking away a privilege, points, or reward)
Use time out.
Limit the number of distractions by establishing isolated work/study area.

Evaluation
Use peer tutor, paraprofessional, or volunteer to work with student to review for test.
Allow test items to be signed to the student and the student to respond in sign.
Allow tests to be taken with teacher of students who are deaf or paraprofessional.
Provide extra time to complete tests, quizzes.
Allow test items to be read to the student.
Provide additional explanation of test questions and instructions.
Provide a study guide with important vocabulary or facts needed for tests and quizzes.
Allow student to use notes, study guide, or textbook on tests.
Evaluate daily work and participation in addition to tests.
Use projects or portfolios in lieu of tests.
Provide graphic cues (i.e., arrows, stop signs) on answer forms.
Modify tests to match student abilities (i.e., matching, multiple-choice questions, true/false questions, short answer questions, as compared to essay questions).
Modify vocabulary used in test items to match student abilities.
Modify the number of test items.
Provide short tests on a more frequent basis.
Chart progress or lack of progress.
Teach test-taking skills.

GRADING
Use IEP as the criteria for grade.
Develop contract as basis for grade.
Use a pass/fail system.
Write descriptive comments and give examples regarding student performance.
Use a checklist of competencies associated with the course and evaluate according to mastery of the competencies.

Adapted from Luckner & Denzin (1998).

early childhood and elementary years will experience greater difficulty taking control of their lives and assuming the role of successful adults in our society (Field, Martin, Miller, Ward & Wehmeyer, 1998). The role of the itinerant teacher of students who are deaf or hard of hearing is to provide students who are deaf or hard of hearing opportunities to gain the knowledge, skills, and experiences that will help them assert their individuality and achieve their goals. Concomitantly, itinerant teachers should consult with families and educators about the importance of helping students become more self-determined. One specific activity that itinerant teachers can initiate is having students plan and facilitate their IEP meeting. Additional examples of content related to self-determination that can be integrated into students IEPs include

1. decision making/ problem solving;
2. setting goals, short term and long term;
3. taking risks;
4. assertive communication;
5. self-evaluation skills;
6. improving study habits;
7. preparing for and taking tests;
8. developing and fostering friendships;
9. getting around the community;
10. Deaf studies;
11. career awareness; and
12. postsecondary education options.

Closely aligned with self-determination is the construct of self-advocacy. Self-advocacy refers to an individual's ability to identify the supports needed to succeed and to communicate that information effectively to others, including teachers and employers (Friend & Bursuck, 2002). The development of self-advocacy skills allows students to become actively involved in identifying and meeting their educational, social-emotional, and career goals. Students who possess effective self-advocacy skills are aware of their strengths and weaknesses and the potential effects of these strengths and weaknesses on their performance. In addition, they are able to identify the support that they will need to succeed and have developed the appropriate communication skills to express their needs in a positive and assertive manner.

Helping students to become more self-aware and also providing them with information and training that will allow them to self-advocate is important if we want students to make successful transitions in life (Luckner, 2002). Examples of skills in the area of self-advocacy that can be integrated in students' IEPs during their elementary and secondary programs include

1. recognizing when he or she needs help;
2. knowing when and how to request help;
3. expressing needs effectively;
4. conflict resolution;
5. knowing appropriate accommodations and modifications;
6. actively participating in setting, establishing, and discussing IEP and transition goals;
7. understanding legal rights while in school, postsecondary education, or work;
8. meeting with medical personnel and asking relevant questions; and
9. identifying and accessing local, state, regional, and national resources.

Practical Suggestions for Itinerant Teachers

Itinerant teaching requires professionals to travel to different schools to work with students and to interact with a wide variety of school personnel. Accordingly, itinerant teachers are required to individualize their service delivery strategy depending upon the students they work with as well as the general education teachers, interpreters, note takers, administrators, and families they encounter. This variety of students and adults makes the job exciting as well as challenging. To successfully address the challenges, itinerant teachers need to be flexible and have an assortment of tools to draw from. Following are some practical suggestions that can be added to the itinerant teacher's box of tools (Bullard, 2003; Luckner & Miller, 1993; Smith, 1997).

- The building principal is usually the individual who establishes the climate of the school. At the beginning of the year make an appointment with the principal to discuss the needs of the student with a hearing loss, your role, and special arrangements you may need. On a regular basis, stop in and visit with the principal to provide him or her with an update and the progress being made. If the principal is generally unavailable, an occasional quick note may suffice.
- Offer to provide staff development to the teachers, paraprofessionals, and to the parent group.
- Try to have a mailbox at every site and let secretaries, teachers, interpreters, and administrators know it is there.
- The first meeting with general education teachers is critical. It should be friendly, informative, and brief.
- Have a custom ear mold made. The district audiologist or a hearing aid dealer can do this. The personal ear mold allows itinerant teachers to listen to students' hearing aids or auditory training units and narrow down possible problems.
- Develop handouts and a list of websites for general education teachers, interpreters, note takers, administrators, and families on hearing loss and on ways to adapt instruction to meet the needs of students who are deaf or hard of hearing.
- Have business cards printed and get in the habit of leaving them with people.
- Become skilled at using word-processing programs and make form letters for everything. Adapt the letters in accordance with your needs.
- Hide an extra key on the car and keep an atlas handy in case of possible detours.
- Continually update the phone list of students, families, resources, and school personnel.
- Establish a system whereby someone from the school is responsible to contact the itinerant teacher when students on his or her caseload are ill or a special activity is planned during regularly scheduled time.
- Make time to engage teachers, administrators, and school personnel in conversations on a personal level. Praise and positively reinforce teachers, administrators, and other staff who work with students who are deaf or hard of hearing whenever possible.
- Develop a cassette or compact disk (CD) book library for long drives. Make use of the local library; they have a growing number of valuable cassettes and CDs.
- Use insulated bags to pack creative, healthy lunches for the car. Eating at fast food restaurants isn't good for the pocketbook or waistline.

- Often, the itinerant teachers' car is their office and faculty room. A car with four doors and a locking trunk is beneficial. Additionally, an AAA policy and adherence to regular maintenance checks and oil changes is essential. Worst-case scenario equipment for the car include a gallon of water, blankets, a small shovel, flares, high-energy snacks, a pair of slacks and sneakers, an umbrella, and a poncho for rainy days.
- Help get students involved in extracurricular programs that exist in school and the community. Find out about and inform families about beneficial summer programs.
- Develop and keep updated a list of resources, such as agencies, service clubs, volunteers, and organizations in the community that can be shared with families and other educators.
- Make time to meet regularly with other itinerant teachers.
- When possible, consider the following points when developing a schedule: (a) Schedule secondary students before elementary students. Secondary schedules are more rigid than elementary. (b) Avoid scheduling once a week students on Mondays or Fridays (holidays). (c) Try to see students during times when making up work they may miss will not be a major problem.
- Put together a color-coded notebook on each student to help organize information.
- Make use of the district's e-mail and voice mail system so that regular communication can be maintained.
- Remind supervisors that driving time is not preparation time.
- Keep a portable tape recorder in the car for recording notes.
- Provide a copy of your schedule to each teacher and to each school secretary so that they know when you are available at the school and where you are at other times during the week.
- Cloth totebags and plastic crates or containers are useful for organizing materials that cannot be left on site.
- When transporting computer software, keep it in a cooler so it won't become damaged in very hot or cold weather.

Summary

The majority of students who are deaf or hard of hearing currently attend school with their hearing peers. Many of these students receive special education services from an itinerant teacher of students who are deaf or hard of hearing. A variety of trends suggest that this approach to service delivery is likely to continue in the near future.

In this chapter the differences between itinerant teaching and teaching in a self-contained setting or resource room were presented. Roles, responsibilities, and important competencies for working as an itinerant teacher were delineated. The importance of collaborating and consulting with educators and families was highlighted and guidelines for providing direct instruction to students were offered. A menu of accommodations and modifications was provided, and the importance of helping students who are deaf or hard of hearing develop the skills to be self-determined and able to self-advocate was emphasized. Finally, a list of practical suggestions was provided to help address the unique aspects of itinerant teaching.

In closing, it is vital to accentuate the point that the population of children and youth who are deaf or hard of hearing is composed of a very diverse group of individuals. Although education of students who are deaf or hard of hearing in general education settings can provide them with wonderful opportunities for friendships, intellectual challenges, positive self-esteem, and the appropriate attitude, knowledge, and skills to succeed in postsecondary and/or career endeavors, it is also important to understand that there may be negative consequences that occur as a result of placing students who are deaf or hard of hearing in general education classrooms where they do not succeed. Lack of academic progress and/or friendships may lead to isolation, frustration, ridicule, and a compromised life.

As professionals responsible for providing direct instruction to students as well as consultation and collaboration with educators and family members, we must also monitor and evaluate students' progress, share data with the other team members, and advocate for a quality educational program for each student and his or her family. What is appropriate and beneficial for one student may be inappropriate and harmful for another student. The diverse needs and aspirations of the population of students who are deaf or hard of hearing suggests they are best served in a variety of settings, including the opportunity to receive quality services in general education settings. At the same time, forcing students and families to place students who are deaf or hard of hearing in general education classrooms without appropriate services is wrong and likely to be harmful.

As we look to the future, it grows increasingly clear that the challenge for itinerant teachers, as well as all service providers, is to continue to refine our ability to deliver quality services to students regardless of where those services are provided. Simultaneously, we need to work with families and students to make well-informed decisions about what they want and need and then collaborate with team members to build and deliver programs that help students achieve their greatest potential.

References

Algozzine, B., & Maheady, L. (1986). When all else fails, teach. *Exceptional Children, 52,* 487–488.

Bullard, C. (2003). *The itinerant teacher's handbook.* Hillsboro, OR: Butte Publications.

Calderon, R., & Naidu, S. (2000). Further support for the benefits of early identification and intervention for children with hearing loss. *The Volta Review, 100*(5), 53–84.

Chorost, S. (1988). The hearing-impaired child in the mainstream: A survey of the attitudes of regular classroom teachers. *The Volta Review, 90*(1), 7–12.

Conway, L. (1990). Hearing-impaired children in the mainstream. In M. Ross (Ed.), *Issues related to classroom management* (pp. 131–157). Parkton: York Press.

Easterbrooks, S. R. (2002). Annotated bibliography of cochlear implant research and publications, *Communication Disorders Quarterly, 24*(1), 31–34.

Field, S., & Hoffman, A. (1996). *Steps to self-determination: A curriculum to help adolescents learn to achieve their goals.* Austin, TX: PRO-ED.

Field, S., Martin, J., Miller, R., Ward, M., & Wehmeyer, M. (1998). *A practical guide for teaching self-determination.* Reston, VA: The Council for Exceptional Children.

Friend, M., & Bursuck, W. D. (2002). *Including students with special needs: A practical guide for classroom teachers* (3rd ed.). Boston: Allyn and Bacon.

Holden-Pitt, L., & Diaz, J. A. (1998). Thirty years of the annual survey of deaf and hard-of-hearing children & youth: A glance over the decades. *American Annals of the Deaf, 143*(2), 72–76.

Johnson, C. D., Benson, P. V., & Seaton, J. B. (1997). *Educational audiology handbook.* San Diego: Singular Publishing Group.

Luckner, J. L. (1991). Consultation skills for teachers of students with hearing impairments. *The Volta Review, 93*(7), 311–322.

Luckner, J. L. (2002). *Facilitating the transition of students who are deaf or hard of hearing.* Austin, TX: PRO-ED.

Luckner, J. L. (2004). Building general education environments that maximize students success." In R. Rittenhouse (Ed.), *Deaf education at the dawn of the 21st century: Old challenges, new directions* (pp. 105–149). Hillsboro, OR: Butte Publications.

Luckner, J., & Denzin, P. (1998). In the mainstream: Adaptations for students who are deaf or hard of hearing. *Perspectives in Education and Deafness, 17*(1), 8–11.

Luckner, J., & Howell, J. (2002). Suggestions for preparing itinerant teachers: A qualitative analysis. *American Annals of the Deaf, 147*(3), 54–61.

Luckner, J., & Miller, K. J. (1993). On the road: Meeting the challenge of itinerant teaching. *Perspectives on Education and Deafness, 11*(4), 16–18.

Luckner, J. L., & Muir, S. (2001). Successful students who are deaf in general education settings. *American Annals of the Deaf, 146*(5), 450–461.

Martin, F. N., Bernstein, M. E., Daly, J. A., & Cody, J. P. (1988). Classroom teachers' knowledge of hearing disorders and attitudes about mainstreaming hard-of-hearing children. *Language, Speech, and Hearing Services in Schools, 19*, 83–95.

Mastropieri, M., & Scruggs, T. (2000). *The inclusive classroom: Strategies for effective instruction.* Upper Saddle River, NJ: Merrill.

Meadow-Orlans, K. P., Mertens, D. M., & Sass-Lehrer, M. A. (2003). *Parents and their deaf children: The early years.* Washington, DC: Gallaudet University Press.

Moores, D. F. (2001). *Educating the deaf: Psychology, principles, and practices* (5th ed.). Boston: Houghton Mifflin Company.

Nowell, R., & Innes, J. (1997). *Educating children who are deaf or hard of hearing: Inclusion.* (ERIC Document Reproduction Service No. ED 414 675)

Pipp-Siegel, S., & Biringen, A. (2000). Assessing the quality of relationships between parents and children: The emotional availability scales. *The Volta Review, 100*(5), 237–249.

Rosenshine, B. V. (1986). Synthesis of research on explicit teaching. *Educational Leadership, 43*(7), 60–69.

Smith, M. D. (1997). *The art of itinerant teaching for teachers of the deaf & hard of hearing.* Hillsboro, OR: Butte Publications.

U.S. Department of Education. (2002). *To assure the free appropriate public education of all children with disabilities: Twenty-fourth annual report to Congress on the implementation of the individuals with disabilities act.* Washington, DC: Author.

Ward, M. J. (1998). *The many facets of self-determination.* (Transition Summary 5, pp. 2–3). National Information Center for Children and Youth with Handicaps. Washington, DC: Office of Special Education Programs of the U.S. Department of Education.

Yarger, C. C., & Luckner, J. L. (1999). Itinerant teaching: The inside story. *American Annals of the Deaf, 144*(4), 309–314.

Yoshinaga-Itano, C. (2003). From screening to early identification and intervention: Discovering predictors of successful outcomes for children with significant hearing loss. *Journal of Deaf Studies and Deaf Education, 8*(1), 11–30.

Websites Valuable to Itinerant Teachers

gri.gallaudet.edu/~catraxle/ACADEMIC.html#consider
The Gallaudet University Research Institute's review of assessment instruments traditionally used with students who are deaf or hard of hearing to assess academic, readiness, and language skills.

caid.org/CAID-swim.html
Council of American Instructors of the Deaf Success Within the Mainstream special interest group.

www.nclid.unco.edu
Home page of the National Center on Low-Incidence Disabilities.

www.hearinglossweb.com
Hearing Loss Web provides information on events, issues, medical topics, resources, and technology related to hearing loss.

www.shhh.org
Self Help for Hard of Hearing (SHHH) is an organization for people with hearing loss that provides information, education, advocacy, and support.

www.nichy.org
Home page of the National Dissemination Center for Children with Disabilities.

center.uncg.edu
Home page for the Collaborative Early Intervention National Training e-Resource for professionals serving families with infants and toddlers who are deaf or hard of hearing.

CLAUDINE STORBECK

LUCAS MAGONGWA

Teaching About Deaf Culture

CULTURE PERVADES OUR EVERYDAY LIFE: everything we do, say, and experience. It is an integral part of who we are and yet something much neglected within the current educational system. In preparing to work with deaf and hard of hearing students, we believe it essential for professionals to reflect on the effects that culture has on the school curriculum and to reflect on the necessity of becoming aware of and gaining insight into the personal culture and paradigms of the self as educator. We hope to lead the reader to an understanding that becoming truly inclusive and multicultural within deaf education means first introducing a rich Deaf cultural studies program into the curriculum and second infusing Deaf culture content throughout the curriculum and the school culture itself.

We use a multicultural framework (Banks, 1994) because the Deaf community—despite a shared Deaf identity based on shared experiences—is enormously diverse (Padden & Humphries, 1988, p. 4). To effectively meet the needs of our Deaf learners, we argue that schools for deaf students need be responsive to the multicultural needs of the Deaf community. For schools to become culturally inclusive, a host of changes needs to occur, such as "changes in the curriculum; the teaching materials; teaching and learning styles; the attitudes, perceptions, and behaviours of teachers and administrators; and in the goals, norms, and culture of the school" (Banks, 1994, p. 4). At the same time, however, schools need to assist communities, families, and the individual learners they serve to become more inclusive of cultural diversity in order to ensure a sustainable Deaf cultural studies program.

Why Deaf Cultural Studies

Deaf cultural studies, the study of Deaf people, their way of life, and their history, among other things, can be seen as part of a specific area of study, which Banks (2003) refers to as ethnic or cultural studies (including women's studies and Chicano stud-

A special word of thanks to Tom Humphries, coauthor of *Inside Deaf Culture* and *Deaf in America: Voices From a Culture*, and Barbara Gerner de Garcia, a leader in the field of multicultural issues and deafness, for their valuable comments and input on earlier drafts of this chapter.

ies, to name a few). Deaf and hard of hearing learners, regardless of their academic placement—residential/day school, self-contained class, or resource room—have a right and a need to know their Deaf heritage. We argue that this is a right because deaf students rarely have opportunities to understand themselves as a linguistic and cultural group, which is seen as crucial in their development of identity. Additionally we propose that deaf and hard of hearing learners also have a need to develop an understanding of their Deaf culture and how it relates to their home culture (and thus the language) of their family, which in the large percentage of cases is the hearing community. This in turn is a necessity for a growing understanding of themselves as part of a broader diverse community (nationally and globally), which will lead to the development of Deaf education as inclusive and multicultural. To this end, we propose that deaf and hard of hearing children be exposed to a rich and diverse Deaf cultural studies curriculum to prepare them effectively to take their rightful place in society. In this chapter we discuss the components of such a curriculum and their implications within the various educational settings.

The aim of this chapter is not to teach about Deaf culture (this topic is well-documented by experts in the field of Deaf culture such as Padden, Humphries, Ladd, and Bahan, to name but a few), but to discuss how and why it should infuse the total school curriculum. Additionally our aim is for the reader to gain deeper insight into the cultural and identity development of deaf and hard of hearing learners because it is an essential aspect of effectively serving the needs of deaf learners. However, as Welch (2000, p. 4) has expressed, "while attention to the importance of Deaf Culture (its history, values, and commitments) is crucial in preparing teachers who will work with Deaf students, uniform definitions which exclude or seek to downplay issues of race, ethnicity, gender, class, and sexual orientation provide these same teachers with only a partial understanding of that culture." Therefore, we discuss Deaf culture as an integrated holistic school subject, as well as challenge the status quo in terms of current curricula. Many of the examples we use will be African. African society, like American society, is multicultural and multilingual. However, we believe that the international universal perspective we bring to the chapter is applicable to both the U.S. and international Deaf education communities.

Before we discuss the proposed Deaf cultural studies curriculum, it is essential first to have a shared understanding of deafness, culture, and community. Let us begin with a question: If you were to ask a hearing friend to stop for a moment and consider how he or she would define "deafness," the large majority of people would define it as a hearing loss and a related inability to communicate and speak effectively. If, however, we were to ask Deaf and hard of hearing people to define deafness, they would most often refer to deafness in terms of their way of life: their culture, their communication, and their community. In short, Deaf people do not view themselves as disabled; rather, they identify themselves as being part of a linguistic and cultural minority group, the Deaf community. In addition to their Deaf identity, Deaf people often also refer to the home culture into which they were born, for example, Xhosa or Jewish culture, which will be reflected in the additional language and community groups with which they may identify. It is thus evident that cultural identity is complex and each individual has more than one cultural reference point. We thus acknowledge that when discussing the needs of deaf and hard of hearing learners, multiple perspectives exist and need to be addressed.

The Notion of Community

The notion of community is one that we all use every day, and yet it is quite difficult to define because it is used in various ways. Social scientists, for example, refer to towns and cities as communities, but they have also referred to prisons, religious groups, and corporations as communities (Higgins, 1987). Other terms that are often used are *the international community* or *the business community* (Thornton & Ramphele, 1988). If one considers the latter two examples and tries to answer the following questions, one begins to see just how complex the notion of community really is. For example, when people refer to "the business community," do they mean small businesses or large corporations? When they refer to "the international community," are you and I, as individuals, part of "the international community" or are only countries or their leaders part of this community (Storbeck & Morgans, 2001)?

One use of "community" is to refer to a group that shares a set of characteristics; for example, some people talk about the "white community" or "the black community." In this case they are using the term "community" as a euphemism for "race," because they prefer not to talk about race. Others talk about communities in terms of language or religion: the "Portuguese community," the "Zulu community," or the "Jewish community." Once again the complexity of the issue becomes evident when we ask the question, is there only one Zulu or Jewish community? Do we not need to distinguish between, for example, a poor Zulu community living in rural KwaZulu-Natal (South Africa) and a wealthier group of IsiZulu speakers who live in Johannesburg, speak many languages, and send their children to private schools? Do these two groups of people belong to the same Zulu community?

Another understanding of "community" is that of people who live close together. A community center would be one such example, because it can be used by people who live close to it, no matter what language they speak or what religion or race they are. Thus, some IsiZulu-speaking people and some Jewish people might consider themselves to be part of the same community if they live near each other, send their children to the same schools, and share similar interests. Perhaps a school can be considered to be a community, which exists as part of other, larger communities. One might consider oneself to be part of a community of "teachers of deaf and hard of hearing students," whether one is deaf or hearing, black or white, Sesotho, or French- or English-speaking. When considering these questions, one realizes that one characteristic may not suffice to define a community.

To discuss the "Deaf community," it is important to develop some shared ways of discussing the concept of community. One way to define a community would be that it is a group of people in social interaction who share one or more commonalities. The commonalities could be shared experiences, shared goals, shared language, and identification with one another. These commonalities then usually lead to and strengthen participation in the social activities of the group (Storbeck & Morgans, 2001).

Communities thus develop because of common ties leading to "more or less intense social interaction among their members, which inevitably produce social boundaries defining them and giving them identity" (Thornton & Ramphele, 1988, p. 38). No matter what the binding factors are, Thornton and Ramphele argue that communities have the following characteristics in common:

- The boundaries of communities are symbolic and exist by virtue of people's belief in them.
- Communities are dynamic and are always in a constant state of flux, even when they are apparently very stable.
- Community is the unpredictable product of history and of people. It is not the same thing as the category created by government or statisticians for reasons of their own.

An additional set of important facts that is often lost in discussions of communities is that members of a community do not always agree with each other, that communities interact with each other, and that people often move freely among communities. Thus, communities are social organizations created and believed in by people that provide them with a sense of belonging and identity. When referring to the Deaf community we need to recognize that the Deaf person's sense of belonging gives reality to the concept of a Deaf community and subsequently the development of the deaf child's identity cannot be separated from the acknowledgement of the Deaf community.

The Deaf Community

The Deaf community can be defined as a group of Deaf and hard of hearing people who have shared goals and have identified responsibilities to one another. Like any community, for example, the Sesotho or French community, the Deaf community is bound by its unique language (sign language) and has a unique culture, and membership of the community is regulated by a set of boundaries (Thornton & Ramphele, 1988).

Membership is thus not achieved through birth or right but is ascribed once a set of unnamed criteria is met, which are in themselves often in a state of flux. Researchers have discussed various criteria in relation to the Deaf community: Baker-Shenk and Cokely (1980) identify four criteria (audiological, linguistic, social, and political) and Schein (1989) identifies five components as defining factors in determining the Deaf community: demography, alienation, affiliation, education, and milieu. Schein highlights two central forces at play in creating this Deaf community: the centrifugal force pushing Deaf and hard of hearing people away from the hearing majority (through alienation and discrimination) and the centripetal force pulling Deaf and hard of hearing people toward each other because of their shared experiences and affiliation with each other. Finally, the Deaf community may include people who are themselves not deaf but who actively support the goals of the Deaf community and work with (rather than for) Deaf people (Padden & Humphries, 1988, p. 92).

A shared community leads to a shared way of thinking about and doing things. We call this the development of a culture and the subsequent development of a Deaf identity.

The Notion of "Culture"

As with the notion of community, the notion of culture is complex and difficult to define, and it holds different meanings for different people. For some people, culture is an overarching concept that distinguishes humans from animals (Geertz, 1993). In this sense, culture is what goes beyond nature to make us human. Thus, a cultural product or form can be anything that is made by humans, both practical and impractical, for example, buildings, music, language, mathematics, ideas, clothes, beliefs, and so forth. Geertz's definition of culture is as follows:

> Culture is the pattern of meanings embodied in symbolic forms, including actions, utterances and meaningful objects of various kinds, by virtue of which individuals communicate with one another and share their experiences, conceptions and beliefs.

In other words, a key aspect of culture for Geertz is that culture enables people to make meaning of their experience, both individually and collaboratively. We can say that culture is a way of enabling us to make sense of our worlds, through language, ideas, beliefs, and ways of thinking.

For Thornton (1988, p. 24) culture is a resource on which we draw to be able to live in and make sense of the world: "culture is the information which humans are not born with but which they need in order to interact with each other in social life" and it is learned "during the long process of education, socialisation, maturing, and growing old." In comparing culture with other resources such as energy, sunlight, food, and air, Thornton argues that it is both similar and different. Unlike other resources, culture can never be "used up," but can only "grow, change or even disappear in use; it is people who create cultural resources and control access to them." Like other resources, culture "cannot belong exclusively to any particular individual or group of individuals" because "all groups and individuals must have access to at least some of these resources to survive." At the same time, "although culture is an essential resource, this does not mean that all people have equal access to all of culture, or even access to all of the cultural resources that they might need and desire" (Thornton, 1988).

The speakers of a particular language may form an ethnic group whose "culture" (i.e., resources for and ways of making sense of the world) goes beyond their language. Their ways of making meaning may be similar to or different from the resources of speakers of other languages. Some people want to talk of "South African culture" or "African culture" to denote the shared ways of making sense that South Africans and Africans may have. Still others talk of "youth culture" or "gay culture," denoting the ways in which young people or gay people make sense of the world. The notions of community and culture are not always positive: they can be used in destructive ways, for example, as they were under apartheid in South Africa (and in other countries where oppression is still rife today).

The key concept here is that culture is not static and is not bound by time and place. Culture is dynamic, interactive, and changeable by the very people who are necessary for its transmission (Storbeck & Morgans, 2001). Culture can be seen as a way of keeping communities together or creating the boundaries and the social cohesion through the meanings that it enables or inhibits. Furthermore, culture is the imagining and re-imagining of communities that people put into place as a continual and dynamic process, which is why communities are continually formed and transformed.

What Is Deaf Culture?

We now turn to the idea of Deaf culture and ask the question, what is Deaf culture? A simple answer would be the ways in which Deaf people make sense of their experience and the resources that they draw on to do this. However, the more we learn about Deaf people, Deaf communities, and the implications of deafness within individual contexts, the more we realize that to answer this question is a very complex task. Part of the complexity of answering this question lies in what Ladd called "the plurality of deafness" (Ladd, 2003, p. 406), which we will address in the next section.

To date, proponents of Deaf culture have identified it as a linguistic minority culture within the larger community (Woodward, 1989; Padden & Humphries, 1988; Higgins, 1987). This argument comes out of the historical context of asserting Deaf people as whole people with ways of understanding and making sense of the world, of interacting and making meaning. This model is preferred to models of Deaf people as deficient, disabled, and lacking aspects of culture that other people have. Previously we have defined what it means to belong to the Deaf community, and we have shown how Deaf culture and the Deaf community are interlinked. We have argued that these are not static entities, but that they grow and change just as other communities and cultures do, and that people, both hearing and Deaf, migrate among cultural communities all the time (Thornton & Ramphele, 1988; Ladd, 2003).

Additionally Deaf history plays an important part in Deaf culture. It is transmitted mostly through an "oral tradition" (through sign language) from one generation of Deaf people to the next. Deaf people engage in storytelling, performances, and many other forms of cultural transmission through the medium of sign language. The stories they tell are part of Deaf literature, which is key to the identity and culture of Deaf people. These stories are the common lived experiences (most often of oppression and marginalization) shared by Deaf people the world over. This oppression and discrimination (based on auditory profile) is referred to as audism (Humphries, 1977; Gertz, 2004). This form of discrimination is one factor that leads to the strength and unity within the Deaf community. Despite these shared experiences even within the Deaf community, there are people who have been more or less oppressed in other aspects of their lives: for example, black Deaf people, especially in South Africa (but also in most white-majority countries); gay Deaf people; and Deaf women. Thus, to develop a Deaf culture curriculum that is fully empowering we need to recognize and understand how the Deaf community (and each unique individual) interacts with other communities, particularly when they have common membership.

Being Deaf in a Multicultural Society— The Plurality of Deaf Cultures

Despite the general assumption that deafness is the core identity of Deaf people, there are indeed "multiple selves" at play, which prompts questions about how these multiple selves (e.g., Deaf/Italian/white/Catholic/female) affect the life of the individual (Welch, 2000, p. 16). It is thus becoming more evident that members of the Deaf community are indeed far less homogeneous than initially acknowledged; yet, Deaf education curricula remain largely unresponsive to the multiple identities (and thus educational needs) of Deaf learners.

One example of an additional identity is membership in the black Deaf community: Dunn (1992) argues that black Deaf American youth often identify more with their black, hearing peers than with their white Deaf peers. However, Dively (1999, pp. 390–395) reports that although "Native Deaf individuals indicated that they were proud of who they were as Native Deaf people and proud of their Native heritage," many had difficulty participating in their native community's ceremonies and subsequently maintaining a native identity. For this reason Taylor (1997, p. 114) in her book *Buddhas in Disguise* states that "being deaf can overshadow the strict social barriers of ethnic identities" and that many ethnic families fear this estrangement from their children. Because of the failure of current Deaf studies curricula to consider that Deaf children simultaneously exist in the Deaf community and their families, this estrangement continues to occur. The inclusive curriculum will create the possibility that someone can be Deaf *and* another identity, as opposed to polarizing the identities. It is essential that this pride in and social importance of the plural identity and diverse heritages of Deaf children are acknowledged and reflected in the curriculum.

Despite major variables of identity such as race, ethnicity, and gender, Banks (1994, p. 88) reminds us that "individuals belong to these groups at the same time," that each of the variables "influences the behaviour of individuals," and that the variables seldom if ever work independently but rather simultaneously. Figure 1 is a depiction of this plurality of the Deaf identity. Any one of the variables can be "fronted" depending on the context in which the person moves (e.g., a Deaf woman would front her gender identity in a meeting with Deaf men but would probably front her linguistic and Deaf identity among a group of hearing colleagues). This plurality then meets in the center, the confluence of all the diverse cultures, thus forming the person's unique Deaf identity. This plurality of identity is further supported by Welch (2000, p. 19) when she proposes that "each participant in a classroom (both teachers and students) is a collage of social identities." This collage of social identities is often fluid and is sure to have one or two variables that are inevitably stronger than others (race and deafness, for example) within this synergy. Thus, despite the primary identity evident within the Deaf community (the Deaf identity), it is becoming more evident that

Figure 1
Plurality of the Deaf identity

Language identity

Gender identity

Racial identity

Ethnic identity

Religious identity

Physical identity

(Diagram adapted from Banks, 1994, p. 89; Baker-Schenk & Cokely, 1980; and McIlroy, 2004).

Deaf culture is affected by the plurality of an individual's cultures. For this reason it is crucial for the educator and practitioner in deafness to both recognize multiple identities and facilitate their development and maintenance.

When considering this plurality of Deaf identity, the question thus arises of whether Deaf culture as a curriculum subject is sufficient and how we can effectively empower Deaf learners to take their rightful places in society as confident individuals in whom the Deaf identity is just one of their "multiple selves."

In countries such as South Africa, Canada, and the United States, there is growing acknowledgment of the multiplicity of languages and cultures that surround our children. Thus, South African Deaf children born into a Zulu family will need to—if they are to take their rightful place in a South African Zulu society—know all about their Zulu heritage, history, way of life (including *lobola*, a special ceremony; rites of passage; and funeral and wedding ceremonies), as well as know (at least in part) the language IsiZulu.[1] At the same time the child will need to learn about deafness, Deaf

---

[1] *Lobola* is the gift (money or cattle) that the bridegroom gives the bride's family.

culture, and South African Sign Language, as well as acquire literacy in the majority language of English to become employable. Learning the language and understanding the culture of the general hearing community (which may overlap in part with the Zulu culture) is also essential in surviving in a hearing world.

This multicultural acceptance and understanding of diversity is essential, because intercultural differences and misunderstandings occur among the Deaf community and other communities. In the South African black community, for example, eye contact between a young child and an adult (initiated by the child) can be seen as a sign of lack of respect; similarly, facial expressions and use of hand movements and gestures in public can be seen as inappropriate in some communities. In the same way, a very religious family saying prayers or meditations may find the open eyes of a Deaf person disrespectful or the physical contact when getting attention—especially between boys and girls—inappropriate; however, if clarified, these diverse communities can make adjustments and compromises to ensure dual respect and acceptance. Although these problems would seem readily apparent, Deaf children and adults daily experience problems in situations such as these.

One example of a Deaf studies curriculum is the Kendall Curriculum Guide (Miller-Nomeland & Gillespie, 1993). It covers a broad range of topics from ASL to Deaf culture to issues of communication, identity, and social change. These are, however, all still focused on one single vision of the Deaf experience, and we suggest that these topics be enhanced with a more inclusive multicultural and multilingual approach.

The Deaf Studies Curriculum

When designing a Deaf studies curriculum in an inclusive multicultural way, much can be learned from experts in multicultural/multiethnic education. One such example would be Banks' framework for multicultural curriculum reform (1994, pp. 206–210). In this framework, Banks refers to four approaches to including cultural content into the curriculum: the contributions approach, the additive approach, the transformation approach, and the social action approach. He sees a gradual cumulative development from the first to the fourth level; however, he also acknowledges that the approaches can be mixed or blended, and it is this blended approach to curriculum reform that we propose. This blend can be implemented through both a separate course on Deaf cultural studies and fully integrating and infusing Deaf culture into the whole curriculum, thus creating a Deafcentric curriculum—including content, visual learning and teaching styles, and Deaf indigenous teaching and learning practices. Additionally, as discussed at the outset, the multicultural inclusive framework that recognizes and implements Deaf learners' plurality of identities needs to be at the core of the four levels of curriculum transformation as discussed in the following sections (Banks, 1994).

Contributions Approach

This approach can be an important first step in the child's creation of a Deaf consciousness, which "is necessary for anyone to become a full-fledged member and to participate in social change that benefits his/her own community" (Gertz, 2004, 183). Banks refers to this approach as the "heroes and holidays" approach, which for the Deaf community means exposing deaf students to key Deaf role models.

Science

Introduce learners to famous Deaf scientists such as Konstantin Tsiolkovsky, "the father of the space age" (Carroll & Mather, 1997, p. 132); John Goodricke, an astronomer; and Thomas Edison, inventor of the light bulb (for more, see Lang, 1996).

Social Sciences

Examples of Deaf leaders and politicians are Francis Humberstone Mackenzie (member of the British parliament in the late 18th century), Antonio Magarotto (founder of the World Federation of the Deaf), and Wilma Niewoudt Druchen (member of the South African parliament in 2002).

Extracurricular Activities (Sport, Art, Music, and Dance)

Deaf learners need to know that they can aspire to swim like Olympic silver medalist Terrence Parkin (from South Africa), paint like Juan Fernandez Ximenes de Navarette (from Spain), sculpt like Douglas Tilden, or get involved in the theatre like Bernard Bragg (both from the United States). Additionally, although deaf learners may not have a direct interest in music, they may be interested to know that the famous composer, Ludwig van Beethoven, was deaf.

These role models need to be both international and national (allowing deaf learners the opportunity to learn about the larger Deaf community and the Deaf community of their own country). The role models should be selected with cognizance of the multiple identities children bring to the learning environment; for example, in addition to those people presented as examples of Deaf role models, minority deaf children (such as Hispanic or black deaf children) need exposure to Deaf role models from similar backgrounds. Hairston and Smith (1983) confirm the necessity of exposing deaf children (and in particular minority deaf children) to effective role models when they state that "Black deaf children have never had the opportunity to talk with or meet Black deaf adults during their formative years. They undergo the challenge of having to get along in a hearing environment without the role models who can ease their adjustment, give them pride, encouragement, and offer a few tricks of the trade on 'getting through'" (p. 57).

Additive Approach

The second approach allows for culturally appropriate Deaf role models, texts, and issues to be included in the regular curriculum. In art and literature, examples of Deaf art, Deaf poetry, and other literature may be included, as well as poetic comparisons between oral and visual rhyming, for example. In history, for example, when discussing key events in history, Deaf history can and should be integrated (e.g., in South Africa after the first democratic elections in 1994, there was a powerful move within the Deaf community mirroring that of black South Africans' struggle for self-control and representation that led to the 1995 election of the first Deaf director of the national Deaf organization and the subsequent inclusion in the World Federation of the Deaf).

Another way to infuse the general curriculum with Deaf culture would be to include Deaf examples in mathematics and accounting problems. (For example, there are two TDDs and four more need to be purchased; how many will they have? How will the depreciation of the equipment affect the school budget?) Additionally, school plays and publications need to include appropriate adaptations such as flashing lights, the sign language alphabet, and so forth.

Transformation Approach

This approach is fundamentally different from the previous two in that it "is not the addition of a long list of ethnic groups, heroes and contributions, but the infusion of various perspectives, frames of reference, and content from various groups that will extend students' understandings of the nature, development and complexity of society" (Baker, 1994, 208). Some examples are the following:

- Various perspectives on key events in history or Deaf history can be included as part of the formal Deaf cultural studies curriculum, for example, discussing the effects of World War II on Deaf people or discussing the birth of the "great debate" and the perspectives of the various role players (hearing people, Deaf people, educators, parents, etc.).
- Discuss how various minority communities use art and literature to explore their struggle and use it as a form of protest (e.g., a film on audism developed by the Deaf studies department at Gallaudet University).

This approach is the first to directly challenge the dichotomous and hierarchical approach to cultures—us vs. them; our culture vs. their culture—and introduces learners to diverse perspectives and insights.

Social Action Approach

In addition to all of the elements in the transformation approach, this fourth approach to curriculum reform encourages learners to act upon their new-found knowledge. They are given a social problem, such as prejudice against Deaf people in the workplace or discrimination in schools, and are encouraged to engage critically with the problem, do research, "analyze their values and beliefs, synthesize their knowledge and values, and identify alternative courses of action, and finally decide what, if any, actions they will take" to address the issue concerned (Banks, 1994, p. 209). This would require Deaf students to identify areas of discrimination that they have faced (audism, Humphries, 1977; dysconcious audism, Gertz, 2004) and their subsequent effect on their education, employment, and so forth. Additionally the social action approach would require students to reflect on their beliefs and the values of the oppressive community, and identify a course of action to take. It is thus clear that in addition to merely giving information, the social action approach has as its goals "to teach students thinking and decision-making skills, to empower them, and to help them acquire a sense of political efficacy" (Banks, 1994, p. 209).

We propose that a Deaf cultural studies curriculum, in addition to being a separate curriculum with specific time and space, also be integrated in a holistic manner into the general curriculum and subsequently be woven into the daily school experience of the learners. Additionally, one of the biggest challenges with transforming the curriculum in this way is the integration of the subject into the total school culture through teachers (and principals and administrators) who both recognize and acknowledge the effects that their own belief systems have on the transformation process.

Issues in Pedagogy

To implement a truly transformative Deaf cultural studies curriculum in schools for deaf students (making use of all of the levels discussed previously), teachers need to know more than just Deaf culture and how to sign fluently. Teachers of this curriculum need to know and understand their values and beliefs as well as their prejudices, stereotypes, and misconceptions, because these "values and perspectives mediate and interact with what they teach and influence the way that messages are communicated and perceived by their students" (Banks, 1994, p. 159). When teachers present the curriculum, it is also essential for them to consider the "design of pedagogy to teach that knowledge" (Banks, 1997, p. 35) and to ensure that rather than perpetuating inequality and oppression (even if it is in favor of the previously marginalized), the goal is to allow the curriculum and the self (as educator) to become "agents of liberation and empowerment" (Banks, 1994, p. 160).

This will mean that in the class, the deaf students should learn how to "create voices, learn to hear their own voices and ... to compel others to listen" (Humphries, 1996, p. 353) and be challenged to listen to the diverse voices of others.

Conclusion

This chapter has given an overview of Deaf culture and what we believe to be essential in preparing deaf learners for adulthood. We have made reference to multilingualism and multiculturalism, not to sideline or question the validity of Deaf culture as an essential part of the curriculum but to enhance the curriculum into what we believe is an honest response to a diverse world.

This chapter acknowledges that there are those Deaf and hard of hearing people who choose not to be fervent activists in their efforts as Deaf people because often they would rather front their racial or linguistic culture (and identity). This point does not mean that they either reject or ignore their Deafness, but that only it is not the central feature of how they see themselves. The individual journey in search of identity needs to be accepted and encouraged.

Finally, we propose that the Deaf cultural studies program in schools not merely focus on the "teaching of facts, but on transforming students' own constructions and interpretations" (Ladd, 2003, p.425). To do this, teachers move beyond decisions of "what to teach" and grapple with issues of "how they teach" as well (Welch, 2000, p. 22).

Author's Note

This chapter is written from an inclusive multicultural perspective because both authors were born and raised in countries of great diversity. Lucas Magongwa is Deaf, was born in Mokopane in the Limpopo Province of South Africa, and is an African born from the Ndebele tribe that lives in the middle region of Limpopo. Lucas is a fluent user of six languages, which was particularly beneficial when he was appointed the first Deaf school principal in South Africa (in a multicultural school for deaf students). Claudine Storbeck is hearing, was born in Johannesburg, and is part of the English-speaking South African community. She initiated the first teacher training program for teachers of deaf students in South Africa and although she does not consider herself a South African Sign Language interpreter, her contribution to the interpreting profession is acknowledged by the South African Deaf community. Claudine is fully trilingual.

Both authors have extensive experience within the multicultural and multilingual deaf education context and have consulted and worked within the Deaf and hearing communities in deaf education—related fields during the past two decades. Lucas and Claudine have hosted international conferences on deaf education and, most important, they have both taught in schools for deaf students and thus know the challenges that teachers of deaf students face daily.

The authors are the coordinating team of the Centre for Deaf Studies and Deaf Education at the University of the Witwatersrand, Johannesburg, South Africa, where they embrace multilingualism and multiculturalism as they offer services to their diverse audience nationally and internationally.

References

Baker-Shenk, C., & Cokely, B. (1980). *American Sign Language: A teacher's resource text on grammar and culture.* Washington, DC: Gallaudet University Press.

Banks, J. A. (1994). *Multiethnic education: Theory and practice* (3rd ed.). Boston: Allyn and Bacon.

Banks, J. A. (1997). *Educating citizens in a multicultural society.* New York: Teachers College Press.

Banks, J. A. (2003). *Teaching strategies for ethnic studies* (7th ed.). Boston: Allyn & Bacon.

Bragg, L. (Ed.) (2001). *Deaf world: A historical reader and primary sourcebook.* New York: New York University Press.

Carroll, C., & Mather, S. M. (1997). *Movers and shakers: Deaf people who changed the world.* San Diego: DawnSignPress.

Dively, V. L. (1999). Contemporary native Deaf experience. In L. Bragg (Ed.), *Deaf world: A historical reader and primary sourcebook.* New York: New York University Press.

Dunn, L. (1992). Intellectual oppression of the black deaf child. In D. Garretson (Ed.), *Viewpoints on deafness: A deaf American monograph*, Vol. 42. Washington, DC: National Association of the Deaf.

Geertz, C. (1993). *The interpretation of cultures.* London: Fontana.

Gertz, G. (2004). Dysconscious audism: What is it? In *Deaf studies today: A kaleidoscope of knowledge, learning and understanding.* Conference Proceedings.

Hairston, E., & Smith, L. (1983). *Black and deaf in America.* Silver Spring, MD: TJ Publishers.

Higgins, P. C. (1987). The Deaf community. In P. C. Higgins & J. E. Nash (Eds.), *Understanding deafness socially.* Springfield, IL: Charles C. Thomas.

Humphries, T. (1977). *Communication across cultures (deaf/hearing) and language learning.* Unpublished doctoral dissertation, the Union Institute, Cincinnati, OH.

Ladd, P. (2003). *Understanding deaf culture: In search of deafhood.* Sydney: Multilingual Matters Ltd.

Lang, H. G. (1996). The deaf experience in the history of sciences. In R. Fischer & T. Vollhaber (Eds.), *Collage: Works on international deaf history.* Hamburg: Signum Press.

McIlroy, G. (2004). *An investigation of the impact of inclusive education on deaf identity.* Master's proposal, the University of the Witwatersrand, Johannesburg, South Africa.

Miller-Nomeland, M., & Gillespie, S. (1993). *Kendall Demonstration Elementary School: Deaf studies curriculum guide.* Washington, DC: Pre-College Programs, Gallaudet University.

Padden, C., & Humphries, T. (1988). *Deaf in America: Voices from a culture.* London: Harvard University Press.

Schein, J. (1989). *At home among strangers.* Washington, DC: Gallaudet University Press.

Storbeck, C., & Morgans, H. (2001). *Sign language for education: Theory and practice II.* B.ed. honors course module, School of Education, University of the Witwatersrand, Johannesburg, South Africa.

Taylor, I. (1997). *Buddhas in disguise: Deaf people of Nepal.* San Diego: DawnSignPress.

Thompson, J. B. (1990). *Ideology and modern culture: Critical social theory in the era of mass communication.* Cambridge: Polity.

Thornton, R. (1988) Culture: A contemporary definition. In E. Boonzaier & J. Sharp (Eds.), *South African keywords: The uses and abuses of political concepts.* Cape Town, South Africa: David Philip.

Thornton, R., & Ramphele, M. (1988). The quest for community. In E. Boonzaier & J. Sharp (Eds.), *South African keywords: The uses and abuses of political concepts.* Cape Town, South Africa: David Philip.

Welch, O. M. (2000). Building a multicultural curriculum: Issues and dilemmas. In. K. Christensen (Ed.), *Deaf plus: A multicultural perspective.*

Woodward, J. (1989). How you gonna get to heaven if you can't talk with Jesus? The educational establishment vs. the deaf community. In S. Wilcox (Ed.), *American deaf culture: An anthology.* Silver Spring, MD: Linstok Press.

T H O M A S   W.   J O N E S

J U L I E   K.   J O N E S

K A R E N   M.   E W I N G

Students With Multiple Disabilities

LEARNERS WITH MULTIPLE DISABILITIES present such significant challenges to educators that—at first glance—the prospect of designing curriculum for them could appear overwhelming. The task need not be daunting, however. Knowledge in four broad areas can guide the development of valid, cohesive, and effective curricula for students with multiple disabilities:

- a positive understanding of the challenges involved,
- valid assumptions about the students' abilities and instructional variables,
- inclusive approaches to curriculum design, and
- the scope and sequence of relevant curricular areas.

Challenges

Educators sometimes view disabilities and the resulting challenges as the most significant factor in designing curriculum and intervention for students with multiple disabilities. Curriculum content for students with multiple disabilities, however, rarely is determined by disability diagnoses, IQ, or test scores. Nevertheless, understanding the disability-related challenges involved in planning curriculum for this population can avoid pitfalls and lead to effective intervention. Several interrelated challenges are involved (Jones & Jones, 2003).

Multiplicity

Deaf students with multiple disabilities have the educational needs of deaf students plus the educational needs associated with one or more additional disabilities. In addition, the interaction of the disabilities creates educational needs that are not characteristic of any single disability. For example, a deaf student with mental retardation has learning needs that neither a typical curriculum for deaf students nor a typical curriculum for students with mental retardation would address (Jones, 1984).

Heterogeneity

Most schools in the United States today serve students with a wide range of ethnic backgrounds, learning styles, family support systems, and educational histories. Students with multiple disabilities bring to the educational setting not only all of these variables but also those associated with their combination of disabilities (Jones, 1984). As a consequence, effective curricula for students with multiple disabilities must be individualized and unique.

Low Incidence

Compared with single disabilities, the overall incidence of multiple disabilities is low. As a subcategory of students who are deaf or hard of hearing, the number of students with multiple disabilities is extremely small (Holden-Pitt & Diaz, 1998). Holden-Pitt and Diaz report approximately 7,000 deaf students with multiple disabilities, for example, compared with almost 3 million students with learning disabilities and 612,000 students with mental retardation (U.S. Department of Education, 2002). Consequently, few curriculum guides, professional materials, and training opportunities are available to teachers working with this population (Jones & Jones, 2003).

Diagnostic Delays

The diagnosis of second and third disabilities is often more difficult than diagnosing a single disability (Jure, Rapin, & Tuchman, 1991; Moeller, 1985), and parents and professionals often delay recognizing or accepting diagnoses of additional disabilities (Meadow-Orlans, Smith-Gray, & Dyssegaard, 1995; Schuyler & Rushmer, 1987). Consequently, appropriate intervention may be implemented too late to be effective. The result can be developmental delays that curriculum planning should address.

History of Failure

Each of these factors can postpone intervention or cause it to be ineffective. As a consequence, many students with multiple disabilities experience failure for a significant period of time (Jones & Jones, 2003). As part of the curriculum development process, educators should consider the potentially deleterious effects of failure experiences on skills, behavior, and self-esteem.

Assumptions

Assumptions about learners and their environments can guide curriculum development and ensure that the resulting courses of study are valid and meaningful. Similarly, certain positive assumptions about deaf students with multiple disabilities can make the curriculum design task for this complex population both manageable and effective. Each of the following has specific implications for the scope and sequence of an individualized curriculum and the selection of specific educational objectives for deaf students with multiple disabilities.

Every Child Can Learn

Although this assumption may seem self-evident, educators might not believe it when facing a student whose disabilities are multiple and severe (Ewing & Jones, 2003). Individuals with significant needs are capable of learning and learning well (Orelove & Sobsey, 1996). Educators who recognize this fact will ensure positive learning environments for each individual. The assumption that every child can learn implies that intervention and curriculum design should begin with the student rather than with predetermined content. It also indicates the need to consider nonacademic areas and to task-analyze objectives into small manageable steps.

Students With Multiple Disabilities Are Unique

The heterogeneity and low incidence of students with multiple disabilities, described previously as challenges for educating them, ensure that each has a unique combination of needs and abilities (Jones, 1984). This assumption implies that curriculum designed for these students should be individualized, with content, objectives, scope, and sequence tailored to each student.

Educational Outcomes Should Be Functional

Goals for students with multiple disabilities—like those for all students—should enable them to function as productively and independently as possible in the mainstream of society. This assumption requires that each student's curriculum be future oriented, practical, and meaningful (Carpenter, 1995).

Intervention Should Be Compensatory, Rather Than Remedial

Remedial curricula focus on correcting or ameliorating the child's disability—auditory training and physical therapy are familiar examples. In contrast, compensatory curricula emphasize utilizing the child's strengths to acquire skills that the disability would seem to prevent—a child who does not have functional language, for example, might be able to learn to use a picture menu to order in a restaurant.

Peer Acceptance and Social Relations Are Essential for All Students

The skills that most learners with multiple disabilities need most—linguistic skills and social skills—are best learned from peers. In addition, all children yearn for peer acceptance. Children who from an early age are included with peers of all ability levels gain invaluable linguistic and social skills that will affect their lives positively. Peer tutors, mentors, and models provide very powerful learning opportunities for children with multiple disabilities. A curriculum that emphasizes social skills will help the students succeed in the general school setting, as well as in the larger community and society, and prepare them for successful adulthood (Ewing & Jones, 2003).

The Transdisciplinary Model Prevents Fragmentation

Numerous service providers from different disciplines plan curriculum and other aspects of intervention for students with multiple disabilities and their families. In contrast to other team models, the transdisciplinary model has the most potential for coordinating and integrating this diverse expertise to plan intervention for complicated children with multiple disabilities (Orelove & Sobsey, 1996). Using a transdisciplinary model, curriculum planners share information and skills collaboratively across traditional disciplinary boundaries (Ewing & Jones, 2003).

Families Are Critical for Success

Just as many different professionals working in isolation do not optimally benefit the child, curriculum design for students with multiple disabilities is incomplete without the child's family. Families often know the child best, especially when communication issues occur. Family input helps define valid long-range goals, and the home environment provides fodder for functional curriculum goals and objectives (Ewing & Jones, 2003).

Approaches to Curriculum Design

Two common approaches to determining curriculum for students with multiple disabilities do not satisfy the assumptions described previously. In norm-based approaches, the child's overall developmental level, instructional level, or test performance typically leads to placement in a preexisting curriculum. In criterion-based approaches, the child's performance within a predetermined hierarchy of tasks is used to establish objectives for advancing the child's performance through the hierarchy. Although these approaches may have elements of individualization and functionality, they often result in curricula that are fragmented, meaningless, and ineffective.

As described previously, curriculum for deaf students with multiple disabilities should be individualized and functional, and its design should involve families and professionals in disciplines relevant to the child's needs. Three approaches, in particular, provide a method for determining educational objectives that are meaningful and appropriate, regardless of the student's age or functioning level: person-centered planning, ecological assessment, and adapting a general education curriculum.

Person-Centered Planning

Person-centered planning is a process that results in individualized programs that are designed to meet each student's unique needs (O'Brien & Lovett, 1992). It involves bringing together the child, the child's family and friends, and professionals involved with the child. Together, they participate in a series of meetings to learn as much as possible about the child and to plan for positive outcomes for the child. The process should capture in writing what is important both to and for the child. Likes and dislikes, routines, capacities, talents, hopes, fears, and desires for the child should be discussed. The outcome should be a plan for making the desires happen and commitment to implementing the plan. Several approaches to person-centered planning are available. These include (a) McGill Action Planning System (Forest & Pearpoint, 1992); (b) Individual Service Design (Forest & Pearpoint, 1992); (c) Essential Lifestyle Planning (Smull & Harrison, 1992); (d) Personal Futures Planning (Mount & Zwernik, 1988); (e) Whole Life Planning (Butterworth et al., 1993); and (f) Group Action Planning (Blue-Banning, Turnbull, & Pereira, 2000). Although each has slightly different ways of executing the process, all result in clear articulation of the each child's unique qualities and realistic and positive outcomes for the child. A person-centered plan crystallizes the goals and objectives for an appropriate individualized education plan. Because the plan includes implementation strategies, it ensures that the goals and objectives will be achieved.

Ecological Assessment

Unlike traditional approaches to determining curriculum, which focus on the child's performance levels, ecological assessment focuses on the environments in which the child exists.

The process yields individualized educational objectives that meet the assumptions described previously (Jones & Ross, 1998). Four broad steps are involved:

1. List the subenvironments in which the student is functioning. These typically include various areas of the school (e.g., classroom, hallway, cafeteria), home (e.g., family room, kitchen), and community (e.g., grocery store, doctor's office).
2. Inventory the activities that typically occur in each subenvironment (e.g., selecting food, paying, eating, socializing, etc., in the school cafeteria).
3. For each inventoried activity, list the skills typically needed to perform the activity (e.g., paying for food may require recognizing the amount due, selecting an appropriate amount to give the cashier, and pocketing the change).
4. Prioritize all of the inventoried skills across activities and subenvironments for the learner.

Only the first and fourth steps consider the learner for whom the curriculum is being designed. The second and third steps focus on what most people do in each subenvironment.

An educator—or a transdisciplinary team—who completes this process will have a long list of meaningful objectives. Prioritizing them for the assessed student ensures that the resulting curriculum is meaningful to the student and will lead to increased independence. The curriculum designer can group the objectives into domains, and instruction can proceed.

Adapting a General Education Curriculum

Teachers working with students with multiple disabilities often adapt curriculum to meet the needs of students with multiple disabilities. Strategies such as cooperative learning, demonstration, peer tutoring, and small-group instruction have enabled students with multiple disabilities to become successful members of inclusive classroom communities (Downing, 2000; Jones & Ross, 1998).

Although little or no research has been conducted on deaf students with multiple disabilities using the general curriculum, a parallel can be drawn from general special education literature (Ewing & Jones, 2003). Future research in this area is indicated. Special education research documents the advantages of the general education curriculum in inclusive settings for students with disabilities and their peers without disabilities. Benefits for students with disabilities include increased language and pronounced academic gains. Their peers demonstrate greater acceptance and understanding of peers with disabilities (Downing, Eichinger, & Williams, 1997). Similarly, Rafferty, Piscitelli, and Boettcher (2003) reported gains in language development and social acceptance. Freeman and Alkin (2000) found much higher academic performance for students with mental retardation in inclusive settings using the general curriculum compared to segregated special education classrooms following a special education curriculum.

Students with multiple disabilities have the right not only to access a general education curriculum but also to have that curriculum adapted to maximize their opportunities for learning. Planning for the student with multiple disabilities should begin before the curriculum is implemented to ensure that adaptations are effective. The preparation for adaptations should include a careful assessment of the individual student, with ecological assessment or person-centered planning as discussed previously. Only after the individual needs of the student are clear can educators identify the adaptations needed in the existing curriculum.

Numerous variables may be manipulated to individualize curriculum and instruction. The following curriculum components are examples:

1. *Materials for study.* Teachers can use textbook and other materials with levels of difficulty matched to the child's instructional level. In addition, rather than standard materials, they can choose from a wide array of materials, including those that provide an experiential knowledge base through literature, art, music, newspapers, journals, and magazines.
2. *Method of study.* Thematic instruction and cooperative learning are among the most effective strategies for diverse learning needs in small or large groups of students (Fuchs & Fuchs, 1997; Slavin, 1995).

3. *Pace of instruction*. Variations in pace may help accommodate the wide range of ability levels that result when students with multiple disabilities are included in the general education curriculum with their nondisabled peers. This may include slowing the pace of instruction for some students so that they can experience success in mastering portions of the curriculum. In contrast, some students with hyperactivity or attention disorders may benefit from an increased instructional pace (Munk & Repp, 1994).

4. *Learning focus*. Learning should identify and focus on shared values, attitudes, and the problem-solving process that are most relevant and interesting to all students, including those with disabilities.

5. *Instructional setting*. Teachers should not limit themselves to classroom instruction but should provide as many opportunities as possible for students to acquire skills in the community and other nonschool environments.

6. *Evaluation of learning*. To make learning more relevant for students, the curriculum should include structured evaluation and self-evaluation opportunities. Teachers can provide such learning experiences by using authentic assessment strategies (Grenot-Scheyer, Abernathy, Williamson, Jubala, & Coots, 1995).

Curriculum Content for Students With Multiple Disabilities

For a variety of reasons, many students with multiple disabilities have special educational needs that go beyond the scope and sequence of the general education curriculum. These include the areas of literacy and functional academics, communication and language, social and behavioral skills, motor skills, and life skills.

Literacy and Functional Academics

Literacy and other academic curricula can take many forms for deaf students with multiple disabilities. Some may able to complete the typical literacy and academic curricula offered to their peers without multiple disabilities. Others may need instructional or response modifications (e.g., using a switch-activated computer or a Braille writer) but no curricular modifications.

Other deaf children with multiple disabilities need literacy and academic curricula that support successful functioning in daily life activities. Developing such functional curricula begins with studying each child's personal plan—developed during person-centered planning meetings—to identify the child's current and future skill needs. Ecological assessments conducted to support each child's personal plan will also identify needs. Finally, comparing these needs against the general education curriculum available to the child will result in an individualized, functional curriculum that can address a child's needs as they interact and learn with other deaf children. *Choosing Options and Accommodations for Children* (COACH) (Giangreco, Cloninger, & Iverson, 1993) provides a process for addressing functional academic needs within general classroom settings that is adaptable to classrooms for deaf children with multiple disabilities.

The content for a functional literacy or language arts curriculum should address socialization, recreation, vocational, safety, and daily life skills needs. Such a curriculum could include areas such as reading and writing one's name and other personal information, reading and applying schedules, reading recipes and making shopping lists, reading for household tasks such as laundry, reading product warning labels or environmental signs, and reading menus (Browder & Snell, 2000; Ford et al., 1989; Westling & Fox, 2000).

A student's age, years remaining in school, functioning level, and student and family desires should be considered when developing a functional literacy or language arts curriculum (Browder & Snell, 2000; Westling & Fox, 2000). Instruction in reading a list of sight words from a science or social studies unit can enable the student to participate more meaningfully alongside peers. Learning to read favorite website names on the list of "bookmarks" permits students to return to these favorite sites while surfing the Internet, perhaps with friends. Mastering sight words from one of the standard lists (e.g., Dolch, 1948) might be appropriate for a younger child because the words on these lists are often useful in daily life activities, such as following recipes, using television listings, and checking weather information (Browder & Snell, 2000; Ford et al., 1989; Westling & Fox, 2000). Reading instruction should focus on comprehension, not simply word recitation, so that reading is meaningful. Embedding reading instruction within practical learning activities ensures such comprehension (Browder & Snell, 2000; Westling & Fox, 2000).

Pictures can be as important as reading words for many children with multiple disabilities. Picture menus can permit independent food selection in a restaurant. Reading product labels can permit independent shopping in the market. Daily life tasks, such as brushing teeth, doing laundry, or reading recipes, can be translated into a series of pictures or picture symbols to permit independence (Robertson, Gravel, Valcante, & Mauer, 1992). Reading pictures in magazines can be a very enjoyable recreational activity. Pictures can support a level of independent functioning that might not be possible if only written words were used.

Writing is also an important part of a functional academic curriculum for deaf children with multiple disabilities. Being able to write simple notes can support independence and socialization. If physical disabilities impede writing with pen or pencil, a computer and printer can be used. Words and phrases can be available via commercial or individually developed software so that spelling is unnecessary. Writing can also be accomplished with pictures and symbols. Product labels can be scanned, sized, and printed from a color printer to make shopping lists, for example. Magazine pictures or picture symbols can be grouped to write a story.

Functional mathematics also is an important part of functional academics. A functional mathematics curriculum would include counting and applying written numerals with quantity concepts, reading costs, making purchases, making basic calculations with or without calculators, telling time, applying basic time-management skills, and measuring (Browder & Snell, 2000; Westling, & Fox, 2000).

For younger children, functional social studies and science curricula can draw from general education curricula. Learning about one's family and community, for example, as well as about cultures of the various children in the class, will be meaningful for young deaf children with multiple disabilities as well as their peers. A functional social studies curriculum for older elementary, middle, and high school age children might include learning about making rules to govern how we live and work, or our local, state, and national leaders and how we elect them. Although not to the depth that their peers without disabilities might study these topics, the study will provide opportunities to interact and participate with these peers and can lead to gains in communication and social skills. For example, a functional science curriculum might focus on learning names (e.g., spider, beetle, bug, worm, earthworm, or body parts) or learning to associate dress with weather while the remainder of the class might be studying the unit in depth.

Communication and Language

The ultimate goal of a communication curriculum is to provide learners with effective communication systems (Kaiser, 1993). Deaf children with multiple disabilities need the same kinds of experiences and interactions that all children need to acquire such systems (Ewing & Jones, 2003). Facilitating their communication and language skill acquisition, however, requires tailoring the experiences to accommodate each student's very unique needs. This often means using modalities other than vision, the primary modality used to teach deaf children, because the children's other disabilities—autism, impaired vision, cerebral palsy, cognitive impairments, or brain injury—may interfere with processing information presented through vision channels (Jones & Jones, 2003). In many cases, combining modalities may enable children with multiple disabilities to acquire both receptive and expressive language skills.

A number of disabilities, including cognitive delays, autism, cerebral palsy, and some learning disabilities, affect children's abilities to pay attention. Increased time to attract and maintain attention during communicative interactions beyond that typically required for deaf students may be necessary. Also, some students may need additional time to process incoming information and form responses. Reinforcing the incoming information with pictures or words may aid comprehension. Children who are deaf-blind require longer processing time when using a visual or tactile modality to receive information. Deaf children who have attention deficits may require increased time to acquire and maintain their attention for communication or—alternatively—they may require an increased pace of communication (Munk & Repp, 1994).

Augmentative communication approaches play a key role in communication systems for students whose mental or physical disabilities limit the movements needed to sign intelligibly. The use of augmentative communication is not limited to deaf children with disabilities such as cerebral palsy, autism, or mental retardation. Some children without a categorical disability diagnosis may have a type of motor apraxia that makes forming signs difficult. Including some type of augmentative communication in their communication systems permits these children to express themselves more fully.

Students using augmentative communication systems may communicate by selecting objects, pictures, picture symbols, textured symbols, or printed or brailled words to communicate. They may communicate by touching, looking at their selection (eye-pointing), handing their selection to a communication partner (symbol exchange), or by choosing their selection when a device or someone else offers choices (scanning or stepping). For further information see Reichle, York, and Sigafoos (1991).

The augmentative communication vocabulary can be organized and displayed in a variety of ways. Children in wheelchairs, for example, often have augmentative communication boards or electronic communication devices attached to the trays of their wheelchairs. Children who are mobile might carry their symbols in a special bag, notebook, or communication wallet containing their pictures or symbols.

A variety of portable electronic communication devices that speak the selections are available. Although the deaf child might not hear the selection, these devices have a variety of advantages. Children who are not mobile can use such devices to call hearing peers or teachers to them to initiate communication, an important communication goal for many deaf children with multiple disabilities. Spoken communications are beneficial to hearing communication partners, especially peers and strangers, who may not readily understand the chosen symbols without interpretation.

Social and Behavioral Skills

Social and behavioral skills (e.g., friendship, community membership, turn taking, seeking and gaining attention, play, cooperation, transitioning, and conversation skills) are often overlooked for children with multiple disabilities. Teachers who incorporate social and behavioral goals throughout the curriculum, however, provide their students with lifelong benefits in many areas of functioning.

Social competence must be explicitly taught. Published sources, such as the "Social Cues Questionnaire" (Gray, 1993) can provide guidance for the areas that should be addressed. Careful observation by members of the transdiciplinary team also may yield social skills goals.

Rubin and Rose-Krasnor (1992) found that children with disabilities must have access to their nondisabled peers in order to develop social skills. In mixed-ability classrooms, cooperative learning strategies have enabled students with disabilities to make gains in peer relations, academics, and social skills (Fuchs & Fuchs, 1997) and have increased social competence in students both with and without disabilities (Slavin, 1995). Curriculum guides for teaching social skills to diverse groups of learners provide suggestions and activities that facilitate mutually enjoyable and reciprocal play among children, while expanding each member's social and symbolic play repertoire (Wolfberg, 1999). Short stories describing a situation, concept, or social skill are meaningful to individual children. Called "social stories," this tool can be integrated throughout the curriculum from preschool through adulthood (Gray, 2000).

Historically, teachers have emphasized behavior as a way of maintaining order within the classroom. A student exhibiting behavior that was considered "out of the norm" was viewed as a child who needed to be brought under control. Disruptive behavior, however, may be one of the most effective communication tools that children with multiple disabilities have at their disposal. Communication difficulties correlate highly with problem behaviors (Durand, 1990). Rather than viewing behavior as a problem to be eliminated, teachers should determine the function that the behavior serves for the child (Durand, 1990). Problem behaviors—like communication—can serve many functions. The function is valid for the student and has been learned, which means that appropriate replacement behaviors can also be learned. Some possible functions of behaviors are (Alberto & Troutman, 2006) these:

- to gain attention from teacher, parent, or peer;
- to acquire something tangible (e.g., object, activity, or event);
- to obtain sensory stimulation (e.g., visual, auditory, olfactory, gustatory, or kinesthetic stimulation),
- to escape from inappropriate or demanding tasks (e.g., social interaction, attention, activity, event, or object); and
- to escape from internal stimulation that is painful or discomforting.

"Functional assessment" provides a method for determining the function of a problem behavior. Teachers, parents, and professionals can conduct such functional assessments to identify replacement behaviors that will provide students with socially appropriate means to meet their needs without having to resort to problem behaviors. The Motivational Assessment Scale (Durand & Crimmins, 1990) can be used to determine the functional significance of behaviors. Once educators determine the functions of problem behaviors, they can design positive behavioral supports increase the student's prosocial behavior and improve the student's quality of life (Falvey, 1997).

Motor Skills

Given adequate nutrition, a safe environment, access to proper activities and experiences, and good health, children's gross and fine motor development follows a typical sequence (Finnie, 1997). Curricula designed to support young children's physical development provide ample opportunities for children to walk, run, skip, jump, climb, throw, carry, balance, build, cut, draw, work with puzzles, and use modeling clay. As the children engage in these activities, they also learn valuable language, social, and communication skills and enhance their concept development.

The goals of a motor skills curriculum for deaf children with multiple disabilities should provide activities to facilitate acquisition of gross and fine motor skills necessary for functioning in all aspects of their daily lives. The exact skills that the curriculum will focus on will depend on each child's needs and any needed modification to the child's mode of executing these skills. In addition, the student might be older but still developing motor skills generally associated with younger children. Ambulation skills are a good example.

Walking, running, skipping, and hopping are forms of ambulation. Some are more recreational (e.g., jumping or hopping) whereas others enable movement from place to place. A deaf child with multiple disabilities might need a walker whereas another might need a wheelchair to move from place to place. A motor skills curriculum for children with such adaptive aids might involve providing activities that permit the children to practice and refine their modified ambulation skills. One child might practice learning to control a motorized wheelchair on a computer during computer time and later practice with the actual wheelchair in the classroom and school. Another student might practice very refined wheelchair control while competing in a basketball game with classmates. Softball games might be modified so the child who uses a walker can still "run" the bases with the walker.

In general, work on motor skills can be integrated into other activities (Campbell, 1995). All activities involve motor skills, so integrating motor work throughout the day is natural. Cutting strips of paper to learn and practice cutting makes little sense in isolation. Cutting strips of paper and then making a paper chain to decorate a bulletin board does. Locating and then cutting pictures from magazines to illustrate a story integrates functional reading and language along with fine motor work. Involving classmates makes the activity an excellent social experience as well. Writing the story might mean using a switch to select letters or words as the computer scans operating an augmentative communication program—the fine motor activity of writing for one deaf child with multiple disabilities.

Life Skills

Students with multiple disabilities, like all students, attend school to gain the necessary skills for lifelong learning and successful community membership. Much of the information that schools typically provide is academic instruction geared toward the goals of attending college or vocational school in the postsecondary years. Students with multiple disabilities also need preparation for life after school but a typical academic education may not meet their needs. Instead, they may benefit from curriculum content that addresses life skills. Life skills contain several key areas of learning, including vocational preparation, recreation and leisure education, community living, and health and sex education. A life skills curriculum fosters independence as well as prepares students for life after the classroom.

Only 15.6% of people with disabilities who have less than a high school diploma participate in today's labor force (National Center on Secondary Education and Transition, 2004). Vocational education, however, should increase that percentage. Such a curriculum may include prevocational skills that could be applied to many different jobs, independent living skills, community-based work experiences, and job coaching.

The Individuals With Disabilities Education Act requires that plans for transition to life after school should begin by age 14 (Hasazi, Furney, & DeStefano, 1999). Such planning provides information and guidance for vocational programming. Transdisciplinary teams should work to maintain high expectations and to afford students sufficient opportunities to acquire vocational education, service learning, community work experience, and adult living skills (Johnson, Sharpe, & Stodden, 2000). Ideally, vocational education begins in elementary school. Students with multiple disabilities should have classroom and school jobs to perform with their nondisabled peers. Community-based vocational training experiences can begin in the middle school years. By the time the students reach high school age, transition planning focused on a specific community-based job and independent living services programs should ensure that the students are able to integrate into the community with as much independence as possible.

In addition to generally enhancing the quality of a person's life, the ability to occupy one's leisure time in a socially valued and acceptable manner may have a significant impact on where a person with disabilities lives, success on the job, and the quality of relationships that develop with family, neighbors, colleagues, and others in the community (Ford et al., 1989). Students with multiple disabilities should be offered the same recreational opportunities and experiences as their nondisabled peers. A varied recreation and leisure repertoire offers many advantages to students, including increased social skills and friendships, independence, physical fitness, and self-esteem.

The process of developing a leisure education curriculum should begin by assessing the student's recreation needs and preferences. Assessments should accentuate abilities, potential, and preferences rather than skill deficits or functional limitations (Schleien, Green, & Heyne, 1993). Several useful assessments include the Home Leisure Activities Survey (Wuerch & Voeltz, 1982), Client Home Environment Checklist (Wehman & Schleien, 1981), and Student Interest Survey (Wuerch & Voeltz, 1982). Recreation and leisure skills should be identified and incorporated into the student's individualized education plan and taught in a variety of naturally occurring settings with peers.

Community living skills rarely are included in the general education curriculum. Students with multiple disabilities will benefit from having community living goals incorporated throughout their education, however. These skills include travel, community safety, grocery shopping, general shopping, eating out, and using community services. Each area requires the student to perform tasks outside of the school setting. Therefore, instruction and practice in the community environment is critical not only for acquiring skills but also for generalization to occur.

Health and sex education concepts can be more abstract than some other curricular areas, which can cause students with multiple disabilities to have difficulty acquiring knowledge in these important areas. Many general education curricula include health courses, and many school systems offer limited sex education courses. Students with multiple disabilities can benefit from this instruction when certain adaptations are made to the curriculum. These include (Muccigrosso & Scavarda, 1991) the following:

- simplified but age-appropriate reading materials or media that do not require reading, hearing, or vision, depending on the student's level of ability and combination of disabilities;
- a variety of concrete teaching strategies to reinforce the information presented (e.g., written materials, audiovisual materials, role playing, interactive games, etc.);
- learning strategies that closely approximate real life;
- opportunities for interaction with nondisabled peers and role models; and
- repeated opportunities for ongoing learning.

Many books, videotapes, pictorial stories, and other learning materials are specifically designed to provide sex education to students with disabilities. Health and sex education should be incorporated into the student's curriculum beginning in the elementary school.

Conclusion

Deaf and hard of hearing students with multiple disabilities present many challenges to educators. Curriculum planning can meet these challenges if it is person centered and compensatory and includes transdisciplinary teams and parents. Appropriate planning will result in curricula for these complex students that are individualized, person centered, functional, and—most important—effective.

References

Alberto, P. A., & Troutman, A. C. (2006). *Applied behavior analysis for teachers*. Upper Saddle River, NJ: Prentice-Hall.

Blue-Banning, M. J., Turnbull, A. P., & Pereira, L. (2000). Group action planning as a support strategy for Hispanic families: Parent and professional perspectives. *Mental Retardation, 38*(3), 262–275.

Browder, D. M., & Snell, M. E. (2000). Teaching functional academics. In *Instruction of students with severe disabilities*. Upper Saddle River, NJ: Prentice-Hall.

Butterworth, J., Hagner, D., Heikkinen, B., Faris, S., DeMello, S., & McDonough, K. (1993). *Whole life planning: A guide for organizers and facilitators*. Boston: Children's Hospital and University of Massachusetts at Boston.

Campbell, P. H. (1995). Supporting the medical and physical needs of students in inclusive settings. In N. G. Haring & L. T. Romer (Eds.), *Welcoming students who are deaf-blind into typical classrooms*. Baltimore: Paul H. Brookes.

Carpenter, B. (1995). Across the lifespan: Educational opportunities for children with profound and multiple learning difficulties. *Early Child Development and Care, 109*(3), 75–82.

Dolch, E. W. (1948). *Problems in reading*. Champaign, IL: Garrard Press.

Downing, J. E. (2000). *Including students with severe and multiple disabilities in typical classrooms: Practical suggestions for interventionists*. Baltimore: Paul H. Brooks.

Downing, J. E., Eichinger, J., & Williams, L. J. (1997). Inclusive education for students with severe disabilities: Comparative views of principals and educators at different levels of implementation. *Remedial and Special Education 18*(18), 133–143, 165.

Durand, V. M. (1990). *Severe problem behaviors: A functional communication training approach*. New York: Guilford.

Durand, V. M., & Crimmins, D. B. (1990). Assessment. In V. M. Durand (Ed.), *Severe behavior problems: A functional communication training approach* (pp. 31–82). New York: Guilford Press.

Ewing, K. M., & Jones, T. W. (2003). An educational rationale for deaf students with multiple disabilities. *American Annals of the Deaf, 148*(3), 267–271.

Falvey, M. A. (1997). *Community-based curriculum: Instructional strategies for students with severe handicaps*. Baltimore: Paul H. Brookes.

Finnie, N. R. (1997). *Handling the young cerebral palsied child at home*. Woburn, MA: Butterworth-Heinemann Medical.

Ford, A., Schnorr, R., Meyer, L., Davern, L., Black, J., & Dempsey, P. (1989). Recreation/ leisure. In *The Syracuse community referenced curriculum guide for students with moderate and severe disabilities*. Baltimore: Paul H. Brookes.

Forest, M., & Pearpoint, J. (1992). MAPS: Action planning. In J. Pearpoint, M. Forest, & J. Snow (Eds.), *The inclusion papers: Strategies to make inclusion work* (pp. 52–56). Toronto: Inclusion Press.

Freeman, S. & Alkin, M. (2000). Academic and social attainments of children with mental retardation in general education and special education settings. *Remedial and Special Education, 21*(3), 3–18.

Fuchs, D., & Fuchs, L. S. (1997). Peer-assisted learning strategies: Making classrooms more responsive to diversity. *American Educational Research Journal 34*(1), 174–206.

Giangreco, M. F., Cloninger, C. J., & Salce Iverson, V. (1993). *Choosing options and accommodations for children*. Baltimore: Paul H. Brookes.

Gray, C. (1993). Social cues questionnaire. In *Taming the recess jungle*. Arlington, TX: Future Horizons.

Gray, C. (2000). *The new social story book*. Arlington, TX: Future Horizons.

Grenot-Scheyer, M., Abernathy, P. A., Williamson, D., Jubala, K., & Coots, J. (1995). Elementary curriculum and instruction. In M. A. Falvey (Ed.), *Inclusive and heterogeneous schooling: Assessment, curriculum, and instruction* (pp. 319–340). Baltimore: Paul H. Brookes.

Hasazi, S. B., Furney, K. S., & DeStefano, L. (1999). Implementing the IDEA transition mandates. *Exceptional Children, 65*(4), 555–566.

Holden-Pitt, L., & Diaz, J. A. (1998). Thirty years of the annual survey of deaf and hard-of-hearing children and youth: A glance over the decades. *American Annals of the Deaf, 143*(2), 72–76.

Johnson, D. R. (2004). *Current challenges facing the future of secondary education and transition services for youth with disabilities in the United States* (National Center on Secondary Education and Transition Report). Minneapolis: University of Minnesota Press.

Johnson, D. R., Sharpe, M. N., & Stodden, R. (2000). The transition to postsecondary education for students with disabilities. *IMPACT 13*(4), 1–2.

Jones, T. W. (1984). A framework for identification, classification and placement of multihandicapped hearing impaired students. *Volta Review, 86*(2), 142–151.

Jones, T. W., & Jones, J. K. (2003). Educating young deaf children with multiple disabilities. In B. Bodner-Johnson & M. Sass-Lehrer (Eds.), *The young deaf or hard of hearing child: A family-centered approach to early education*. Baltimore: Paul H. Brookes.

Jones, T. W., & Ross, P. A. (1998). Inclusion strategies for deaf students with special needs. *Endeavor, 37*(1), 2–22.

Jure, R., Rapin, I., & Tuchman, R. F. (1991). Hearing impaired autistic children. *Developmental Medicine and Child Neurology, 33*(12), 1062–1072.

Kaiser, A. P. (1993). "Introduction: Enhancing children's communication." In A. P. Kaiser & D. B. Gray (Eds.). *Enhancing children's communication: Research foundations for intervention* (vol. 2). Baltimore: Paul H. Brookes.

Meadow-Orlans, K. P., Mertens, D. M., Sass-Lehrer, M. A., & Scott-Olson, K. (1997). Support services for parents and their children who are deaf or hard of hearing: A national survey. *American Annals of the Deaf, 142*(2), 278–288.

Meadow-Orlans, K. P., Smith-Gray, S., & Dyssegaard, B. (1995). Infants who are deaf or hard of hearing, with and without physical/cognitive disabilities. *American Annals of the Deaf, 140*(3), 279–286.

Moeller, M. P. (1985). Developmental approaches to communication assessment and enhancement. In E. Cherow (Ed.), *Hearing-impaired children and youth with developmental disabilities: An interdisciplinary foundation for service* (pp. 171–198). Washington, DC: Gallaudet University Press.

Mount, B., & Zwernik, K. (1988). *It's never too early, it's never too late: An overview on personal futures planning.* St. Paul, MN: Governor's Council on Developmental Disabilities.

Muccigrosso, L., & Scavarda, M. (1991). *Double jeopardy: Pregnant and parenting youth in special education.* Reston, VA: Council for Exceptional Children.

Munk, D. D., & Repp, A. C. (1994). The relationship between instructional variables and problem behavior: A review. *Exceptional Children, 60*(March–April), 390–401.

National Center on Secondary Education and Transition. (2004). Challenges facing the future of secondary education and transition services for youth with disabilities in the United States. Retrieved November 8, 2004, from http://www.ncset.org/publications/discussionpaper/

O'Brien, J., & Lovett, H. (1992). *Finding a way toward everyday lives: The contribution of person centered planning.* Harrisburg, PA: Pennsylvania Office of Mental Retardation.

Orelove, F. P., & Sobsey, D. (1996). *Educating children with multiple disabilities: A transdisciplinary approach.* Baltimore: Paul H. Brookes.

Rafferty, Y., Piscitelli, V., & Boettcher, C. (2003). The impact of inclusion on language development and social competence among preschoolers with disabilities. *Exceptional Children, 69*(4), 467–479.

Reichle, J., York, J., & Sigafoos, J. (1991). *Implementing augmentative and alternative communication.* Baltimore: Paul H. Brookes.

Robertson, W. H., Gravel, J. S., Valcante, G. C., & Mauer, R. G. (1992). Using a picture task analysis to teach students with multiple disabilities. Teaching Exceptional Children, 24(4), 12–15.

Rubin, K. H., & Rose-Krasnor, L. (1992). Interpersonal problem-solving and social competence in children. In V. B. van Husselt & M, Hersen (Eds.), *Handbook of social development: A lifespan perspective*, (pp. 283–323). New York: Plenum.

Schleien, S. J., Green, F. P., & Heyne, L. A. (1993). Integrated community recreation. In M. E. Snell (Ed.), *Instruction of Students With Severe Disabilities* (pp. 526–555). New York: Merrill.

Schuyler, V., & Rushmer, N. (1987). *Parent-infant habilitation: A comprehensive approach to working with hearing-impaired infants and toddlers and their families.* Portland, OR: IHR Publications.

Slavin, R. E. (1995). *Cooperative learning: Theory, research, and practice.* Boston: Allyn and Bacon.

Smull, M. W., & Harrison, S. B. (1992). *Supporting people with severe retardation in the community.* Alexandria, VA: National Association of State Mental Retardation Program Directors.

U.S. Department of Education. (2002). *To assure the free appropriate education of all chil-*

dren with disabilities: Twenty-fourth annual report to Congress on the implementation of the Individuals with Disabilities Education Act. Retrieved March 14, 2004, from http://www.ed.gov/about/reports/annual/osep/2002/toc-execsum.pdf

Wehman, P., & Schleien, S. J. (1981). *Leisure programs for handicapped persons: Adaptations, techniques, and curriculum.* Austin, TX: PRO-ED.

Westling, D. L., & Fox, L. (2000). *Teaching students with severe disabilities.* Upper Saddle River, NJ: Prentice-Hall.

Wolfberg, P. J. (1999). *Play and imagination in children with autism.* New York: Teachers College Press.

Wuerch, B., & Voeltz, L. (1982). *Longitudinal leisure skills for severely handicapped learners: The Ho'onoea curriculum component.* Baltimore: Paul H. Brookes.

BARBARA GALE BONDS

School-to-Work Transitions

T HE TRANSITION FROM SCHOOL to work should be part of a lifelong process of learning for every student and all curricula should provide educational experiences to pave the way for this process. *School-to-work* (STW) is an umbrella term for activities, experiences, and opportunities that prepare students for the world of work and includes youth apprenticeships, mentoring, internships, job shadowing, career exploration, and integration of academic and vocational curriculum. This chapter provides background on STW, laws shaping requirements for STW programs, and research supporting STW components that can help shape the STW curriculum. Recommendations are provided for curricular elements of an STW program, and trends in STW are forecast.

Two significant developments in federal legislation have implications for facilitating the STW process for deaf students. The first is the well-known Education for All Handicapped Children Act and its subsequent reauthorizations as the Individuals With Disabilities Education Act (IDEA). The second impetus has come from the School-to-Work Opportunities Act (STWOA) of 1994 (Public Law 103-239), which allows access to funds to establish statewide STW opportunity systems. STWOA is a federal law executed by both the U.S. Department of Education and the U.S. Department of Labor.

In 1994, as part of the national movement for educational reform, Congress passed the STWOA, which recognized the importance of including every student from kindergarten through grade 12, with special focus on the needs of women, minorities, and disabled individuals. Linked with IDEA, STWOA requires that educational programs have STW transition plans for all disabled students 16 years of age and older. STWOA also stipulates that trade school or college, as well as work, is to be considered employment and as part of a transition. Thus, transition plans can ensure better preparation for both college and work. If a student enters the world of work, transition opportunities are state- and locally based and are seen as incorporated into school, family, business, and community partnerships. These partnerships, along with effective staff development for teachers, professionals, and industry participants, and willing and motivated students, promote successful transitions into the world of work.

This chapter is based on Bonds, B. (2003). School-to-work experiences: Curriculum as a bridge. *American Annals of the Deaf,* 148(1), 38–48.

IDEA has helped to promote academic and career development of students who are deaf or hard of hearing. Individualized education programs (IEP) are required under this act for all students with disabilities who are receiving services in school. An IEP outlines all the academic services a student will receive, including the transition plan for students age 16 years or older. Transition plans detail specific programs, activities, and services that address the obstacles that youth with disabilities face as they make the transition to work.

School-to-Work Terminology

Terms related to STW are defined in laws requiring STW transition preparation. *Transition* involves service routes to the individual's movement from high school to employment, a comprehensive approach to educational program development, and an alignment of student goals with educational experiences and services (Warger & Burnette, 2000). *Transition services,* as defined by IDEA, are coordinated sets of activities for students with disabilities. They must be designed within an outcome-defined process and promote movement from high school to post-school activities such as postsecondary education, vocational training, integrated employment, continuing and adult education, adult services, independent living, and community participation. Services must be based on the individual's needs, preferences, and interests. They can include instruction, related services, community experiences, development of employment and other postsecondary adult living objectives, and daily living skills. *Transition planning* must begin when a student reaches age 14 years and by age 16 years should contain a statement of transition services, including a statement of interagency responsibilities or other needed linkages. Students should be invited to attend their IEP meetings to consider transition needs.

The U.S. Office of Special Education Programs (OSEP) advocates *student-centered transition planning*. Self-determination skills are considered fundamental to student participation in their own IEPs (Kohler, 1998). This ensures that goals for transitional services are valued and attainable.

School-to-Work Curricular Influences

Opportunities for career preparation can make the transition from school to work easier for high school students. In America, the success of the STW program depends on national and state funding in coordination with local business and community opportunities. Students who are deaf and hard of hearing can benefit from STW programs if appropriate support services are in place to smooth the transition between school and the workplace. Work is understood to include college and trade school placement.

STW is a system that provides career awareness, career exploration, and career preparation. This system can coordinate STW programs for an entire state or be limited to a single school district. The STW initiative has revived an interest in educational reform. STW has become a part of a broader, national movement for educational reform, which has also included the Goals 2000: Education America Act and the National Skill Standards Act of 1994. STWOA allows access to funds to develop and establish statewide STW opportunity systems.

STW is for all students. Activities should begin in kindergarten and continue through 12th grade. STWOA makes specific references to students with disabilities, individuals from minority groups, and women. It recognizes the importance of including these individuals in STW initiatives by increasing opportunities for them to prepare for careers that are not traditional for their race, gender, or disability.

STW has become an umbrella term for many activities, experiences, and opportunities that prepare students for the world of work. School-based instruction and experiences focus on academic and occupational skills standards. Work-based instruction focuses on the workplace experience, structured training, mentoring, and apprenticeships at various job sites. A variety of activities builds and maintains bridges among school, work, and other adult environments.

America's STW systems incorporate principles of flexibility, high academic and skill standards, and wider opportunities for all students. They are designed to provide equal benefit to a wide range of youth, including students with disabilities, school dropouts, and academically talented learners. This is a challenge for all states, and changes occur slowly. Misunderstandings about STW for "non-college-bound" students stunt progress. States receive program reports and site visits from federal representatives to ensure that appropriate programs are in place. Trade school or college placement should be considered full- or part-time employment.

As part of the STW initiatives, all students choose a career major by the start of 11th grade. The system builds incrementally, becoming richer and more challenging as the student matures. Linkages occur with postsecondary education in 2-year institutions, with dual enrollment and credit for attending classes at community colleges. Linkages to 4-year colleges are just beginning. Perhaps this is because few teacher-preparation institutions include STW concepts in their program of study.

The Need for School-to-Work Planning

Effective transition programs include longitudinal planning, emphasis on careers rather than disability labels, work-based learning, connections to community resources, and sustained involvement of employers. There is wisdom in beginning early. Planning must begin early and continue throughout the academic experience. The IEP transition plan can begin as early as age 14 years. This process is effective when influenced by students, as well as families and other significant adults at home, school, and work. One tenet of the program is that rather than concentrate on the disability label, students focus on career majors, and as a result tend to achieve better employment outcomes. Career exploration, assessment, job shadowing, internships, and paid work experiences at employer work sites are all a part of work-based learning. Paid work is especially critical. Family support, living arrangements, income, peer interactions, and other factors can significantly affect post-school outcomes.

Strategies for serving youth with disabilities, including students who are deaf or hard of hearing, focus on partnerships, clearly defined roles and responsibilities, and student self-determination. Programs for youth with disabilities work best when treated as part of the existing STW system. Full integration within the school offers these students access to the same range of services and opportunities provided to all students.

STW is most effective when individual planning and career development activities are considered. When student preferences are the focus of the transition plan, students experience the process of decision making directly, which builds their self-esteem and helps them develop their ability to work and live independently.

STW is not a series of year-long programs. The transition plan in the IEP can sharpen the focus on how services today can apply to the workforce demands of tomorrow. High standards must guide transition programming and be used to assess individual and program performance. An array of interpersonal skills is required for success at work. Youth should be allowed to develop these skills in order to become actively engaged in all aspects of community life and to focus on lifelong learning and social integration. The same opportunities should be offered to students who are deaf or hard of hearing as are available to all other youth.

Transition Teams

The transition plan should involve teamwork, with student involvement, family support, and collaborative teams including the student, family, special education teacher, transition specialists, service providers, vocational rehabilitation (VR) counselors, adult service providers, employers, postsecondary education program representatives, and community supporters or advocates. Within the STW program, all partners are responsible for the student's success.

Employers and labor groups can have a part in STW programs. Unions, businesses, and governments can work together as equal partners with the education system. They are charged with transforming workplaces into active learning environments, thus enabling all systems to offer work-based learning to all students.

STW allows for opportunities for staff development that permit teachers and other education professionals to experience internships with outside employers. Such experiences enable education professionals to share information about contextual learning, portfolio assessment, and new uses of technology.

Employers are willing to invest time and resources if they perceive direct benefit. They can be afforded opportunities to influence curriculum, directly train prospective employees, and receive effective consultation in work force preparation. Parents, teachers, counselors, service providers, and students themselves are equal partners in the development of the IEP and the transition plan. Continual contact with each other allows partners to prevent duplication of services, to coordinate services, and to foster support from all partners.

STW programs often require the services of a transition specialist. Transition specialists can offer career guidance and counseling to students and their parents. They can provide assistance to businesses that require aid in adapting their workplaces to meet the needs of these youth. Teachers have to learn how to teach advanced skills while holding students to high standards, and parents must be taught how to help their children take advantage of this wide range of options. Transition specialists can help each in turn. These specialists can also work with VR counselors, when needed, to provide background information and support in the STW process.

The role of the VR counselor varies with every state and locality, but minimally the role should include early interaction, thus benefiting the student in the transition process. The VR counselor needs to be able to sign directly to students. Although initial contact should occur earlier than 11th grade, about half of visits occur during that year (Allen, Rawlings, & Schildroth, 1989).

College-Bound Planning

College-bound planning can also be an important part of any transition plan. This is especially significant because deaf and hard of hearing individuals benefit significantly from attending and graduating from college. For example, Boatner, Stuckless, and Moores (1964) reported that 78% of young deaf adults in New England in the labor market were employed, and 30 years later Holt, Hotto, and Cole (1994) reported that 79% of Deaf adults in the United States were employed, reflecting little change. However, the data for college graduates are much more positive. After leaving NTID, 94% of 1999 graduates who chose to enter the workforce found employment (Simone & Davila, 2000). Only 4% of Gallaudet University alumni with bachelor degrees and 2% of those with graduate degrees reported themselves as unemployed in 1999 (Lam et al., 2000).

Schroedel and Geyer (2000) recommended career counseling before college entry. (They noted that 70% of deaf students drop out before completing college.) They added that students should be advised of their earning potential and encouraged to enter fields tagged for success. Students need to make some of these choices as early as ninth grade, they said. Schroedel and Geyer also noted that to continue making career progress, workers need to develop certain skills. These include using interpersonal competencies to strengthen the quality of on-the-job communication, expanding workplace networks to become good at requesting accommodations, gaining access to mentors, and acquiring the capabilities needed for success in seeking promotions. Schroedel and Geyer also emphasized the importance of obtaining the training needed to get a license or certificate, learning new work skills, improving current work skills, and augmenting reading and writing abilities to enhance prospects for career enhancement.

In a 1999 alumni survey (Lam et al., 2000), Gallaudet University found that when deaf high school graduates enter college or another postsecondary educational institution, they do so with the expectation that they will enjoy higher earnings and greater job satisfaction after college. From 1990 to 1999, 28% of Gallaudet University's graduates earned bachelor's degrees in business administration, economics/finance, or psychology. Although only 25% of alumni of private colleges receive advanced degrees, 43% of Gallaudet undergraduates continue on to attain an advanced degree. The median salary for Gallaudet graduates with a bachelor's degree was estimated at $39,000 a year.

In its annual report for fiscal year 2000 (Simone & Davila, 2000), the Rochester Institute of Technology estimated that NTID graduates earned 36% more in their lifetimes than those deaf students who drop out or who do not attend college. No specific salary estimates were reported. More than one third of NTID graduating students were reported to enter jobs in science and engineering, and one quarter each in business and visual communications. According to the annual report, NTID alumni were also employed as counselors, teachers, and social workers. Seventy-three percent of male graduates held degrees in business, science, applied science, and technology and engineering, whereas about 42% of women had graduated in these same four areas of study. Among female graduates, 58% had earned bachelor's degrees in imaging arts and liberal arts; 27% of male graduates had.

By 2000, it was projected that 50% to 55% of deaf and hard of hearing people with high school diplomas would be entering the job market or college (Foster, 1992). The other students would receive certificates (10% to 20%) or drop out of school before graduation (25% to 30%). STW programs are designed to ease the transitions of students such as these.

School-to-Work Assessment

Some form of testing is a part of every curriculum. Teachers and counselors need to be sure to use testing appropriately. Formal and informal tests can be used.

Two vocational tests are commonly used with students who are deaf or hard of hearing. The Transition Competence Battery for Deaf and Hard of Hearing Adolescents and Young Adults, is a standardized test used to measure the work and social skills necessary to work and live successfully in the community. It was designed for deaf or hard of hearing individuals who primarily use sign communication or who possess limited English-reading skills. This test assesses job-seeking skills, work adjustment skills, job-related social skills, money management skills, health and home skills, and community awareness skills (Luckner, 1999). The Transition Planning Inventory, or TPI (Clark & Patton, 1997), is also used, which includes forms concerning the student and the student's home, as well as a school profile and a form for recommendations of further assessment.

Other instruments include achievement tests, interest surveys, and social-emotional tests. Because of the availability of norms for students who are deaf, the Stanford Achievement Test is used by many counselors and teachers as an academic achievement test. The Valpar Component Work Sample System and the Wide Range Interest-Opinion Test (WRIOT) measure vocational skills and interests. With videotaped standardized instructions, both the Valpar series of tests and WRIOT can be administered nonverbally. (Deaf norms are available for the Valpar series.) For social-emotional assessment, the Meadow-Kendall Social-Emotional Assessment Inventory for Deaf and Hearing Impaired Students was developed specifically for use with deaf students and was validated on a national representative group of deaf youth (Allen, Rawlings, & Schildroth, 1989).

Curriculum Strategies

Many believe that the purpose of contemporary American schools is to prepare young people for their future economic roles (Engel, 2000). Curriculum has been devised that reflects this goal, with very specific skills and knowledge sets.

New scientific discoveries transform jobs, lives, and the shape of public issues. Preparations for the future must link to the economy, technologies, and the kind of education needed by a rapidly changing workforce. In 1999 alone, employers spent more than $62.5 billion on upgrading basic skills of their employees. These skills should have been acquired during school years. It is projected that jobs in the health sciences and computer industries requiring mathematics and science skills will increase by 5.6 million by 2008 (National Center for Education Statistics, 1998). Curriculum must be adopted, similar to the general education curriculum, that offers deaf and hard of hearing students opportunities equal to those of their hearing peers. Instruction must occur to better prepare deaf and hard of hearing students and workers for work and for life. Efforts need to focus on ensuring adequate education and job training so that deaf and hard of hearing students can make the STW transition to more satisfying lives.

Curriculum must be influenced by individual student needs. The ERIC/OSEP Special Project (2000) suggests beginning instruction as early as possible, even in elementary school; being prepared to support students with sensitive issues (reading about one's disability can be unsettling but working through the discomfort can be beneficial); ensuring that students know what their disability means (i.e., encouraging them to talk about it and thus to become comfortable with it); scheduling time to develop skills related to participation on a regular basis (i.e., through IEP training); teaching IEP participation skills as a semester course (students need sufficient time to master the skills in order to take an active role); using motivational techniques to interest students (e.g., asking adult role models to make classroom presentations); and communicating with families and letting parents know the school's intentions. With informed participation in the IEP and transition planning process, students should feel accomplished and empowered.

Cummins and Sayers (1997) found that students need to develop their literacy skills by means of analysis and resolution of local and global problems. They need to be multilingual, with computer literacy one of the language skills to be achieved. Critical thinking and problem-solving skills, along with basic literacy and numeracy skills, were as necessary as citizenship, research, and analysis skills in encouraging students to engage in learning in ways that would promote productive engagement in society in the future.

Pressley and Woloshyn (1995) outlined specific curriculum strategies that work when teachers are getting started on something new. They suggested selecting only a few cognitive strategies to teach, and perhaps to teach the strategies one at a time.

Teachers should make sure that scientifically validated strategies are used. These are procedures that students can use to help them understand and address higher-order tasks in areas such as reading comprehension and writing. Teachers should try to ensure that the skill or knowledge being taught is presented in tandem with other areas of the curriculum to provide reinforcement and applicability in other thinking areas. Teachers should begin with materials already provided in the regular classroom and work slowly, providing students with plenty of information about very specific contexts, with many opportunities to experience guided practice. Teachers should model the strategy being taught, explain extensively how the skill or learning can be applied across the curriculum, question for student understanding, and review the material with students to ensure that no misunderstandings occur. The students should have the chance to learn cooperatively, in groups. This way, individuals have the chance to explain their thinking skills and to benefit through interpersonal interaction mirroring their intellectual skills. A range of materials should be used in teaching different skills and knowledge sets.

Motivation is a key element that must be present for students to apply recently acquired skills. If students are encouraged to try, even if they fail they can learn that even failures can be an investment in future successes. All students must be convinced that they can be efficient information processors. They need to be able to believe they can grow up to be engineers, scientists, and business leaders, fulfilling important roles in the community. One way they can become these successful people is to learn the academic strategies used by them and to acquire the reading, writing, and problem-solving strategies these people know. They need to know that what is being taught in school is important to know now and in the future.

What is taught? When is it taught? Early in the STW process, field trips and career fairs introduce students to the world of work. In junior high school or middle school, the focus shifts to career exploration, working with guidance counselors and teachers to focus on career options, job shadowing, and mentoring experiences. Apprenticeships and internships integrate STW into the high school. School districts can work with postsecondary institutions to refine the skills of both students and teachers.

In STW, students explore all aspects of the industry of their choosing, which means exposure to each component of an industry, including areas such as sales and marketing, management and finance, technical skills, labor and community issues, health and safety, and environmental issues. Career majors help guide students, allowing for maximum exposure to an industry, but students can change majors during high school. Career majors can include arts and communication, business and management, health occupations, human services, manufacturing and engineering technologies, and natural resources.

Suggested School-to-Work Objectives and Activities, by School Level

Preschool

Objective: appreciate all types of work
Activity: career trips

Elementary School

Objectives: develop positive work habits, learn about different jobs, develop independence skills at home and school
Activities: explore technology, read books about different jobs that are available

Middle School/Junior High School

Objectives: career exploration and transition planning to understand the school-to-work transition process; to develop interests, aptitudes, and preferences; and to explore work, independent living, and community opportunities
Activities: visit high school, vocational-technical schools, career fairs; begin learning about money and budgeting; begin job shadowing opportunities; explore local transportation availability; practice conflict resolution strategies; generally broaden experiences in the community

High School

Objectives: career exploration and transition planning, developing realistic employment goals, working in the community, using assistive technology and community support services
Activities: develop the IEP and transition plan, participate in work experiences, explore job placement services, practice independent living skills, take standardized tests, develop academic skills, explain one's disability and the accommodations needed for particular situations, explore options for postsecondary education, involve adult services, practice interviewing, complete résumé, use online services, develop job-seeking skills, register to vote, get driving license, increase community partnerships

A guide to apprenticeships or internships can be helpful. For development of STW transition apprenticeship programs that are both equitable and excellent, five criteria must be met:

1. Apprenticeships should be accessible to all youth, regardless of their postsecondary goals or the absence or presence of conditions of disability.
2. Apprenticeships should be individualized according to the needs, interests, and abilities of each student.
3. Instructional content in STW apprenticeships should prepare all students to meet the generic problem-solving demands of college or work.

4. A combination of classroom, community, and job environments will work well to produce graduates who are mature, responsible, and motivated.

5. Successful completion of apprenticeships should lead to receipt of recognized credentials authorizing entry into career opportunities or postsecondary education programs, placement or acceptance in postsecondary vocational and education programs, placement in competitive or supported employment, or participation in continuing and adult education, adult services, and independent living in community settings. (Mithaug, 1994, p. 2)

Each task should be taught visually, clearly communicated, related to experiences where the student is currently operating, and then made more challenging to raise the student's skill level upward. Education and training for a job should occur in situations similar to those that will be experienced in the real world, with frequent feedback and opportunities for improvement. Work experiences should include field trips, job shadowing, school-based learning, apprenticeship and internships, cooperative education, work-study or part-time job placements, and technical preparation in community or vocational-technical schools. Students also need to prepare for postsecondary education, distance learning, community programs, and other options.

Successful adult functioning includes many domains. Work involving these domains should be included in the high school curriculum. Daily living, physical and emotional health, relationships and social interactions, employment, further education, transportation, finances and money management, leisure, and community participation are all important enough to be included in the STW curriculum at almost every level.

Students who are deaf or hard of hearing often lack interaction skills, responsible behaviors, mediated experiences, and independent learning skills; these gaps may become barriers to employment after high school.

Communication is the key if deaf and hard of hearing students are to be able to learn, compete, and work to their highest capacity. Communication must be the cornerstone for all transition-preparedness programs. "It is incumbent upon us to increase our efforts to ensure that deaf children can grow up to enjoy all of the benefits of literacy" (Moores & Miller, 2001, p. 80). Deaf workers often use a language that is different from that of their English-speaking coworkers and supervisors. Currently, the world's language of commerce is English. "Students who...write in English are thinking in English" (Mayer & Akamatsu, 2000, p. 399). Either workers must be competent in reading, writing, and speaking English, or they must be supported with on-the-job compensations for the differences in language. Often a worker must be able to read, write, and understand reports, manuals, forms, e-mail, written communications, educational materials, safety brochures, and many other information materials, or there may be an increased risk of danger on the job. Some texts are frozen and can be learned and used in different situations. By learning and practicing these texts, workers can become competent users of the forms and sentences included in them.

Workers who are deaf or hard of hearing may attempt to avoid careers that involve a lot of reading and writing. In this capacity, they become underutilized and underemployed, and face a decreased potential for a good quality of life as a result. Recent

(1991–1999) bachelor's degree recipients from Gallaudet University were surveyed for literacy skill requirements on the job. More than 70% reported that writing skills (formal and informal) were very important in their job; more than 80% reported the same of reading skills (Lam et al., 2000).

Without a college education or training, people who are deaf or hard of hearing often must take unskilled or semiskilled jobs. With continued education, they tend to enter into professions similar to those of their hearing peers. Literacy requirements on the job heavily influence job retention and promotion of deaf and hard of hearing workers. Salary differences were noted in the 1999 Gallaudet University alumni survey (Lam et al., 2000) and the 2000 Rochester Institute of Technology annual report (Simone & Davila, 2000), specifically in careers of equal duration; hearing peers tended to earn larger salaries than peers in the same job who were deaf or hard of hearing. If literacy skills are not strong, perhaps support services such as interpreting and note taking can be provided to help eliminate language barriers. Deaf and hard of hearing workers would feel a great difference in job self-confidence and workplace acceptance if they could teach sign language classes for coworkers and supervisors. Hearing workers would also benefit from learning about Deaf culture, and the door would be opened to greater mutual understanding and greater assistance for the deaf or hard of hearing worker.

Recommendations

The five recommendations provided here focus on curricular elements of a STW transitional program. Using appropriate assessment methods, following the strengths and interests of the student, taking advantage of every opportunity, keeping expectations high, and maintaining a sense of reality can all help during the STW transition process.

First, schools should ensure that testing is appropriate for deaf students, and that these students are adequately tested on the desired competencies. Tests should measure students' goals and current levels of functioning and provide insights into how to bridge the two. Informal assessments should be used such as person-centered planning based on the preferences and strengths of the student, developed specifically so that the IEP goals, objectives, and action statements can easily be implemented (Luckner, 2002). To optimize student performance, test-taking skills may need to be taught.

Second, the interests and strengths of the student should be followed. The transition plan should be the result of teamwork, with collaborative teams including the student, the family, the special education teacher, transition specialists, service providers, VR counselors, adult service providers, employers, postsecondary education program representatives, and community supporters or advocates. Interest surveys, parent surveys, and skill surveys can be used to determine and update student interests. Flexibility should be built in to allow for changes in the transition plan that would permit exploration of new avenues of career interest.

Third, whether in elementary school, middle school, high school, or beyond, students should be enlisted in every meaningful opportunity to learn job skills. Activities outside school and school alternatives should be used if available.

Fourth, expectations should be kept high. With low expectations, one can expect low results. Emphasizing the high status of deaf people in the workforce may raise self-expectations of students who are deaf. Teachers should open students' eyes to future needs in technical, scientific, and medical fields to help prepare them to win jobs in those areas. Curricular supports can be built in that can help students meet these high expectations. Effective transitions are based on mastery of fundamental academic skills. Teachers should begin with that area.

Fifth, teachers need to maintain a sense of reality. An appropriate work ethic is rewarded, but there is no "free lunch." Working toward a meaningful career leads to dignity and a more enriched life and will also result in better-prepared future generations.

Conclusion

Education today must prepare citizens for the future. With technological change constantly affecting people's lives, teachers working with students who are deaf or hard of hearing must be particularly diligent in preparing these students. Through emphasis on the need for cooperation in a global economy, students can be better integrated into the world of work. Workers must be prepared to constantly update and reeducate themselves for the acquisition of new skills. Lifelong learning must be a goal for every teacher and student, and the curriculum provided during educational experiences should pave the way to attainment of this goal. Students who are deaf or hard of hearing should be given numerous opportunities, early and often, to develop vocational skills and knowledge. A teacher who does so gives the gift of a more enriched life to every student.

References

Allen, T. E., Rawlings, B. W., & Schildroth, N. N. (1989). *Deaf students and the school-to-work transition*. Baltimore: Brookes.

Boatner, E., Stuckless, E., & Moores, D. (1964). *Occupational status of the young adults of New England and the need and demand for a regional technical-vocational training center*. West Hartford, CT: American School for the Deaf.

Bullis, M., Davis, C., Bull, B., & Johnson, B. (1997). Expectations versus realities: Examination of transition plans and experiences of adolescents who are deaf and adolescents who are hearing. *Rehabilitation Counseling Bulletin, 40*(4), 251–264.

Clark, G., & Patton, J. (1997). *Transition planning inventory*. Austin, TX: PRO-ED.

Cummins, J., & Sayers, D. (1995). *Brave new schools: Challenging cultural illiteracy through global learning networks*. New York: St. Martin's Press.

Engel, M. (2000). *The struggle for control of public education: Market ideology vs. democratic values*. Philadelphia: Temple University Press.

ERIC/OSEP Special Project. (2000, spring). New ideas for planning transitions to the adult world [Electronic version]. *Research Connections in Special Education, 6. Retrieved* from http://ericec.org/osep/recon6/rc6sec1.html

Foster, S. (1992). Accommodation of deaf college graduates in the work place. In S. Foster & G. Walter (Eds.), *Students in post-secondary education* (pp. 210–235). London: Routledge.

Holt, J. A., Hotto, S. A., & Cole, K. (1994). *Demographic aspects of hearing impairment: Questions and answers* (3rd ed.). Washington, DC: Gallaudet University.

Individuals With Disabilities Education Act Amendments of 1997, Pub. L. 105–17, 20 U.S.C. §1400 *et seq.* (1999).

Kohler, P. (1998). Implementing a transition perspective of education. In F. Rusch & J. Chadsey (Eds.), *Beyond high school: Transition from school to work* (pp. 179–205). Belmont, CA: Wadsworth.

Lam, K. S., King, J., Skilton, J. C., Galvan, D., Rawlings, B., & Johnson, R. C. (2000). *Gallaudet University alumni survey 1999.* Washington, DC: Gallaudet University.

Luckner, J. L. (1991). *The SCANS report.* Washington, DC: U.S. Department of Labor, Secretary's Commission on Achieving Necessary Skills.

Luckner, J. L. (1999, July). *Seeking access to the global community: Students with additional disabilities.* Paper presented at the annual meeting of the Convention of American Instructors of the Deaf, Los Angeles.

Luckner, J. L. (2002). *Facilitating the transition of students who are deaf or hard of hearing.* Austin, TX: PRO-ED.

Luckner, J. L., & Muir, S. (2001). Successful students who are deaf in general education settings. *American Annals of the Deaf, 146*(5), 450–461.

Mayer, C., & Akamatsu, T. (2000). Deaf children creating written texts: Contributions of American Sign Language and signed forms of English. *American Annals of the Deaf, 145*(5), 394–403.

Mithaug, D. E. (1994). *Equity and excellence in school-to-work transitions of special populations* (Center Focus No. 6). Berkeley, CA: National Center for Research in Vocational Education, University of California. Also available at http://ncrve.berkeley.edu/CenterFocus/cf6.html

Moores, D. F., & Miller, M. S. (2001). Literacy publications: *American Annals of the Deaf* 1996 to 2000. *American Annals of the Deaf, 146*(2), 77–80.

National Center for Education Statistics. (1998). *Projections of education statistics to 2008.* Washington, DC: U.S. Department of Education.

National Commission on Excellence in Education. (1983). *A nation at risk: The imperative for educational reform.* Washington, DC: U.S. Government Printing Office.

Pressley, M., & Woloshyn, V. (1995). *Cognitive strategy instruction that really improves children's academic performance* (2nd ed.). Cambridge, MA: Brookline Books.

School-to-Work Opportunities Act of 1994, Pub. L. No. 103-239, 20 U.S.C. § 6161 *et. seq.* (1994).

Schroedel, J. G., & Geyer, P. D. (2000). Long-term career attainments of deaf and hard of hearing college graduates: Results of a 15-year follow-up survey. *American Annals of the Deaf, 145*(4), 303–313.

Simone, A. J., & Davila, R. R. (2000). *Rochester Institute of Technology, thirty-fourth annual report (fiscal year 2000).* Rochester, NY: Rochester Institute of Technology.

Warger, C., & Burnette, J. (2000). *Planning student-directed transitions to adult life.* (Report No. E593). Reston, VA: ERIC Clearinghouse on Disabilities and Gifted Children. (ERIC Document Reproduction Service No. EDO 00 2).

Internet Resources for School-to-Work Transitions

Center for Self-Determination
http://www.self-determination.org

ERIC Clearinghouse on Disabilities and Gifted Education
http://ericec.org

Model Transition Projects: The Transition Institute
http://www.ed.uiuc.edu/sped/tri/projwebsites.html

National School-to-Work Office
http://www.stw.ed.gov

National Transition Alliance for Youth With Disabilities
http://www.dssc.org/nta

National Transition Network
http://www.ici.coled.umn.edu/ntn

Quintessential Career and Job-Hunting Resources Guide
http://www.stetson.edu/~rhansen/careers.html

School-to-Work Site Devoted to Students With Disabilities
http://www.ici.coled.umn.edu/schooltowork/default.html

Showing the Children of Today the Possibilities of Tomorrow!
http://www.iwc.com/careertv/

So You Want to Be A . . .
http://student.studentcenter.com/inside/bea/bea.htm

Transition Research Institute
http://www.ed.uiuc.edu/SPED/tri/institute.html

PART THREE

Instructional Considerations Across the Curriculum

MARGERY MILLER

Individual Assessment and Educational Planning: Deaf and Hard of Hearing Students Viewed Through Meaningful Contexts

I N THIS CHAPTER, several issues are addressed. Among these are the usefulness of verbal measures of intelligence and the limitations of sole reliance on performance, or nonverbal, measures. Also, three prototypical models of development are proposed. Within this framework we discuss norms, test modifications, accommodations, and overall fairness.

Attempts to provide meaningful and valid assessments for deaf and hard of hearing children have met with limited success over the years. Initially, deaf children were tested orally to determine their overall level of verbal and nonverbal (performance) "intelligence," regardless of whether they were able to understand the questions by lipreading or "speechreading" the spoken words and sentences presented on the examiner's lips. This was a dark era in the history of psychological and psychoeducational testing and the evaluation of deaf children. Far too often deaf individuals tested under these conditions were incorrectly labeled as mentally retarded and were even placed in institutions for the retarded. At best, the intellectual abilities of deaf children were consistently underestimated, and this continued into their adult lives.

Through the efforts of psychologists familiar with the potential language differences and complex and varied developmental issues related to language, communication, and conceptual development of people who are deaf, the focus of psychological assessments for deaf children evolved into one that concentrated solely on measuring nonverbal "performance" intelligence. This yielded Performance (nonverbal) Intelligence Quotients (PIQs), which seemed to provide a more valid and appropriate measure of the intelligence of children who were deaf and hard of hearing. This eliminated the confounding variables of lipreading, language differences, and communication modality, and deaf children were suddenly viewed as having intellectual functioning that fell, more or less, within the normal limits of expectations for children within their various age ranges.

Verbal and Performance Measures of Intelligence

For a period of time, it was considered unprofessional and inappropriate to suggest that tests of verbal intelligence be used with deaf children. The mistakes of the past were still fresh, and people believed that even if using performance intelligence tests alone was an incomplete (and often misleading) measure of a deaf child's intellectual functioning, at least it was not an inaccurate measure of intelligence. An inaccurate measure, as previously mentioned, could return the field to the dark abyss when numerous deaf children were classified as verbally and globally retarded because the verbal and nonverbal (performance) scores were added together and deaf children thus had depressed global IQ scores. Although this new dependence on nonverbal or limited verbal measures was, in fact, a much better alternative to what had previously been used by psychological assessment specialists, it created its own problems relative to the accurate description of a deaf child's overall functioning in cognitive, linguistic, and academic achievement areas.

Numerous studies describe the incidence of "additional disabilities" among the Deaf population. A survey of more than 36,000 deaf and hard of hearing school-age children (Gallaudet Research Institute, 2003) reported that approximately 40% were identified as having multiple disabilities and approximately 70% had "functional disabilities," including disabilities involving expressive and receptive communication, maintaining attention, and reasoning skills. This report may very well underestimate the numbers of deaf children with both "additional disabling conditions" and "functional limitations" because numerous assessment protocols for deaf children do not use language-based measures and thus potentially miss identifying deaf children who have language disabilities. Because numerous disabilities manifest themselves in the verbal area as well as in the nonverbal area of intellectual development, this exclusive reliance on performance measures meant it was now possible for a deaf child or adolescent who was assessed nonverbally to have performance IQs well within the normal limits but be significantly deficient in advanced signed, cued, or spoken communication and academic performance relative to deaf peers. Many of these children were placed in regular classes for deaf children with generically trained teachers of deaf students who lacked the specialized training to work with deaf children with multiple disabilities. These children may be viewed by parents and some professionals as not working up to their full potential, as measured by the nonverbal tests of intelligence, or as having behavioral disorders, because they do not behave well enough or pay attention long enough to benefit from instruction. Occasionally, professionals more correctly identify the nature of observed disabilities and determine that there is some kind of language delay or language-processing disorder. However, they may not fully understand the nature of the language-processing deficits because of the limited verbal assessment options available for use with deaf children.

Based on experiences working with deaf children at a residential school, and seeing evidence of intact verbal intellectual development in nondisabled deaf children, Miller (1985) developed an experimental procedure for assessing the verbal intelligence of deaf children. This study examined deaf children in middle school and junior high who did not have a formally identified disability in their assessment reports. It is important to note that the sample included children who might have had functional limitations such as language delay or disorders through signed communication and academic difficulties not expected from a deaf child of that age. That is, unless there was formal documentation of a disability, the child was included in the sample for this research study. This is mentioned because if that had not been true, the scores received by the deaf children in the study may have been higher.

Miller (1985) used several native American Sign Language (ASL) users (Deaf adults from Deaf families using ASL) as consultants during the translation process. There were three separate sets of translations. The first set of translations was a Signed English version of selected verbal scale subtests of the WISC-R. This was a word-for-word signed translation. The second set of translations was in ASL, with a few adaptations. These few sign language adaptations were necessary because of the nature of some linguistic aspects of ASL and to preserve the integrity of some test items. For example, if the ASL sign revealed the answer, another procedure was used for that item (e.g., if the question asked how many pennies were equal in value to a nickel, the procedure would show an actual nickel instead of signing the term because the sign reveals the answer). The third set of translated items was in Pidgin Sign English, now referred to as Contact Signs. This translation kept the items in English order but it used many ASL constructions.

In general, the results demonstrated that when deaf children have access to the questions, they are able to respond verbally (in this case, with all subjects using signs as their primary means of communication) in ways that were previously thought to be impossible on formal tests of verbal intelligence. Although the scores were slightly lower for deaf children ($\overline{X}$ = 97.8) than for their hearing peers ($\overline{X}$ = 100), the practical significance was minimal. Although one could reasonably argue that the tests were not identical, the important point is that it is possible to incorporate verbal measures of intelligence and linguistic functioning to yield more complete and appropriate assessments of deaf children. Comparing deaf children's performance to a hearing norm sample is but one small way to utilize the scores. Comparing a deaf child with other deaf children of a similar age is equally beneficial and more meaningful in some instances.

Assessing the verbal skills of deaf children in meaningful, valid, and reliable ways is a difficult task that must take numerous factors into consideration, but it is feasible. Maller (1996) argued that verbal intelligence test items were not consistently valid for use with deaf children because both the sequences of the items and the correlation of these scores with academic achievement were not necessarily uniformly valid for this population. The item sequence, although it is not exactly the same for deaf and hearing children, is largely adequate because of the ceiling or discontinue rules. That is, even if the child is exposed to an item that may be at a higher developmental level for a deaf child than for a hearing child, or vice versa, the error received on that item will not typically prevent this person from receiving scores on later items on the subtest.

Miller (1985) found only one or two items that would not have been presented to deaf children because they were beyond the ceiling or discontinue rule point.

This is a problem that should and must be addressed by the field for each and every test; however, it should not slow the search for appropriate ways to measure the verbal intelligence of deaf children and to develop normative data on both the Deaf and the Deaf with multiple disabilities population. These two distinct groups, (a) deaf children and adolescents and (b) deaf children and adolescents with multiple disabilities, must have relevant comparison groups for norm development that are representative of themselves, of the other group of deaf students, and of the total deaf student population so that meaningful distinctions and comparisons can be made. Without these norm group distinctions, depressed cognitive, linguistic, and academic achievement scores will be incorrectly attributed to deafness instead of to the varied disabling conditions often accompanying a child's deafness, especially for children whose deafness is secondary to specific etiologies that carry greater risks for disabling conditions.

It should be clear that we do not want to assess the validity of verbal tests of intelligence used with deaf children based on correlations with English literacy skill attainment levels. This would be similar to looking for strong correlations between the measured intelligence of children with learning disabilities and their academic achievement, knowing that the very nature of certain learning disabilities causes a discrepancy between measured intelligence and academic achievement. A more reasonable view of developing validity studies for the verbal intelligence test scores of deaf children is to correlate their raw scores and standard scores with age instead of with academic achievement. This comparison should demonstrate the test's ability to detect increasingly higher levels of verbal intelligence as students become older.

The expected outcome from these studies would show a significant number of deaf children who have strong verbal fluency and verbal intelligence, as measured by verbal subtests and through informal communicative interchanges, but who have not attained similar English literacy proficiency levels, as measured by academic achievement and written English language usage tests, even when compared with deaf peers. Similarly, there will be a significant number of deaf children who will have strong verbal skills both "through the air" (signs, speech, or cues), as measured by verbal tests of intelligence, and who demonstrate English literacy proficiency on selected tests of reading and writing. It is exactly this kind of differentiation that the assessment specialist must make.

When a print literacy lag is noted relative to a higher obtained verbal intelligence measure, a critical question must be answered: Are the literacy skills of a particular deaf child related to an overall lack of verbal fluency and conceptualization, or is this a deaf child with superior signed verbal conceptualization (as measured by verbal tests of intelligence that do not involve English in print) who is experiencing delays or deficits in the area of English language skill development in print? If the latter is the case, what are the variables contributing to this discrepancy, and how can they be remedied for this child? Also, are these delays in literacy development similar to those of other nondisabled deaf children or are they significantly greater? That would possibly indicate a reading or writing learning disability, reflect a faulty instructional approach for this particular child, or suggest a delay in language exposure that could not be compensated for at this point in time.

Verbal tests of intelligence are a necessary component of a complete psychological and psychoeducational assessment for deaf children (Braden 1991, 1994). These tests are likely to correlate much more strongly with academic achievement than do nonverbal performance tests of intelligence, as is true with hearing children. According to Braden (1991, p. 61), "nonverbal tests are still critical for differentiating deafness from mental retardation, but the exclusion of verbal IQ tests from educational practice and research seems most unfortunate." Braden (1991) and Moores (1990) reported that scores on the verbal subtests of IQ instruments were more highly correlated with academic achievement than were nonverbal subtests. The verbal IQ scores and selected academic achievement scores were fairly well correlated for deaf and hard of hearing children (Braden, 1994; Maller & Braden, 1993). Verbal fluency is a prerequisite for acquiring increasing academic achievement levels with increasing increments of age and instruction for all children, and therefore should be formally measured and analyzed for all children, including deaf and hard of hearing children.

Misuse of Tests

The literature is rife with suggestions for testing deaf children that may result in significantly underestimating their intelligence levels. Instead of accommodating the testing needs of deaf children, these testing approaches accommodate the weak sign language skills of the examiners and their lack of expertise in understanding developmental issues of deaf children. For example, in Sattler and Dumont's *Assessment of Children: WISC-IV and WPPSI-III Supplement* (2004), examiners are encouraged to give the nonverbal subtests with instructions provided in deaf children's "native language or preferred mode of communication, such as American Sign Language" (p. 383). The authors go on to say that if examiners are unable to use sign language, they should use modifications such as writing out the instructions for each subtest on a piece of paper and having the child read the instructions, or saying the instructions out loud while the child looks at the examiner's face. They suggest showing "urgency" through nonverbal body gestures as well as showing the stopwatch to indicate that responses are timed and thus the child should know to respond quickly. Although these instructions certainly make sense on one level, it would be refreshing to see such well-respected authors say something to the effect that if examiners are unable to communicate in the deaf child's mode of communication or language, then it is inappropriate and perhaps even unethical to test the deaf child. Instead, a referral should be made to a psychologist who possesses these necessary communication skills and who has training and/or experience in interacting with and assessing deaf children and their linguistic environments.

Although the field is now asking important questions concerning the validity, reliability, and practical applicability of the psychological and psychoeducational measurements used to evaluate deaf children, few improvements have been made. The following factors account for this slow progress:

1. Difficulty deciding who should be included in the "deaf" normative sample—all deaf children, deaf children without disabilities, deaf and hard of hearing

children, deaf children who use ASL or manual codes on English, deaf children who use cued speech, deaf children whose parents are hearing, pre- or postlingual deaf children, and so forth.

2. Difficulty determining appropriate translation protocols. Should items be translated into ASL (even though very few deaf children use ASL as their first language), Signed English, Contact Signs, Cued Speech, or all of them? If multiple translation processes are used, how would consistency and equivalency of item difficulty be determined in psychometrically and practically applicable ways?

3. Difficulty locating sufficient numbers of practicing psychologists who possess superior signed communication skills and who are capable of using a variety of sign language or other visual systems (Signing Exact English [SEE], Signed English, Cued Speech) or languages (ASL) to present items and accurately comprehend the verbally expressed responses of the deaf children.

4. Difficulty selecting tests with items that can be translated easily into sign language without losing the item discrimination feature of certain higher-order items. It may be difficult to match the ASL translation to the intended item discrimination status (e.g., 9 year olds should not be able to answer the question but 12 year olds should be).

5. Difficulty getting agreement in the field about which tests require "deaf norms" and which tests should use so-called "hearing norms" or the norms described in the test manual.

6. Difficulty viewing measured intelligence as it should be viewed—merely as an estimate of the *current* level of functioning—instead of as a fixed measure of overall ability and "potential." If viewed as a fixed ability score, assessment specialists are reluctant to use certain verbally laden intelligence tests because of what is known about delayed access to language stimulation. Delayed access can result from delayed identification of the hearing loss, delayed sign language or cued speech skills of the parents, or improper educational programming.

7. Difficulty getting test publishers to fund the development of large-scale test adaptations and population sampling for deaf and hard of hearing children because of the low incidence nature of deafness.

8. Difficulty keeping up with the revisions of tests in the assessment field.

9. Difficulty envisioning standardized procedures that could be used by most of the psychologists currently serving deaf students.

10. Inappropriate suggestions by leaders in the assessment field that assessment specialists should continue to use nonverbal measures with deaf children because of misinformation about "verbal problems" or because of the communication complexities (Sattler & Dumont, 2004; Smith, 2002; Smith & Stovall, 2002).

Constructing an Assessment Framework

The problems of assessing deaf children's language development are due to the lack of assessment materials normed on deaf students and the inability of many examiners to fully communicate with and analyze the communication of deaf children (Easterbrooks & Baker, 2002). If the assessment field is to move forward in meaningful ways, it is important to develop a general assessment framework that can be used with all deaf and hard of hearing children. This framework must have enough flexibility and rationality to fit the varying assessment and intervention needs of this heterogeneous population, including the necessary psychometric standards and guidelines for translating test data into meaningful intervention and/or programming strategies and approaches.

Deaf and hard of hearing infants, toddlers, children, and adolescents have developmental assessment issues that are not so different from their hearing peers. However, when establishing an assessment framework, theoretical templates, and evaluation protocols, one must call to mind the general nature of expected normal development for one particular age range on one particular measure of developmental behavior, taking into consideration the potential effects of both internal (within the child) and external (in the child's environment) factors.

Even though deaf and hard of hearing children may possess very different and unique external factors, assessment specialists still need to keep in mind the normal course of development of a typical deaf child who has no developmental disabilities (such as mental retardation, visual impairment or blindness, neurological damage or dysfunction, language disorder, learning disability, perceptual—motor-processing disorder, physical disability, and psychological or behavioral disorders) and who has been in a linguistically enriched environment from birth.

Typically, assessment specialists have in mind a deaf child of linguistically competent deaf parents, a child who has been in an educational program where experts are trained in deaf education and related specialty areas. This prototypical deaf child serves as the model of expected normal development and developmental milestones for the initial foundation layer of the assessment framework. Other deaf children will be compared to this ideal model of development and ideal level of environmental richness, and measured in ways that can estimate their similarities to or differences from this ideal model.

The second stage of building the assessment framework involves examining the demographic variables relating to young deaf children. Some of the key variables and characteristics include age at onset of deafness; age at identification of the hearing loss; age when formal instruction by trained Deaf educators took place; degree of the hearing loss; audiological status of the parents; linguistic environment at home and at school; number of siblings or other nonparent relatives who are deaf and who consistently are available to communicate with this child; etiology of deafness (genetic, in vitro complications, birth trauma, illness, unknown, etc.); parental ability to communicate fully with the deaf child; presence or absence of disabling conditions (visual impairment, mental retardation, autistic spectrum disorder, neurological impairment, medical disabilities, severe emotional disturbance, etc.); use of and benefit from auditory amplification; the number of times the communication approach used with a child has been changed; the number of years the child has been using the current communication approach or modality; and the language used in the home. Considering these variables, both internal and external, the assessment specialist should be able to identify "deaf only" and "deaf and disabled" children who have received excellent programming from an early age and those who have received little or inappropriate educational programming.

The fact that fewer than 10% of all deaf children will have an ideal linguistically enriched environment means that a second guiding foundation or template must be established. In this second framework, the deaf child with no additional disabilities who has a fairly "typical" life experience with hearing parents (relevant to age at onset of hearing loss, age at identification of hearing loss, educational programming, and the typical slower rate of parental acquisition of advanced signed communication abilities) is used as the second prototypical model of development in young deaf children. Thus, deaf children with hearing parents will be compared to this set of developmental expectations, so that the lack of complete access to language stimulation will be taken into account when viewing and interpreting the child's overall development. This mental template will assist the assessment specialist in determining if the deaf child appears to be progressing well, given a diminished amount of early language access, or if the developmental pattern is more indicative of a disabling condition accompanying the deafness, such as mental retardation, autistic spectrum disorder, a language-processing deficit, or other condition that may disrupt the normal course of development.

As full access to appropriate educational programming becomes established and maintained for the deaf child with hearing parents, the overall assessment framework and the template of developmental norms must change. That is, the template of developmental norms for the prototypical deaf child with deaf parents becomes the model for all deaf children. Clinical observations often show that deaf children who have no disabling conditions and have involved and attentive hearing parents tend to "catch up" developmentally and have the potential for academic success similar to deaf children (with no disabling conditions) with deaf parents.

Designing Meaningful Assessments: Purposes and Pitfalls

As noted earlier in this text, the Individuals With Disabilities Education Act (IDEA) and related laws require that all public schools in the United States must individualize educational programs and personalize the various types of accommodations, according to the unique needs of each child (Pullin, 2002). Although assessment specialists are required to make reasonable accommodations for students with disabilities, and deaf children are categorized as disabled for special education purposes, the law and school district policies are often vague and confusing. Additionally, IDEA and the Americans With Disabilities Act (1994) also specify certain activities that educators and other school professionals must undertake, including discussing and considering the various accommodations that would be considered reasonable for the specific individual with a specific disability (Pullin, 2002). That is, one cannot make general accommodation standards for a "disability" but must instead evaluate accommodation needs for specific children.

IDEA does allow for nonstandardized test administration procedures to be used for students with disabilities; however, this nonstandard condition or set of conditions must be fully described in assessment reports, in addition to the descriptions of specific training and qualifications of the assessment professional (Pullin, 2002). For statewide, countywide, or national tests, however, it is unclear how much accommodation a deaf student would qualify for under this law. One of the qualification standards for significant testing accommodations, including exemption from the test, is that the student must have a disability that necessitates a significant alteration of the curriculum, thus presenting a mismatch between what is taught and what is tested (Pullin, 2002; McDonnell, McLaughlin, & Morrison, 1997). If, as with many deaf students, a student is exposed to the same curriculum as hearing students, their right to have significant testing accommodations may be limited under No Child Left Behind mandates. School districts would not have a great deal of latitude in how they would meet the testing needs of these deaf and hard of hearing students. Thus, most deaf students would fall into the school category of students with disabling conditions whose disabilities do not exclude them from standardized test requirements. In these cases, students may be eligible for an alternative method of testing various competencies in addition to specific test accommodations, although the content standards must remain the same (McDonnell, McLaughlin, & Morrison, 1997).

High-stakes testing for promotion or graduation is one area where advocates for deaf children have difficulty gaining a significant number of meaningful accommodations. One area that may have been overlooked is within the laws that require multiple measures. Advocates may be able to argue for equivalent multiple measures for deaf students if the justifications are well thought out. In the disability field, in general, the drive toward developing meaningful and valid alternative measures is proving very difficult and is presenting numerous challenges (Ysseldyke, Olson, & Thurlow, 1997).

One area of concern is the practice of requesting inappropriate accommodations relative to the purpose of a particular test. For example, if a test is given to measure reading and writing skills in English, it is not appropriate to request that passages be signed to deaf students because this accommodation disrupts the intended purpose of the test (Olson & Goldstein, 1997). Obviously, "a reading comprehension score generated without the test taker having read the material must necessarily reflect a different ability than if the test taker had read the material" (Behuniak, 2002, p. 52). However, it would be appropriate to request that the instructions be signed, just as they are read to hearing students. If the goal of the test is to measure reading and writing skills in English, few if any accommodations will be granted, nor would they be appropriate. If, however, the test's purpose is to measure science knowledge, it would be reasonable to remove the reading comprehension component for students with difficulties in reading comprehension by signing the questions. Perhaps the test could be administered in two ways—one using print only and one using a signed version of the test items. This way the results could be interpreted based on the student's ability to demonstrate content knowledge with and without the reading factor as a variable. Both pieces of test data would be of significant importance to program and educational strategic planning for a deaf child. First, results would provide information relative to how future curricular content is best presented to a particular child. Second, the test data would provide information about how best to improve literacy skills to enable the child to acquire knowledge independently, thus untying the deaf child from the dependence on a teacher or interpreter to convey information.

Assessment specialists must be sure that all scores used to evaluate the skills and general development of a student with a disability must be valid, reliable, fair, and an appropriate measure for that child (McDonnell, McLaughlin, & Morrison, 1997). For tests to be deemed fair in this context, a test must be said to operate or function in an equivalent manner for two or more groups (Geisinger, Boodoo, & Noble, 2002). In this situation, it might be useful to show that a test would be able to operate in a similar way for both deaf and hearing students. Geisinger and colleagues describe two types of fairness measures. The first fairness measure compares scores for different groups of people to see if the test can be considered equivalent for the groups. An example would be to see if scores on SATs correctly predict college success for the groups under study. The second fairness measure is traditionally thought of as a test item analysis measure: Researchers would test for score patterns that are similar for both groups in identifying a certain skill or characteristic. This is referred to as a differential item functioning test.

Klimoski (1993) and Klimoski & Palmer (1993) have also referred to a test's "robustness" in determining the appropriateness of a test for individuals with disabilities. A test is said to be robust when it can be adapted and modified for individuals with disabilities and still produce valid results, as formally determined. Thus, robust tests are well suited to accurately measure the skills of both deaf and hearing students.

Behuniak cautions against universal decisions for accommodations based on a specific disability and insists that accommodation decisions be made at the level of the individual: —"A generally allowable accommodation might invalidate the scores for one test even though that accommodation would be fine for many other tests" (2002, p. 46). Behuniak goes on to say that "the applicable principle is that the accommodation should increase examinee access while maintaining or enhancing the validity of the resulting test scores" (p. 46).

Both norm-referenced and criterion-referenced tests will often meet eligibility for accommodations, but criterion-referenced tests often need less accommodation considerations than norm-referenced tests. With criterion-referenced tests, such as mandated by No Child Left Behind, a set of skills or specific behaviors are measured that are desired for students to achieve. Results are usually given in terms of the number of items scored as correct and are typically presented in terms of percentages. Conversely, norm-referenced tests compare the performance of the child being tested with a sample of children (the normative sample) who are considered to be representative of the total school-age population. These scores are usually presented in terms of standard scores, where a student's score is given a relative standing as compared with the reference group (the normative sample). Thus, one can see where the child falls along the continuum of the measured skill attainment level or area of development relative to a comparable peer group.

The difficulty with norm-referenced tests for deaf children is that the normative sample typically consists of hearing children. In many instances this may be quite acceptable from a practical perspective (Braden, 1994), but in other instances, it may be an inappropriate use of norms. Additionally, when tests are modified and standard scores are reported for the individual receiving accommodations, the relative standing within the normative group reflected by the standard score may not accurately reflect the true relative position of that person's performance. "Modifications in test stimuli, test procedures, or response format may reduce the meaningfulness of the test norms, because norm-referenced tests are based on the assumption that the same stimuli were administered in the same way to all examinees. Thus, normative comparisons under conditions of accommodation need to be interpreted cautiously" (Smith, 2002, p. 75). This does not mean that norms cannot be used, but that they must be used only when deemed appropriate and with the strongest degree of caution. Additional measures, formal or informal, that corroborate the findings can support the validity of the test even when given under varying test accommodation conditions (Smith, 2002). There is always the need to maintain a balance between the validity of the assessment and the individual student needs (Behuniak, Perlman, & Qualls, 2002).

Curriculum-based assessment procedures and criterion-referenced tests can be very meaningful for deaf children (Bradley-Johnson & Evans, 1991), in addition to analyses of language samples for form, meaning, and use (Schirmer, 1994). Easterbrooks & Baker (2002) suggest using "checklists, tallies, assessment rubrics, artifacts from a portfolio of products, interviews, and analysis of language samples" (p. 102).

It is always helpful to keep in mind the purposes of the assessment for each child. The purposes can include facilitating educational placement decisions, evaluating progress, determining educational approaches to be used, improving educational and intervention strategies, monitoring progress for individual education plans (IEPs) or family education plans (FEPs), determining eligibility for services, determining if a student has met preestablished minimal competency standards, and assessing the effect that various multiple disabilities are having on the educational and developmental processes. Each assessment should be constructed and interpreted differently based on the purpose of the assessment.

For a valid and meaningful assessment to take place, the examiner must possess knowledge of and have experience with that particular disability (Smith, 2002). Additionally, the examiner must be familiar with and competent in providing the accommodation necessary to assure fair and appropriate testing for that individual and must understand the construct that each test is measuring so that accommodations do not alter the test's ability to measure what it was designed to measure (Smith, 2002). Many professionals involved in the education and assessment of children who are deaf often ignore this fundamental accommodation principle by inappropriately advocating for linguistic modifications on tests of English print literacy.

As if the complications of testing a deaf child from a home where hearing parents use English as the language of communication is not challenging enough, the problems of assessment are compounded when the deaf child comes from a home where another language is the native spoken language used by most members of the family. In addition to determining the language of instruction, the language of assessment, and the language to be used for parent education purposes and sign language classes, psychologists and other assessment specialists should be fluent in both English and the language of the deaf child's family, although this is not always feasible.

The background information for a bilingual deaf child from a Spanish-speaking home, for example, should include a dual measure of language proficiency in English and Spanish, determination of the child's transcultural experiences and cross-cultural capabilities, and a determination of appropriate and linguistically and culturally relevant educational programming (Figueroa, Delgado, & Ruiz, 1984). Figueroa and colleagues emphasize that if an examiner administers a test with signs and spoken Spanish to a child whose language is Spanish, then the child "should be taught in a similarly appropriate language and mode of communication" (p. 144). This is an example where our efforts to establish valid and linguistically appropriate assessment communication guidelines for use with deaf children may have a positive effect on communication decisions for instructional purposes in educational programs.

Moores (2001) describes the assessment process in general as being an inexact science at best. "The problem lies in the necessity of 'measuring' small incidences of behavior over a short period of time in a contrived situation and then making generalizations about how an individual will function in the real world" (p. 171). When one adds the complexities inherent in assessing deaf children with all of these linguistic, cultural, and family communication issues, the task is even more daunting and potentially fraught with error.

Summary

The appropriate assessment of deaf children is a difficult task that must be successfully addressed by psychologists and other psychoeducational assessment specialists who work with deaf and hard of hearing children and their families. It is no longer acceptable to merely point out the problems inherent in current assessment modification and adaptation approaches. Assessment professionals must develop tools that make sense for the largest number of students who are deaf and hard of hearing. Checklists, interview protocols, and formal tests of intelligence, language, behavior, social-emotional development, and other critical areas must be developed and/or adapted from existing instruments. Only assessment specialists who have expertise in the developmental issues of deaf children and who also possess advanced communication capabilities with this group of children should assess their current levels of functioning and make educational placement and intervention recommendations. Deaf children should only be formally assessed by experts in the field who understand developmental expectations for deaf children with deaf parents and deaf children with hearing parents.

Norms must be developed for deaf children and should include at least three distinct subgroups: (a) deaf children with no disabling conditions, (b) deaf children with disabilities, and (c) a combined group of all deaf children. Additionally, normative data needs to be developed for linguistically diverse populations of deaf children, such as Latino children from families using Spanish within the home environment, and for subgroups based on their ability to use residual hearing with amplification sufficient to access spoken language.

Measures of deaf children's receptive, expressive, pragmatic, and related areas of language development must be available to have a complete picture of the overall cognitive, social, academic, and behavioral functioning of this group of children. Too many deaf children with superior language skills and relatively weaker nonverbal, performance skills are in jeopardy of being incorrectly labeled as having reduced intellectual abilities because of the heavy reliance on performance-based tests. Conversely, many deaf children with significant "through the air" (signs, speech, or cues) language delays or disorders are falling through the cracks and not receiving the intensive language intervention they need because they score high on nonverbal tests of performance.

The field must define, describe, and specify measurement approaches necessary to be able to define a language disability, language-based learning disability, and other learning challenges that, when detected, can be addressed in terms of intervention and appropriate programming. Students must not be labeled for the sake of labeling, but so their developmental and educational needs can be met. Assessment specialists must apply what they know about ease of access to communication, language exposure, the contribution to intellectual development that language proficiency makes, and the overall developmental needs of deaf children and advocate for the appropriate selection of communication modalities and languages.

Creative suggestions that do not necessarily fit the traditional psychometric model must be tried and held to stringent test standards based on what is known about the development of deaf children, not hearing children. In some instances comparing deaf children with hearing children may be appropriate; however, instead of advocating for "hearing" norms or merely establishing "deaf" norms, or only including a relatively small number of deaf and hard of hearing children in norm samples of tests designed for hearing children, other options should be reviewed. For example, there is benefit in developing tests or cross-test batteries for deaf children based on the ease with which test items can be signed with increasing complexity and which can differentiate between early and later stages of development. Such tests would not have iconic factors, use the same signs for advanced and basic concepts, or have test items fingerspelled for more advanced words (and thus change a language-based test to a spelling-based or literacy-based test). These tests and or test batteries developed by selecting various language-based items from various test instruments could then be normed on various subgroups of deaf children, as discussed earlier, and a small but representative group of hearing children could then be added to the norm sample at various age ranges to allow comparisons. This way, professionals will not be eternally trying to adapt tests designed for hearing children and then give up when they discover that numerous items and subtests cannot be signed while still maintaining the original intention of the test developers or while still maintaining item discrimination capabilities.

Psychologists need to utilize what is known about higher expectations for educational attainment, high-stakes measurement principles (especially when not to modify key aspects of test administration that would change what is being measured, especially on reading tests), and the known discrepancy between the intelligence of deaf children and the group norms for literacy achievement levels. This knowledge can be used to develop educational programs that provide the greatest opportunity for learning for deaf children. Assessment results should be used to assist educators in understanding the language, learning, social-emotional, and testing needs of each individual child who is deaf or hard of hearing.

The collective voice of generations of Deaf adults should not be ignored, but rather fully incorporated into the frameworks, templates, and structures used by psychoeducational assessment professionals. That is, measures of intelligence should be separated from print knowledge of the language spoken within each country. Deaf children's knowledge of academic content should be tested in numerous ways to avoid confounding print literacy knowledge with content knowledge.

Conversely, it is necessary to continue to measure the pure reading skills of deaf children so that professionals can continue to work on better and more effective strategies for teaching deaf children to read and write the print equivalents of the spoken languages in their countries. Deaf children become adolescents and then adults. Deaf adults should not be forever tied to another person, be it a teacher, parent, spouse, interpreter, peer, television announcer, or their own child (deaf or hearing) for information that will continue to enhance and expand their understanding of the world around them. They deserve the freedom that print literacy provides so that ever-increasing levels of information can be acquired independently.

Assessment specialists cannot afford to alter tests in such a way as to bypass the reading process when trying to test reading or bypass the measurement of verbal (sign language, cues, or spoken language) fluency when trying to get an estimate of a person's ability to develop, understand, and manipulate concepts internally through the use of a language code. Instead, efforts must be redoubled to continue to develop meaningful, relevant, and linguistically and culturally appropriate assessment batteries that make the most sense in practical terms for deaf and hard of hearing children and their families.

References

Americans With Disabilities Act of 1990, 42 U.S.C. § 12101 (1994).

Behuniak, P. (2002). Types of commonly requested accommodations. In R. B. Ekstrom & D. K. Smith (Eds.), *Assessing individuals with disabilities in educational, employment, and counseling settings* (pp. 45–58). Washington, DC: American Psychological Association.

Behuniak, P., Perlman, C., & Qualls, A. (2002). Large-scale educational assessment. In R. B. Ekstrom & D. K. Smith (Eds.), *Assessing individuals with disabilities in educational, employment, and counseling settings* (pp. 135–146). Washington, DC: American Psychological Association.

Braden, J. P. (1991). A metal-analytic review of IQ research with deaf persons. In D. S. Martin (Ed.), *Advances in cognition, education, and deafness* (pp. 56–61). Washington, DC: Gallaudet University Press.

Braden, J. P. (1994). *Deafness, deprivation, and IQ.* New York: Plenum Press.

Bradley-Johnson, S., & Evans, L. D. (1991). *Psychoeducational assessment of hearing impaired students: Infancy through high school.* Austin, TX: Pro-Ed.

Easterbrooks, S. R., & Baker, S. (2002). *Language learning in children who are deaf and hard of hearing: Multiple pathways.* Boston: Allyn and Bacon.

Figueroa, R. A., Delgado, G. L., & Ruiz, N. T. (1984). Assessment of Hispanic children: Implications for Hispanic hearing-impaired children. In G. L. Delgado (Ed.), *The Hispanic deaf: Issues and challenges for bilingual special education* (pp. 124–152). Washington, DC: Gallaudet College Press.

Gallaudet Research Institute (2003, December). *Regional and national summary report of data from the 2002–2003 annual survey of deaf and hard of hearing children and youth.* Washington, DC: GRI, Gallaudet University.

Geisinger, K. F., Boodoo, G., & Noble, J. P. (2002). The psychometrics of testing individuals with disabilities. In R. B. Ekstrom & D. K. Smith (Eds.), *Assessing individuals with disabilities in educational, employment, and counseling settings* (pp. 33–42). Washington, DC: American Psychological Association.

Individuals with Disabilities Education Act (IDEA). (1994). 20 U.S.C. §1400 *et. seq.*

Klimoski, R. J. (1993, August 22). Implications of the ADA of 1990 for the practice of psychology. In S. M. Bruyer (Chr.), *Americans With Disabilities Act and Related Canadian Legislation-Implications for Psychologists.* Symposium presented at the annual meeting of the American Psychological Association, Toronto.

Klimoski, R. J., & Palmer, S. (1993). The ADA and the hiring process in organizations. *Consulting Psychologist Journal, 45,* 10–36.

Maller, S. J. (1996). WISC-III verbal item invariance across samples of deaf and hearing children of similar measured ability. *Journal of Psychoeducational Assessment, 14,* 152–165.

Maller, S. J., & Braden, J. P. (1993). The construct and criterion-related validity of the WISC-III with deaf adolescents. In B. A. Bracken & R. S. McCallum (Eds.), *Advances in psychoeducational assessment: Wechsler Intelligence Scale for children* (3rd ed.; Journal of Psychoeducational Assessment Monograph Series; pp. 105–113). Germantown, TN: Psychoeducational Corporation.

McDonnell, L., McLaughlin, M., & Morrison, P. (Eds.) (1997). *Educating one and all: Students with disabilities and standards-based reform.* Washington, DC: National Academy Press.

Miller, M. (1985). Experimental use of signed presentations of the verbal scale of the WISC-R with profoundly deaf children. In D. Martin (Ed.), *Cognition, education, and deafness* (pp. 187–192). Washington, DC: Gallaudet University Press.

Moores, D. F. (1990). *Dissemination of a model to create least restrictive environments for deaf students* (Final Report, Project No. 84133, Grant No. G008720128). Washington, DC: National Institute on Disability and Rehabilitation Research.

Moores, D. F. (2001). *Educating the deaf: Psychology, principles, and practices* (5th ed.). Boston: Houghton Mifflin.

Olson, J. F., & Goldstein, A. A. (1997). *The inclusion of students with disabilities and limited English proficient students in large-scale assessments: A summary of recent progress* (National Center for Education Statistics, Research and Development Report). Washington, DC: Office of Educational Research and Improvement, U.S. Department of Education.

Pullin, D. (2002). Testing individuals with disabilities: Reconciling social service and social policy. In R. B. Ekstrom & D. K. Smith (Eds.), *Assessing individuals with disabilities in educational, employment, and counseling settings* (pp. 11–31). Washington, DC: American Psychological Association.

Sattler, J. M., & Dumont, R. (2004). *Assessment of children: WISC-IV and WPPSI-II supplement*. La Mesa, CA: Jerome M. Sattler.

Schirmer, B. R. (1994). *Language and literacy development in children who are deaf*. New York: Macmillan Publishing Company.

Smith, D. K. (2002). The decision-making process for developing testing accommodations. In R. B. Ekstrom & D. K. Smith (Eds.), *Assessing individuals with disabilities in educational, employment, and counseling settings* (pp. 71–86). Washington, DC: American Psychological Association.

Smith, D. K., & Stovall, D. L. (2002). Individual norm-referenced ability testing. In R. B. Ekstrom & D. K. Smith (Eds.), *Assessing individuals with disabilities in educational, employment, and counseling settings* (pp. 147–171). Washington, DC: American Psychological Association.

Ysseldyke, J., Olson, K., & Thurlow, M. (1997). *Issues and considerations in alternative assessments* (Synthesis Report 27). Minneapolis, MN: National Center on Educational Outcomes.

Suggested Websites

American Annals of the Deaf
Department of Education
407A Fowler Hall 800 Florida Avenue, NE
Washington, DC 20002
http://gupress.gallaudet.edu/annals/

American Psychological Association
750 First Street, NE
Washington, DC 20002-4242
(202) 336-6000
www.apa.org

Consortium for Equity in Standards and Testing (CTEST)
CSTEEP
Campion Hall
Chesnut Hill, MA 02467
(617) 552-4521
www.csteep.bc.edu/ctest

CTB McGraw-Hill
20 Ryan Ranch Road
Monterey, CA 93940
(800) 538-9547
www.ctb.com

National Association of Test Directors (NATD)
1230 17th Street, NW
Washington, DC 20036
(202) 223- 9485
www.natd.org/

National Association of the Deaf (NAD)
814 Thayer Avenue
Silver Spring, MD 20910
(301) 587-1788
www.nad.org

National Association of School Psychologists (NASP)
4340 East West Highway, Suite 402
Bethesda, MD 20814
(301) 657-0275 (V); (301) 657-4155 (TDD)
www.nasp.org

National Center for Research on Evaluation, Standards, and Student Testing (CRESST)
301 GSE & IS, Mailbox 951522
300 Charles E. Young Drive, North
Los Angeles, CA 90095-1522
(310) 206-1532
www.cresst96.cse.ucla.edu/index.htm

National Deaf Education Network and Clearinghouse
Gallaudet University
800 Florida Avenue, NE
Washington, DC 20002-3695
(202) 651-5051 (V); (202) 651-5052 (TDD)
www.clerccenter.gallaudet.edu

MARC MARSCHARK

CAROL CONVERTINO

DONI LAROCK

Optimizing Academic Performance of Deaf Students: Access, Opportunities, and Outcomes

DESPITE THE EFFORTS OF EDUCATORS AND PARENTS, the academic performance of deaf children frequently lags behind that of hearing peers (Allen, 1986; Lang, 2003; Marschark, Lang, & Albertini, 2002; Traxler, 2000). Although we recognize that such generalizations refer to deaf students as a group, and that some deaf children excel in academic settings, progress in improving educational outcomes has been disappointing across most academic content areas. There is general agreement that such difficulties are not direct consequences of hearing loss (e.g., Marschark, 1993; Moores, 2001), but their solution has been elusive. This chapter explores the possibility that the factors underlying deaf students' academic challenges are more general than has been assumed previously. In particular, the education of deaf children might be more successful if both challenges and strategies for overcoming them are viewed across the curriculum rather than in terms of particular content areas.

Preparation of this chapter was supported in part by grants REC-0207394 and REC-0307602 from the National Science Foundation. Any opinions, findings, conclusions, or recommendations expressed in this material are those of the authors and do not necessarily reflect the views of the National Science Foundation.

179

Access to Learning

Even if childhood hearing loss does not necessarily entail academic difficulty, many of the educational and other developmental challenges facing deaf children relate to their relatively impoverished early language environments, which do follow from their hearing losses. Consider reading, for example. The relatively poor literacy achievement of deaf children is often ascribed to early language delays, with claims that deaf children of deaf parents read better (Padden & Ramsey, 1998; Singleton, Supalla, Litchfield, & Schley, 1998). Jensema and Trybus (1978, p. 17), however, found significant positive correlations between reading comprehension and greater use of spoken language between parents and their school-age children, with smaller, negative correlations between comprehension and sign language use.[1] Moores and Sweet (1990) also found small (−.06 and −.02) negative correlations between ASL fluency and reading and writing, respectively, in a group of 65 deaf students of deaf parents. Although such findings are often ignored, Perfetti and Sandak (2000) have noted that reading optimally depends on spoken language. Nevertheless, there is also compelling evidence that deaf parents and hearing parents who provide their young deaf children with both effective early access to language (when sign language may be more effective) and intensive exposure to print materials tend to have children with better literacy skills (e.g., Akamatsu, Musselman, & Zweibel, 2000; Brasel & Quigley, 1977; Leybaert & Alegria, 2003; Mayer & Akamatsu, 1999; Strong & Prinz, 1997). We thus are in need of empirical studies of reading by children of deaf and hearing parents who vary in their own literacy skills and behaviors, so that the links among parental hearing losses, early exposure to language, and literacy-specific factors can be disentangled.

Jensema and Trybus (1978, p. 19) cautioned that "variables other than communication method are operating to give [deaf children with one or two deaf parents] a performance advantage over [deaf] children with hearing parents." Deaf parents may be more accepting of hearing loss, adept at visual communication, and sensitive to the needs of deaf children, but Moeller (2000) found that deaf children whose hearing parents were very involved in early intervention activities demonstrated language scores comparable to hearing peers, independent of whether they used signed or spoken communication. Bodner-Johnson (1986) investigated family factors in deaf students' academic achievement. Through interviews with parents, she identified two significant predictors: acceptance of the child's hearing loss (including a positive view of the Deaf community) and high expectations for their children. Toscano, McKee, and Lepoutre (2002) similarly found that deaf college students who demonstrated high academic literacy skills tended to have parents who were very involved in their early educations, effective family communication (regardless of mode), early and intensive exposure to reading and writing, and high expectations on the part of their parents. Such characteristics may be more frequent in deaf parents than hearing parents, but they need not be.

Corson (1973) explored parents' expectations for their deaf children and their "opin-

---

1. These relations controlled for the influences of program type, student hearing loss, preschool experience, use of hearing aids, and parental income.

ions of deafness" in addition to children's academic achievement, social adjustment, self-image, speech intelligibility, and speechreading. His study was unique in including not only of children of both deaf parents and hearing parents, but also groups who used either spoken language or sign language with their (deaf or hearing) parents, that is, a complete two (parental hearing status) by two (mode of communication [school]) design. Students who used spoken language attended the Clarke School for the Deaf and those who used sign language attended the American School for the Deaf.

Several of Corson's findings are of particular relevance here. First, deaf children of deaf parents significantly surpassed children of hearing parents in reading, mathematics, and speechreading, regardless of the mode of communication used with their parents. Second, children who used spoken language with their parents significantly surpassed those who used sign language in reading, mathematics, speechreading, and social adjustment, regardless of whether their parents were deaf or hearing. Third, deaf parents were significantly more accepting of their children's deafness than hearing parents, even though they had significantly more negative opinions about deafness. Unfortunately, the confounding of mode of communication and school in Corson's study prevents the definitive identification of the locus of his findings, because families of students who used spoken language (Clarke School) tended to have higher socioeconomic status (SES) than those who signed (American School). Corson thus suggested that SES might have explained the differences in both the social adjustment and academic achievement, although school selection factors seem an equally likely possibility (Stinson & Kluwin, 2003). The study did not include a hearing comparison group, which would have further clarified the findings.

In summary, there is considerable evidence that earlier availability of language enhances language development, which, in turn, should support academic growth during the school years. Yet even though deaf children of deaf parents often demonstrate higher academic achievement than those with hearing parents, they do not gain the levels of hearing age-mates (see Marschark, 1993, pp. 62–65, for a review). Marschark, Sapere, Convertino, and Seewagen (2005a) addressed this issue in relation to their finding that deaf students who had deaf parents learned no more from interpreted classroom lectures than peers with hearing parents, but both groups learned significantly less than hearing peers. They suggested that their findings could indicate (a) that mediated instruction (e.g., via interpreting, captioning, etc.) is insufficient or creates a barrier to deaf students' educational achievement, (b) that deaf students at the college level have insufficient skills or abilities, on average, to benefit from instruction at a level comparable to hearing peers, or (c) that methods of instruction designed for hearing students and presented by a "hearing-thinking" instructor in a setting designed for hearing students may not be optimal or even appropriate for the education of deaf students given currently available support services. Although these alternatives are not mutually exclusive, they clearly have common roots and to the extent that alternatives (a) and (b) are true, they both cause and reflect (c). This situation might be altered by using different instructional and communication methods during the K–12 years, but significant change at the college level seems unlikely. Because this argument is the whole point of this chapter, let us consider several pieces of the academic puzzle, noting their mutual influence and possible synergistic effects as we go along.

What Is So Special About Special Education?

Detterman and Thompson (1997) argued that effective special education methods cannot be developed until we better understand individual differences and the cognitive abilities underlying learning and until educators develop specific and realistic outcome goals. With regard to the inclusive (mainstream) approach to special education, Detterman and Thompson argued: "The most troubling part about this movement...is that there is little or no evidence to indicate that one approach is better than the other.... There is no unified body of research findings that would allow a rational choice among philosophical alternatives" (p. 1084). In their view, the revolutionary (if nominal) change in access to education by children with disabilities has not been matched by change in educational methods—a conclusion that should ring true to anyone involved in the education of deaf students (see Cokely, 2005).

Despite new communication methods, new instructional methods, and new educational alternatives coming into vogue at regular intervals during the past 30 years of the mainstreaming movement, deaf students generally remain behind their hearing peers in academic achievement, with no hint of agreement on the reasons for these differences. Marschark and Lukomski (2001) claimed that this situation follows from the view common to many teachers and other professionals that, hearing and speech aside, "deaf and hard of hearing students are just like hearing students" (Seal, 1998, p. 128). They suggested that although this assumption is consistent with notions of equity and our belief in the potential of deaf learners, its blind acceptance might do deaf students a greater disservice than treating them as though they are different from hearing children. Rather, there are unique interactions among language fluencies, cognitive and academic abilities, assessment methods, and content knowledge that deaf children bring to the learning context. If we want to optimize academic success of deaf students, or just level the playing field, educational methods used in teaching them thus might need to change in some fundamental ways. Some of these changes, however, may not be practical in mainstream settings, because of a lack of knowledge on the part of teachers and interpreters about the cognitive abilities underlying learning by deaf students or their lack of language expertise.

Our concern about the potential and future of deaf education, across the curriculum and across K–12 and postsecondary levels, derives from recent investigations of deaf students' performance in various academic settings and findings concerning interaction among language, cognition, and learning of deaf children and young adults. Looking ahead, although some of the conclusions from these studies may appear frustrating, we believe that their demonstration and the discussion that has followed augur well for our ability to change the historical trend in educating deaf students. Whether we have the will and resources to act accordingly is another question.

Alternative School Settings: Is There a Level Playing Field?

This section considers the relation of language and learning by examining research concerning the comprehension of interpreted lectures by deaf students. The rationale for ordering our discussion in this manner is that it mirrors our own thinking about ways to promote greater educational success by deaf students, first recognizing their readiness to compete in the college classroom, then trying to determine how they "got to where they are," and leading to suggestions of methods by which teachers and support services might better prepare them. Our efforts in this regard have led us to the cognitive and language development literatures, which, as it turns out, mesh well with research on the education of deaf students and in some cases point to ignorance or oversight on the part of those of us who seek to enhance access, opportunities, and outcomes for deaf students.

Is Mainstream Education Equitable and Appropriate?

Those involved in the education of deaf students frequently encounter the suggestion that "mediated instruction," even if provided by superlative interpreters under optimum conditions, could never be comparable to direct instruction by qualified teachers who can effectively communicate directly with their students and share cultural and cognitive organization and knowledge.[2] The point here is not to minimize the problems associated with teachers and interpreters whose lack of communication skills jeopardize the academic futures of the students they serve. Rather, the suggestion is that beyond the quality of communication used in the classroom, deaf students may be underprepared relative to hearing peers in terms of learning strategies and their content and world knowledge, thus placing them at risk in mainstream settings (Marschark, Sapere, Convertino, Seewagen, & Maltzen, 2004; Marschark, Sapere, Convertino, & Seewagen, 2005a). Although we originally thought that communication was the preeminent issue, we are having second thoughts.

Marschark et al. (2005a) reviewed the relatively limited literature concerning deaf students' understanding of interpreted classroom communication in the context of the demands of mainstream education. They noted that the basis for mainstream school placement for deaf children lies in the belief that deaf children can be educated in that environment as well as or better than in special settings. This belief assumes that information communicated by a hearing teacher for a hearing class is equally accessible to deaf students, who, as are described in the following sections, have knowledge structures and learning styles somewhat different from those of hearing peers. Some such differences will turn out to be either trivial or transient in their effects, but others may put deaf students at a serious academic disadvantage

---

2. Given how infrequently this ideal situation occurs (if ever), such claims are gratuitous and perhaps better suited to theoretical discussion than empirical verification. In fact, we now have data indicating that even when interpreters do capture all relevant information (well enough for other interpreters to comprehend near ceiling), deaf college students still learn significantly less that hearing peers.

in mainstream classrooms compared to settings where those special needs are recognized and accommodated.

Faith in mainstream education for deaf students also assumes that for those students who depend on signed communication, sign language interpreting can provide them with access to classroom communication comparable to the access enjoyed by their hearing peers through spoken language. The available evidence, however, casts some doubt on this assumption. Most educational interpreters acknowledge that interpreting in K–12 classrooms, where deaf students are still learning language and are in need of competent language models, tends to be relatively poor (e.g., Winston, 2005). That view is supported by evidence reported by Schick, Williams, and Bolster (1999). They evaluated interpreters' skills in K–12 educational settings and found that less than half of the interpreters performed at a level considered minimally acceptable for educational interpreting.

A series of studies by Marschark and his colleagues has taken a rather different approach, utilizing optimal classroom settings with highly skilled interpreters to assess the comprehension of educational content by deaf students with different language and demographic backgrounds. Across experiments incorporating a variety of student characteristics, interpreter characteristics, and settings, deaf students have consistently scored significantly below hearing peers on comprehension tests of lecture content, even when prior content knowledge is controlled (Marschark et al., 2004, 2005a, 2005b). Lest it be assumed that the issue here is one relating specifically to sign language interpreting, it is important to note that similar findings have been obtained in studies examining deaf students' learning via systems that provide real-time text in the classroom (Stinson, Meath-Lang, & MacLeod, 1981; Stinson et al., 2000).

Studies of this sort, as well as reports of academic achievement by deaf students over the past 30 years, lead us to the conclusion that the mainstream classroom does not provide deaf students with a "level playing field" in their pursuit of academic achievement. It is important that this lack of equity is not the fault of interpreters or captionists. Indeed, the findings of Marschark et al. (2004, 2005a) suggest that no provision of sign language interpreting in the classroom—at least not given the present roles of interpreters and mainstream classroom instructors—is likely to provide educational equity for deaf and hearing students. But, if it is not the medium, where is the impediment to equality of educational opportunity? Simply put, it appears that the conditions of early childhood and K–12 education encountered by most deaf children result in their being less prepared than hearing peers for classroom learning, a gap likely to increase with age. In part, this difference follows from teachers and interpreters having separate, noncollaborative roles and accountability (Ramsey, 1997). At its heart, however, the problem is that deaf students often receive instruction that is inconsistent with their prior knowledge, learning strategies, and language comprehension skills. We thus now turn to a brief treatment of academic achievement by deaf learners, consideration of ways in which they appear to be different than hearing learners, and the implications for future research and practice.

Predicting Academic Achievement in Alternative School Settings

Although a complete discussion of the factors affecting deaf students' performance in various school settings is beyond the scope of this chapter (see Karchmer & Mitchell, 2003; Kluwin, 1992; Kluwin & Gaustad, 1992; Powers, 2003), several issues are noteworthy here because they affect our understanding of deaf students' academic performance in different contexts. Most obviously, students in a particular school setting usually have characteristics that already favorably match that program. Students who enter mainstream programs, for example, often are already functioning at a level that leads parents and educators to assume that they can "handle it." They may have less severe hearing losses, later age of onset, or more parental involvement in their education (Karchmer & Mitchell, 2003; Moeller, 2000). Exposure to signed and spoken communication in mainstream programs also may be more beneficial than the exposure only to spoken language or sign language in separate schools (Akamatsu, Musselman, & Zweibel, 2000). Alternatively, such settings may deny young deaf students access to fluent language models in either spoken or sign modes, creating a barrier to learning. If any one of these variables is individually insufficient to affect achievement, a combination of their effects might be responsible for differences observed between deaf and hearing students' academic success.

Research concerning the academic achievement of deaf children occasionally makes use of classroom-based information (e.g., GPA, specific examinations) but usually relies on standardized tests (Marschark, Lang, & Albertini, 2002). Using such measures, deaf children in mainstream settings typically demonstrate higher levels of achievement than those in special school settings (Stinson & Kluwin, 2003; Lynas, 1986), and students who are partially mainstreamed tend to do better when they spend more hours per week in such settings (Holt, 1994). Few studies have taken into account the many confounds in school placement and standardized test performance as a function of parent preference, school availability, and persistence. When demographic variables are taken into account in such comparisons, however, there still appears to be a slight academic advantage for students in mainstream settings (Furstenberg & Doyal, 1994; Kluwin, 1993). Kluwin (1993), for example, found that deaf students in mainstream high school programs were more likely to be functioning at grade level than those in separate school placements, largely because they took more academic courses. This finding is consistent with the finding among hearing students that the academic rigor of high school courses taken is a much better predictor of college graduation than entrance examination scores, high school grades, or class ranks (Adelman, 1999). Thus, the academic nature and resources of schools must be considered along with the competencies of students, teachers, and interpreters.

One infrequently discussed factor in the academic achievement of deaf students is transfer across school settings. Some deaf students enrolled in special programs move to mainstream programs, and others move from mainstream programs to schools for the deaf or other separate programs. Regardless of whether movement in these two directions is quantitatively the same, the qualitative effects are quite different. Those students moving into the mainstream are likely to be performing at relatively high levels, demonstrating somewhat better literacy skills, and have personal characteristics (e.g., motivation, intelligence, self-esteem) that support their performance in that setting. Movement in that direction thus may lower the mean actual or perceived intellectual/academic "pool" of students left in the special program, even while increasing the mean level of performance of deaf students in the mainstream as a group. Meanwhile, movement of students from the mainstream to schools for the deaf usually involves students whose language abilities, literacy skills, or expected standardized test performance would lower the mean level of performance of deaf students in the regular school classroom. Having fallen behind academically (and perhaps cognitively and socially) in the mainstream, their belated entry into a school for the deaf would lower the overall performance for children in that setting. As a result of this inequity, among others, simple comparisons of the two educational settings are unlikely to give us a true picture of the benefit of these alternative placements, either in general or for any particular student.

Because of the complexity of assessing the value of alternative school placements for deaf students, most of the variability observed in such comparisons is either unexplained or due to individual differences among the students themselves (Karchmer & Mitchell, 2003; Kluwin, 1992; Kluwin & Moores, 1985). Indeed, Karchmer and Mitchell (2003) reported that when other factors are taken into account, placement accounts for as little as 1% of the variability seen in deaf children's academic achievement. Most important, however, deaf students in mainstream settings still tend to lag behind hearing peers in achievement (e.g., Powers, 2003; Wolk & Allen, 1984).

Finally, regardless of school placement, parental and teacher expectations for deaf students—and perhaps students' expectations for themselves—play an important role in academic success. Although there has been little attention given to achievement motivation in deaf children, Stinson (1974, 1978) found that hearing mothers of deaf children did not have as high expectations for their children's achievement motivation as hearing mothers of hearing children. His results reflected the importance of communication between parents and their children, and the way in which interactions in such situations can influence important developmental characteristics of deaf children. It is interesting to note, however, the lack of any more recent empirical research concerning parents' and teachers' expectations for deaf students in academic and social settings. Given the magnitude of changes in educational placement over the past three decades and the continuing debate over its success, examination of relations among expectations and achievement in alternative school placements, including those of deaf and hearing parents and teachers relevant to mainstream and special education settings, seems a potentially important piece of the education puzzle. The lack of such work is even more puzzling.

Educationally Relevant Cognitive Characteristics of Deaf Students

If variability in deaf students' academic performance is largely unexplained, where do we look for ways to improve their lags relative to hearing peers? One possibility is the cognitive processes underlying learning, processes in which deaf students are far more heterogeneous than hearing students (Marschark, 1993; McEvoy, Marschark, & Nelson, 1999). Schick (2005), Tharpe, Ashmead, and Rothpletz (2002), and Marschark (2003) suggested that individuals who are deaf are likely to deal with the world somewhat differently than individuals who are not. They all emphasized that such differences need not imply deficiencies and that not all deaf students necessarily display them; indeed, Schick (2005) and Marschark (2004) emphasized recognition of such differences as an important educational opportunity. Still, the "deaf as different" hypothesis rests on a fine line between a pedagogical view of deaf students as having special, but as yet not fully identified, educational needs and a pathological view of them as in need of "fixing" (Moores, 2001). The education of deaf students is clearly in need of repair, however, and has been for some time. A careful empirical consideration of cognitive differences between deaf and hearing students help to explain data from a variety of cognitive and academic domains. It will be necessary to determine whether hearing loss per se is a causal factor in the differences. Some results suggest that the two groups simply vary in their approaches to cognitive tasks; others indicate an influence of primary mode of communication (speech versus sign) or varying amounts of relevant background knowledge.

With regard to visual processing, for example, deaf signers perform better than either hearing or deaf individuals who use spoken language in their ability to rapidly shift visual attention or scan visual stimuli (Rettenback, Diller, & Sireteanu, 1999), visually detect both motion and sign language in the periphery (Corina, Kritchevsky, & Bellugi, 1992; Neville & Lawson, 1987; Swisher, 1993), and recognize faces (Bellugi et al., 1990). Other investigators have demonstrated that deaf and hearing signers are faster in generating and manipulating mental images than are nonsigning peers (Chamberlain & Mayberry, 1994; Emmorey & Kosslyn, 1996; Emmorey, Kosslyn, & Bellugi, 1993; Talbot & Haude, 1993). The fact that such advantages are not found among deaf individuals who rely on spoken language indicates that the results are more related to the effects of sign language use rather than hearing loss. This situation contrasts with results from memory studies, where differences in mental representation, experience, and organization of knowledge effect performance differences between deaf and hearing individuals. In the domain of short-term or working memory, for example, deaf adults and children tend to recall less from lists of verbal items (text or signs) relative to hearing peers across a variety of paradigms and studies (see Logan, Mayberry, & Fletcher, 1996; Marschark & Mayer, 1998, for reviews). Lichtenstein (1998), Marschark and Mayer (1998), and Wilson and Emmorey (1997) showed that this difference results from the form of mental representation used in memory coding (i.e., speech-based versus sign-based codes), but the relation of such findings to learning still needs to be addressed.

Studies of long-term or semantic memory typically reveal differences in organization and utilization of information in recall of individual items, with potentially related effects in studies of recall from texts and signed passages. Studies utilizing word association tasks have demonstrated considerable overlap in deaf and hearing students' knowledge organization but also have revealed significant differences in the strength and spread of associations among concepts—differences likely to influence comprehension of either signing or reading (e.g., Marschark, Convertino, McEvoy, &

Masteller, 2004; McEvoy, Marschark, & Nelson, 1999). Similar results are obtained in studies examining the organization of recall for words (Liben, 1979) and text (Banks, Gray, & Fyfe, 1990; Marschark, DeBeni, Polazzo, & Cornoldi, 1993), even when text is written in gloss (i.e., "written" British Sign Language, Banks, Gray, & Fyfe, 1990). In those studies, deaf students remembered less than hearing peers, and what they did recall generally consisted of fragments or disconnected words and phrases, whereas hearing students tended to remember semantic information more holistically. Although the specific effects of these findings in the classroom are still uninvestigated, their potential effect on learning appears obvious. Beyond their explanatory power and the warning they carry, however, they also reflect different modes of information processing that could be tapped in educational settings (Marschark, 2004).

Among the information-processing/utilization differences that have been observed across a variety of paradigms are those relating to the ease of processing sequential information versus simultaneously presented material (e.g., Todman & Seedhouse, 1994) and reliance on relational versus item-specific processing (e.g., Marschark, 2003). As in studies of memory, in a variety of problem solving and other academic tasks, deaf students have been found more likely than hearing age-mates to focus on individual item information rather than relations among items (Ottem, 1980; Richardson, MacLeod-Gallinger, McKee, & Long, 1999). Such findings are consistent with earlier studies demonstrating similar performance by deaf and hearing students when tasks involved only a single relevant dimension, but better performance by hearing than deaf individuals when two dimensions and a relation between them had to be considered simultaneously (Ottem, 1980). Focus on individual-item information clearly affects learning and performance in academic domains from mathematics to history, because multiple factors must be considered to understand the causes and outcomes of problems and events.

Another ability at play in academic differences observed between deaf and hearing students is metacognition. To plan the application of knowledge or develop hypotheses, students need to have some awareness of their own cognitive processes (Kruger & Dunning, 1999; Sinkavich, 1995). They need to determine a goal, consider alternative means of achieving it, including barriers and facilitators to success, and perhaps play out various scenarios. This establishment of a mental problem-solving space and reflection on how to bring knowledge to bear on a problem plays an important role in a variety of academic contexts. In reading, for example, we monitor our own comprehension processes, hopefully recognizing when they break down. We notice when we come upon words that we do not know and use context to figure them out. Alternative meanings of ambiguous passages are mulled over, and we use lexical knowledge and contextual inferences to understand them (Oakhill & Cain, 2000).

Studies of metacognition in education have entailed diverse methodologies, from simply asking students "Why did you do that?" or "When you wrote that, what were you thinking?" to more complex tasks that indirectly reveal the use of alternative strategies. Although relatively few studies have examined metacognition among deaf children, what research is available suggests that deaf students are less likely than hearing students to consider alternative approaches to a task prior to undertaking it or while working through it. In domains such as reading and mathematics, deaf students frequently are unaware of their performance, apply strategies that are inappropriate, or fail to apply strategies we know are in their repertoires (Kelly & Mousley, 2000; Marschark & Everhart, 1999; see Strassman, 1997, for a review with regard to reading and Marschark & Mayer, 1998, with regard to memory). Those findings are consistent with the results of Marschark et al. (2004), which demonstrate that hearing students but not deaf students were able to predict their performance on comprehension tests following interpreted classroom lectures.

One likely explanation for many deaf students' failure to apply metacognitive skills appears to have explanatory power with regard to their observed individual-item processing orientation. In a variety of domains, the parents and teachers of deaf students often take a more concrete and directive approach to problem solving, hoping to ensure that their students will have a clear understanding of a particular solution, intention, or strategy, an approach inversely related to ease of communication. Allowing children to discover their own ways of doing things and the relative value of different strategies while discussing them with others is a much more time-consuming activity—especially in the classroom—but it is one that provides for more flexible thinking and the development of metacognition. Oddly, early studies in the area of creativity supported the view that deaf children were concrete and literal in their thinking (i.e., unlikely to be able to master metacognitive skills), leading to teaching techniques that focused on narrower, more limited approaches to thinking and learning (see Blackwell, Engen, Fischgrund, & Zarcadoolas, 1978; Luetke-Stahlman & Luckner, 1991, for examples). This approach created a self-fulfilling prophecy, as the emphasis on literal language discouraged diverse problem solving skills and led to limited metacognitive skills rather than the other way around.

Prescription or Placebo: How Do We Optimize Education for Deaf Students?

The preceding discussion has outlined several differences between deaf and hearing students that both reflect and influence differences in learning. Rather than being intended as an indictment of particular educational methods or a description of a necessary state of affairs, the point has been that offering deaf students access to what appear to be equal educational opportunities may not be the same as offering equity in education. There is a long history in deaf education in which philosophies about communication have created educational structures focused more on political views and administrative expediency than on documented educational value. It is our view that most of these debates have failed to offer prescriptions for improving educational success of deaf students, even if they have provided placebos that make us feel that we are doing something constructive. Claims that "all children are the same" and prior claims that "deaf children are deficient" have equally missed the mark of identifying the needs of deaf learners and shaping educational opportunities to match them. If this discussion of academically relevant differences between deaf and hearing students is to lead to changes, it is incumbent on us to point to directions for possible educational modifications and studies to evaluate their effectiveness. So, let us consider a few possibilities.

Access and Quality in Education Are Not the Same Thing

Access has been the mantra of mainstream education, but it is unclear that this access has been translated into quality education. Stinson and Antia (1999) pointed out that the diversity of settings and students involved in deaf education makes any simple understanding or solutions to the issues facing them unlikely. Clearly, however, simply placing deaf students in public schools does not ensure access to a quality education, regardless of the quality of the classroom for hearing students. Studies involving college-level classrooms have indicated that even with support services such as interpreting or real-time text displays, deaf students are not on an even footing with hearing peers. Regardless of whether the ultimate cause of this discrepancy is a cumulative effect of language deficits (early and/or late), inadequate K–12 educational resources, or something specific to literacy skills, deaf students are not gaining all that their hearing peers are gaining in the classroom.

If deaf students really are faced with poorer quality direct instruction, poorer quality interpreters, or lesser access during the formative educational years, the notion that either a special program or a mainstream program can offer them an equitable and appropriate public education is without foundation. Yet, evaluations of the extent of access and the quality of K–12 education or even of college-level education are not being conducted. At least in part, this gap stems from researchers' not wanting to ask the questions and from administrators' fearing that they will not be able to accommodate the answers. These are questions in need of answers, even if we might not have sufficient resources to implement them. Unless we conduct the necessary research, however, we will miss opportunities for change—or not even know where change is necessary.

Alternative School Placements

Most educational investigators familiar with either deaf students or other students with special needs agree that a broad range of program alternatives are needed to serve the needs of those students. In deaf education, however, the move is clearly in the other direction. Leigh (2003) argued that as universal newborn hearing screening (UNHS) becomes more widely available, the goal should be the placement of young children into programs commensurate with their skills. Such placements are possible not only with regard to signed versus spoken communication, but also within programs favoring one mode or another, depending on the strengths and weaknesses of each child in speech and hearing skills (Blamey, Sarant, & Paatsch, 2006). Leigh noted, however, that UNHS has resulted in most deaf children being placed in auditory-oral programming, with sign-based programs usually held as a placement of last resort. In his view, this result distorts the promise of UNHS and unfairly puts many deaf children at academic risk. More broadly, it deprives the many children who will not achieve spoken language intelligibility of the opportunity to learn language early, naturally, and hence more easily (Yoshinaga-Itano, 2006).

While schools and programs for deaf students have been downsized or closed, a broader look at education in society shows that educators are returning to cloistered and separate educational settings for "special needs" groups. African-Americans, females, and even gay students are being afforded all-inclusive educations in all-exclusive settings. Inclusive education may allow parents and administrators to feel that they have provided equal access to the public school classroom, but it is far from clear that it has provided deaf students with equal access to the curriculum. This situation is particularly evident when newer interpreters and teachers are placed at the elementary level, because it is less demanding than upper grades. Their students may eventually graduate, but it is unlikely that they will do so with the same level of skill and knowledge as hearing peers who have had more complete access to classroom communication and cocurricular activities.

The point here is that neither mainstream placement nor placement in a school or program designed for deaf students offers any panacea. There are sufficient bad examples on both sides, with neither having any general advantage. Unfortunately, the appearance is that decisions about who teaches deaf children, and how, are being made without assessments of what works, where, and for whom. Despite broad agreement that there is no single appropriate educational placement for deaf students, we continue to look for it. If "segregated" education is better for some students, we need to make sure it is of equal quality to that enjoyed by hearing students. If inclusive education is to work, we need to ensure that deaf students not only have access to the classroom, but to the curriculum within it.

Modifying Instructional Methods to Better Serve Deaf Students

Although there is a strong tendency to argue that all children learn in much the same ways, a variety of empirical facts described in this chapter indicate that this is not the case. The goal now should be to determine the extent to which observed differences influence long-term learning and to develop methods to compensate for them or take advantage of them in the classroom. Such differences need not indicate a necessity for separate school placements, with "teachers of the deaf." Most teachers of the deaf lack content training in the courses they teach, so there is no reason to believe that they will offer deaf students much more than a content-knowledgeable public school teacher who has no experience with deaf students. We also recognize the impracticality of attempting to train all public school teachers in methods appropriate for educating deaf students. Although it may be that any method that improves learning by deaf students also facilitates learning by hearing students, there are more efficient alternatives. For example, we could provide incentives for more skilled teachers and interpreters to work in K–12 settings, where their communication proficiencies and experience would provide young deaf children with role models and a solid foundation for future educational success. We could provide interpreters with training concerning the development and education of deaf children, encourage greater collaboration between them and teachers (who could take advantage of that knowledge), and appropriately educate support staff (e.g., tutors or itinerant teachers) to work with teachers on specific instructional strategies congruent with deaf students' cognitive strengths. First, however, we have to recognize and accept those differences that are academically meaningful and develop instructional strategies that take advantage of empirical findings to advance student knowledge.

Marschark, Lang, and Albertini (2002, pp. 199–200) suggested using participative methods for instructing deaf students, some of which were more popular during the 1920s to 1960s than they are now (e.g., learning about geography and culture by planning an imaginary trip) (see also Marschark & Lukomski, 2001). Some methodologies used earlier in schools for deaf students might be more effective now, in concert with early intervention programs for deaf children, even if they were less successful as post hoc remedial strategies. However, there also may be teaching strategies appropriate in self-contained classrooms or schools for deaf children, which are not necessary or effective in mainstream settings (e.g., focusing on language learning with older children). In some cases, they do not have a chance of being used, because teachers in public schools are not trained to teach deaf children and are not attracted to what appear to be simple solutions (e.g., more inclusive classroom interactions, rather than calling on individual children). In other cases, potentially valuable instructional strategies are ignored because they are old, even if they offer new possibilities within the modern classroom (Marschark, Lang, & Albertini, 2002).

The heterogeneity of deaf students also presents a challenge for optimizing education, regardless of whether it occurs in mainstream or separate school settings. How can deaf students have equal access to the curriculum when they are competing with large numbers of students with varying educational needs (see Detterman & Thompson, 1997)? Stone (2000) suggested that there is a paradigm shift occurring in deaf education away from traditional "chalk and talk" instruction toward methods such as cooperative learning, active learning, and deaf-centered curricula, which alter content to better fit the interest and cultural orientations of deaf students. It remains unclear whether "deaf curricula" (or gender-oriented or race-oriented curricula) actually promote greater motivation or learning on the part of deaf students. In the case of parochial schools, religious training and rigorous education are combined with varying but explicit emphasis on one or the other. Such a combination might not be seen as acceptable in a public school setting in the United States because of the "special" nature of government-religion links, but race or disability status may not be any less sensitive or amenable to such educational philosophies. Multicultural curricula do not eliminate information that students need to succeed academically, but encourage students to take greater pride in themselves and their accomplishments and sensitize teachers to cultural and community issues valued by the children they teach.

Changing the Face of Deaf Education

The suggestion that we alter the relationships among interpreters, teachers of the deaf, and support personnel is not made lightly. While looking for solutions, we might also add changing the relationships between schools for deaf students and local public or private schools, and creating partnerships as some have done. In the case of K–12 programs, such partnerships allow deaf students to sample mainstream environments and can educate students and teachers about diversity in education, assuming that the previous access and quality issues can be resolved first. The problem, of course, is how to bring about such changes. More than 25 years of mainstreaming has taught us that simple assimilation is not the answer (Antia & Kreimeyer, 2003; Stinson & Kluwin, 2003).

Education of deaf students, whether in the mainstream or in special programs, appears to have followed a trend in which the higher the student is on the education ladder, the more resources the student receives. Instead, the best and most resources should go to the child in an elementary, middle, or high school setting. If we support students properly in the earlier years, they are more likely to become independent learners in their later careers. This approach also would help to prepare students for the self-reliance and lack of resources they will face once they leave school for the workplace. Whatever approach one wishes to take, greater emphasis must be put on quality and access in the education of younger deaf children, before insurmountable lags in education and achievement have time to develop. Any change—at least on the scale needed—will be costly, but changes earlier will be less so, even if their payoff takes time to accrue.[3]

Back to Basics

The goal of this chapter has not been to suggest that there is any single solution to the challenges facing deaf learners today. If there are educational fundamentals that have worked for generations of hearing schoolchildren, even if they are appropriate today, there is no guarantee that they are the right fundamentals for deaf children or that we know how to teach them in ways that will achieve the same end. Consideration of the current state of knowledge in the field of education, however, does offer some "basics" that should benefit deaf children across a variety of home and school settings. At least four such basics are supported by diverse research and pedagogical literatures.

First, academic achievement tends to be greater in families where parents are more involved in their children's curricular and cocurricular activities. In the case of deaf children, this means that we will have to continue to work to optimize parent-child communication and the rapid acceptance by parents of their children's hearing losses. Those deaf children also will have better relationships with their parents, better communication skills, and better role models, which are all predictors of success (Calderon & Greenberg, 1997). Such interactions begin with early intervention programming and need to be supported throughout the school years. UNHS should facilitate these changes, if we implement it without biases or preconceived ideas of what will be best for "all deaf children."

Second, achievement across the curriculum depends on academic rigor. Rigor is not simply about teaching facts and information, but also about providing the strategies and thinking skills necessary for their acquisition ("learning to fish, rather than getting a fish"). To this end, research clearly demonstrates that we have to enhance early educational practices that will make deaf students more flexible problem solvers, more aware that there are always alternatives, and more likely to make inferences and see relations among concepts.

Third, we have to improve literacy skills. Most of what we know about the world comes from reading, a situation that is not likely to change any time soon regardless of

---

3. Unfortunately, politicians appear to support changes that promise early payoff (i.e., in time for reelection campaigns). Investments in the future are harder to come by, especially in harder economic times.

what technologies might be available. The biographies of most successful deaf people include familiarity and comfort with reading (e.g., Lang & Meath-Lang, 1995). Students who show the greatest penchant for literacy also tend to be those who have had more involved parents (Toscano, McKee, & Lepoutre, 2001) and supportive early educational environments. These basics are far from independent, but despite all of the claims about what makes a deaf student a good reader, there is a surprising lack of research concerning the role of parents as reading models, the importance of reading materials in the home, and early literacy experiences for deaf children. Having deaf parents may not be the answer to literacy for all deaf students, but we need to pay greater attention to those deaf and hearing parents who have produced successful readers and find the "tricky mix" that supported that achievement (Nelson, Loncke, & Camarata, 1993).

Fourth, there is little doubt that early access to language leads to later access to language and to academic access. The fact that, on average, deaf children who have access to sign language early show greater developmental and academic achievement (Calderon & Greenberg, 1997) does not mean that sign language is best for all deaf children, but it does indicate the advantage offered by access to language during the early years. The challenge is to match each child with support and language exposure that offers them optimal access to language, regardless of its mode. The team approach necessary for this change to occur has been absent for many years, but is gaining new momentum with the popularity of cochlear implants and bilingual programming. Yet, evaluations of either cochlear implantation or bilingual programs in terms of academic success are almost nonexistent, with little evidence to support their efficacy or efficiency.

Finally, if there is one basic that supports the preceding four, it is the need for informed research concerning the cognitive abilities underlying learning by deaf children and informed interpretation and application of those findings. As long as philosophies, opinions, and political expediencies guide the education of deaf students, there is little chance of significant improvement. All too often, poor research or anecdote has been taken as offering directions for educational change, and limited research findings have been generalized beyond the bounds of applicability. Collaboration among all those involved in the education of deaf students is the only way to improve the educational success of deaf students, both by planning and supporting investigation and by working together to ensure that deaf children are offered high-quality, accessible academic opportunities. If we cannot succeed, we cannot expect them to.

References

Adelman, C. (1999). Answers in the tool box: Academic intensity, attendance patterns, and bachelor's degree attainment (Publication No. PLLI 1999-8021).Washington, DC: U.S. Department of Education.

Akamatsu, C. T., Musselman, C., & Zweibel, A. (2000). Nature vs. nurture in the development of cognition in deaf people. In P. Spencer, C. Erting, & M. Marschark (Eds.), *Development in context: The deaf children in the family and at school* (pp. 255–274). Mahwah, NJ: Lawrence Erlbaum Associates.

Allen, T. E. (1986). Patterns of academic achievement among hearing impaired students: 1974–1983. In A. N. Shildroth & M. A. Karchmer (Eds.), *Deaf children in America* (pp. 161–206). San Diego, CA: College-Hill Press.

Antia, S. D., & Kreimeyer, K. (2003). Peer interactions of deaf and hard of hearing children. In M. Marschark & P. E. Spencer (Eds.), *Oxford handbook of deaf studies, language, and education* (pp. 164–176). New York: Oxford University Press.

Banks, J., Gray, C., & Fyfe, R. (1990). The written recall of printed stories by severely deaf children. *British Journal of Educational Psychology, 60*, 192–206.

Bellugi, U., O'Grady, L., Lillo-Martin, D., O'Grady, M., van Hoek, K., & Corina, D. (1990). Enhancement of spatial cognition in deaf children. In V. Volterra & C. J. Erting (Eds.), *From gesture to language in hearing and deaf children* (pp. 278–298). New York: Springer-Verlag.

Blackwell, P., Engen, E., Fischgrund, J., & Zarcadoolas, C. (1978). *Sentences and other systems: A language and learning curriculum for hearing-impaired children.* Washington, DC: National Association of the Deaf.

Blamey, P. J., Sarant, J. Z., & Paatsch, L. E. (2006). Relationships among speech perception and language measures in hard-of-hearing children. In P. E. Spencer & M. Marschark (Eds.), *Advances in spoken language development by deaf children* (pp. 85–102). New York: Oxford University Press.

Bodner-Johnson, B. (1986). The family environment and achievement of deaf students: A discriminant analysis. *Exceptional Children, 52*, 443–449.

Brasel, K., & Quigley, S. P. (1977). Influence of certain language and communicative environments in early childhood on the development of language in deaf individuals. *Journal of Speech and Hearing Research, 20*, 95–107.

Calderon, R., & Greenberg, M. (1997). The effectiveness of early intervention for deaf children and children with hearing loss. In M. J. Guralnik (Ed.), *The effectiveness of early intervention* (pp. 455–482). Baltimore: Paul H. Brookes.

Chamberlain, C., & Mayberry, R. I. (1994, May). *Do the deaf "see" better? Effects of deafness on visuospatial skills.* Poster session presented at TENNET V meetings, Montreal, Canada.

Cokely, D. (2005). Shifting positionality: A critical examination of the turning point in the relationship of interpreters and the deaf community. In M. Marschark, R. Peterson, & E. A. Winston (Eds.), *Interpreting and interpreter education: Directions for research and practice* (pp. 3–29). New York: Oxford University Press.

Corina, D. P., Kritchevsky, M., & Bellugi, U. (1992). Linguistic permeability of unilateral neglect: Evidence from American Sign Language. In *Proceedings of the Cognitive Science Conference* (pp. 384–389). Hillsdale, NY: Lawrence Erlbaum Associates.

Corson, H. (1973). Comparing deaf children of oral deaf parents and deaf children using manual communication with deaf children of hearing parents on academic, social, and communicative functioning. Unpublished doctoral dissertation, University of Cincinnati.

Detterman, D. K., & Thompson, L. A. (1997). What is so special about special education? *American Psychologist, 52*, 1082–1090.

Emmorey, K., & Kosslyn, S. (1996). Enhanced image generation abilities in deaf signers: A right hemisphere effect. *Brain and Cognition, 32*, 28–44.

Emmorey, K., Kosslyn, S., & Bellugi, U. (1993). Visual imagery and visual-spatial language: Enhanced imagery abilities in deaf and hearing ASL signers. *Cognition, 46,* 139–181.

Furstenberg, K., & Doyal, G. (1994). The relationship between emotional-behavioral functioning and personal characteristics on performance outcomes of hearing impaired students. *American Annals of the Deaf, 139,* 410–414.

Holt, J. (1994) Classroom attributes and achievement test scores for deaf and hard of hearing students. *American Annals of the Deaf, 139,* 430–437.

Jensema, C. J., & Trybus, R. J. (1978). *Communicating patterns and educational achievements of hearing impaired students.* Washington, DC: Gallaudet College Office of Demographic Studies.

Karchmer, M. A., & Mitchell, R. E. (2003). Demographic and achievement characteristics of deaf and hard-of-hearing students. In M. Marschark & P. E. Spencer (Eds.), *Oxford Handbook of deaf studies, language, and education* (pp. 21–37). New York: Oxford University Press.

Kelly, R. R., & Mousley, K. (2001). Solving word problems: More than reading issues for deaf students. *American Annals of the Deaf, 146,* 253–264.

Kluwin, T. N. (1992). Considering the efficacy of mainstreaming from the classroom perspective. In T. N. Kluwin, D. F. Moores, & M. G. Gaustad (Eds.), *Toward effective public school programs for deaf students: Context, process, and outcomes* (pp. 175–193). New York: Teachers College Press.

Kluwin, T. N. (1993) Cumulative effects of mainstreaming on the achievement of deaf adolescents. *Exceptional Children, 60,* 73–81.

Kluwin, T. N., & Gaustad, M. G. (1992). How family factors influence school achievement. In T. N. Kluwin, D. F. Moores, & M. G. Gaustad (Eds.), *Toward effective public school programs for deaf students: Context, process, and outcomes* (pp. 66–82). New York: Teachers College Press.

Kluwin, T., & Moores, D. (1985). Mathematics achievement of hearing impaired adolescents in different placements. *Exceptional Children, 55,* 327–335.

Kruger, J., & Dunning, D. (1999). Unskilled and unaware of it: How difficulties in recognizing one's own incompetence lead to inflated self-assessment. *Journal of Personality and Social Psychology, 77,* 1121–1134.

Lang, H. G. (2003). Perspectives on the history of deaf education. In M. Marschark & P. E. Spencer (Eds.), *Oxford handbook of deaf studies, language, and education* (pp. 9–20). New York: Oxford University Press.

Lang, H. G., & Meath-Lang, B. (1995). *Deaf persons in the arts and sciences: A biographical dictionary.* Westport, CT: Greenwood Press.

Leigh, G. (2003, December). *Considering the efficacy of sign bilingualism in terms of L1 and L2 proficiency: An Australian study.* Rochester, NY: National Technical Institute for the Deaf, Department of Research Lecture Series.

Leybaert, J., & Alegria, J. (2003). The role of cued speech in language development of deaf children. In M. Marschark & P. E. Spencer (Eds.), *Oxford handbook of deaf studies, language, and education* (pp. 262–274). New York: Oxford University Press.

Liben, L. S. (1979). Free recall by deaf and hearing children: Semantic clustering and recall in trained and untrained groups. *Journal of Experimental Child Psychology, 27,* 105–119.

Lichtenstein, E. (1998). The relationships between reading processes and English skills of deaf college students. *Journal of Deaf Studies and Deaf Education, 3,* 80–134.

Logan, K., Mayberry, M., & Fletcher, J. (1996). The short-term memory of profoundly deaf people for words, signs, and abstract spatial stimuli. *Applied Cognitive Psychology, 10,* 105–119.

Luetke-Stahlman, B., & Luckner, J. (1991). *Effectively educating students with hearing impairments.* New York: Longman.

Lynas, W. (1986). *Integrating the handicapped into ordinary schools: A study of hearing-impaired pupils.* London: Croom Helm.

Marschark, M. (1993). *Psychological development of deaf children.* New York: Oxford University Press.

Marschark, M. (2003). Cognitive functioning in deaf adults and children. In M. Marschark & P. E. Spencer (Eds.), *Oxford handbook of deaf studies, language, and education* (pp. 464–477). New York: Oxford University Press.

Marschark, M. (2004). Developing deaf children or deaf children developing? In D. Power & G. Leigh (Eds.), *Educating deaf students: Global perspectives.* Washington, DC: Gallaudet University Press.

Marschark, M., DeBeni, R. Polazzo, M. G., & Cornoldi, C. (1993). Deaf and hearing-impaired adolescents' memory for concrete and abstract prose: Effects of relational and distinctive information. *American Annals of the Deaf, 138,* 31–39.

Marschark, M., Convertino, C., McEvoy, C., & Masteller, A. (2004). Organization and use of the mental lexicon by deaf and hearing individuals. *American Annals of the Deaf, 149,* 51–61.

Marschark, M., & Everhart, V. S. (1999). Problem solving by deaf and hearing children: Twenty questions. *Deafness and Education International, 1,* 63–79.

Marschark, M., Lang, H., & Albertini, J. (2002). *Educating deaf students: From research to practice.* New York: Oxford University Press.

Marschark, M., & Lukomski, J. (2001). Cognition, literacy, and education. In M. D. Clark, M. Marschark, & M. Karchmer (Eds.), *Context, cognition, and deafness* (pp. 71–87). Washington, DC: Gallaudet University Press.

Marschark, M., & Mayer, T. (1998). Mental representation and memory in deaf adults and children. In M. Marschark & M. D. Clark (Eds.), *Psychological perspectives on deafness: Vol. 2* (pp. 53–77). Mahwah, NJ: Lawrence Erlbaum Associates.

Marschark, M., Sapere, P., Convertino, C., & Seewagen, R. (2005a). Educational interpreting: Access and outcomes. In M. Marschark, R. Peterson, & E. Winston (Eds.), *Sign language interpreting and interpreter education: Directions for research and practice* (pp. 57–83). New York: Oxford University Press.

Marschark, M., Sapere, P., Convertino, C., & Seewagen, R. (2005b). Access to post-secondary education through sign language interpreting. *Journal of Deaf Studies and Deaf Education, 10,* 38–50.

Marschark, M., Sapere, P., Convertino, C., Seewagen, R., & Maltzen, H. (2004). Comprehension of sign language interpreting: Deciphering a complex task situation. *Sign Language Studies, 4*(4), 345–368.

Mayer, C., & Akamatsu, C. T. (1999). Bilingual-bicultural models of literacy education for deaf students: Considering the claims. *Journal of Deaf Studies and Deaf Education, 4,* 1–8.

McEvoy, C., Marschark, M., & Nelson, D. L. (1999). Comparing the mental lexicons of deaf and hearing individuals. *Journal of Educational Psychology, 91,* 1–9.

Moeller, M. P. (2000). Early intervention and language development in children who are deaf and hard of hearing. *Pediatrics, 106,* E43.

Moores, D. F. (2001). *Educating the deaf: Psychology, principles, and practices.* Boston: Houghton Mifflin.

Moores, D., & Sweet, C. (1990). Factors predictive of school achievement. In D. Moores & K. Meadow-Orlans (Eds.), *Educational and developmental aspects of deafness* (pp. 154–201). Washington, DC: Gallaudet University Press.

Nelson, K. E., Loncke, F., & Camarata, S. (1993). Implications of research on deaf and hearing children's language learning. In M. Marschark & D. Clark (Eds.), *Psychological perspectives on deafness.* Hillsdale, NJ: Lawrence Erlbaum Associates.

Neville, H. J., & Lawson, D. (1987). Attention to central and peripheral visual space in a movement detection task: An event-related potential and behavioral study. II. Congenitally deaf adults. *Brain Research, 405,* 268–283.

Oakhill, J., & Cain, K. (2000). Children's difficulties in text comprehension: Assessing causal issues. *Journal of Deaf Studies and Deaf Education 5,* 51–59.

Ottem, E. (1980). An analysis of cognitive studies with deaf subjects. *American Annals of the Deaf, 125,* 564–575.

Padden, C. A., & Ramsey, C. (1998). Reading ability in signing deaf children. *Topics in Language Disorders, 18*(4), 30–46.

Perfetti, C. A., & Sandak, R. (2000). Reading optimally builds on spoken language: Implications for reading and deafness. *Journal of Deaf Studies and Deaf Education, 5,* 32–50.

Powers, S. (2003). Influences of student and family factors on academic outcomes of mainstream secondary school deaf students. *Journal of Deaf Studies and Deaf Education, 8,* 57–78.

Ramsey, C. (1997). *Deaf children in public schools.* Washington, DC: Gallaudet University Press.

Rettenback, R., Diller, G., & Sireteanu, R. (1999). Do deaf people see better? Texture segmentation and visual search compensate in adult but not in juvenile subjects. *Journal of Cognitive Neuroscience, 11,* 560–583.

Richardson, J. T. E., McLeod-Gallinger, J., McKee, B. G., & Long, G. L. (1999). Approaches to studying in deaf and hearing students in higher education. *Journal of Deaf Studies and Deaf Education, 5,* 156–173.

Schick, B. (2005). How might learning through an interpreter influence cognitive development? In E. Winston (Ed.), *Educational interpreting: How it can succeed* (pp. 73–87). Washington, DC: Gallaudet University Press.

Schick, B., Williams, K., & Bolster, L. (1999). Skill levels of educational interpreters working in public schools. *Journal of Deaf Studies and Deaf Education, 4,* 144–155.

Seal, B. C. (1998). *Best practices in educational interpreting.* Boston: Allyn and Bacon.

Singleton, J. L., Supalla, S., Litchfield, S., & Schley, S. (1998). From sign to word: Considering modality constraints in ASL/English bilingual education. *Topics in Language Disorders, 18*(4), 16–29.

Sinkavich, F. J. (1995). Performance and metamemory: Do students know what they don't know? *Journal of Instructional Psychology, 22,* 77–87.

Stinson, M. S. (1974). Relations between maternal reinforcement and help and the achievement motive in normal-hearing and hearing-impaired sons. *Developmental Psychology, 10,* 348–353.

Stinson, M. S. (1978). Effects of deafness on maternal expectations about child development. Journal of Special Education, 12, 75–81.

Stinson, M. S., & Antia, S. D. (1999). Considerations in educating deaf and hard-of-hearing students in inclusive settings. *Journal of Deaf Studies and Deaf Education, 4,* 163–175.

Stinson, M. S., Kelly, R., Elliot, L., Colwell, J., Liu, Y., & Stinson, S. (2000, April). *C-Print, interpreting and notes, and memory of lectures.* Paper presented at the annual meeting of the American Educational Research Association, New Orleans.

Stinson, M. S., & Kluwin, T. N. (2003). Educational consequences of alternative school placements. In M. Marschark & P. E. Spencer (Eds.), *Oxford handbook of deaf studies, language, and education* (pp. 52–64). New York: Oxford University Press.

Stinson, M., Meath-Lang, B., & MacLeod, J. (1981). Recall of different segments of an interpreted lecture by deaf students. *American Annals of the Deaf, 126,* 819–824.

Stone, R. (2000). A bold step: Changing the curriculum for culturally deaf and hard of hearing students. In P. Spencer, C. Erting, & M. Marschark (Eds.), *Development in context: The deaf children in the family and at school* (pp. 229–238). Mahwah, NJ: Lawrence Erlbaum Associates.

Strassman, B. (1997). Metacognition and reading in children who are deaf: A review of the research. *Journal of Deaf Studies and Deaf Education, 2,* 140–149.

Strong, M., & Prinz, P. M. (1997). A study of the relationship between American Sign Language and English literacy. *Journal of Deaf Studies and Deaf Education, 2,* 37–46.

Swisher, M. V. (1993). Perceptual and cognitive aspects of recognition of signs in peripheral vision. In M. Marschark & M. D. Clark (Eds.), *Psychological perspectives on deafness* (pp. 229–265). Hillsdale, NJ: Lawrence Erlbaum Associates.

Talbot, K. F., & Haude, R. H. (1993). The relationship between sign language skill and spatial visualizations ability: Mental rotation of three-dimensional objects. *Perceptual and Motor Skills, 77,* 1387–1391.

Tharpe, A., Ashmead, D., & Rothpletz, A. (2002). Visual attention in children with normal hearing, children with hearing aids, and children with cochlear implants. *Journal of Speech, Hearing and Language Research, 45,* 403–413.

Todman, J., & Seedhouse, E. (1994). Visual-action code processing by deaf and hearing children. *Language and Cognitive Processes, 9,* 129–141.

Toscano, R. M., McKee, B. G., & Lepoutre, D. (2002). Success with academic English: Reflections of deaf college students. *American Annals of the Deaf, 147,* 5–23.

Traxler, C.B. (2000). Measuring up to performance standards in reading and mathematics: Achievement of selected deaf and hard-of-hearing students in the national norming of the 9th Edition Stanford Achievement Test. *Journal of Deaf Studies and Deaf Education, 5,* 337–348.

Wilson, M., & Emmorey, K. (1997). Working memory for sign language: A window into the architecture of the working memory system. *Journal of Deaf Studies and Deaf Education, 2,* 121–130.

Winston, E. A. (2005). Designing a curriculum for American Sign Language/English interpreting educators. In M. Marschark, R. Peterson, & E. A. Winston (Eds.), *Interpreting and interpreter education: Directions for research and practice* (pp. 208–234). New York: Oxford University Press.

Wolk, S., & Allen, T. (1984). A 5-year follow-up of reading comprehension achievement of hearing-impaired students in special education programs. *Journal of Special Education, 18,* 161–176.

Yoshinaga-Itano, C. (2006). Effects of early identification on spoken language development: Patterns and considerations. In P. E. Spencer & M. Marschark (Eds.), *Advances in the spoken language development of deaf and hard-of-hearing children* (pp. 298–327). New York: Oxford University Press.

D A V I D   S .   M A R T I N

Cognitive Strategy Instruction: A Permeating Principle

TEACHING STUDENTS HOW TO THINK at higher levels is not a new emphasis in American education. As early as 1916, John Dewey emphasized the importance of teaching children how to solve increasingly complex problems. This emphasis has had a fascinating history.

Brandt (2001) makes an important distinction among three categories in this domain.

1. Teaching *for* thinking is what a science teacher does when she sets up a laboratory experiment and has groups of students create a hypothesis, collect data, and draw careful conclusions. That teacher is incorporating higher-level cognitive processes and expecting her students to apply them. This kind of teaching is quite old.
2. Teaching *of* thinking is what teachers do when they explicitly label the cognitive processes that they teach—analysis, synthesis, categorization, and the like. In this definition, thinking is a part of the curriculum.
3. Teaching *about* thinking is what teachers do when they ask students to reflect metacognitively on the mental processes that they have used in solving some challenging curriculum problem. This is perhaps the newest of these three techniques.

This chapter advocates the continuation of teaching for thinking, but also explicitly encourages the conscious adoption or adaptation of programs that teach both of and about thinking.

A Rationale

We can identify many reasons why teaching cognitive strategies is important in schools today, including in programs for deaf and hard of hearing students.

First, there recently has been and continues to be an explosion of knowledge, and it is already impossible for anyone to know everything about anything. Still, we must equip students with the skills to find information, judge information, and manipulate information, however it may change. Second, students will grow up in a world where problems abound—on the global level (preserving the environment), on the curriculum level (solving high-level content problems), on the workplace level, and on the personal level (choosing a mate, housing, approaches to personal finance, childrearing, and more). Third, attention to higher-level cognitive processes is actually a memory aid. The ability to organize knowledge into sensible patterns is a higher-level skill. Fourth, students will be able to make difficult choices with a clear rationale. This is especially helpful for determining the correct answers on multiple-choice exam questions and, more importantly, choosing pathways for one's life. Hence, a focus in the curriculum of any subject area that ensures attention to higher-order thinking strategies will serve as a consistent thread for the student's entire intellectual life if it cuts across the various aspects of the curriculum and is not compartmentalized.

Important Ideas

Several critically important ideas form the foundation of the movement to incorporate higher-level thinking strategies into the curriculum. The first of these was actually propounded by Dewey (1916) when he stated that intelligence is not fixed, but rather grows; yet, in spite of his position, for a long time educators and psychologists labored under the idea that intelligence was indeed fixed, undoubtedly somewhat as the result of the emphasis on the measurement of intelligence for various purposes in the early 20th century. However, the idea of dynamic intelligence was firmly established later by the work of Reuven Feuerstein (1980) when he described important educational experiments in Israel and elsewhere that demonstrated the cognitive flexibility of the individual, no matter what age or disability characterized the individual.

A second critical idea was that intelligence is not a single entity but rather multiple entities. Again, the trend for a long time in intelligence testing was to assign a single score (even though the score was actually composed of several different components) to an individual. Howard Gardner's seminal work (1983) in multiple intelligences exploded that myth and helped teachers to see that a student can be intelligent in up to eight different ways (linguistic, logical/mathematical, spatial, musical, bodily/kinesthetic, intrapersonal, interpersonal, and naturalistic).

Still another idea relates back to the teaching *about* thinking. This is metacognition, which is a powerful educational technique in which learners reflect consciously on the mental processes they use, have used, or will use in a problem-solving situation. The rationale is that the learner must become autonomous, and one of the conditions for intellectual autonomy is the ability to think for oneself about what strategies one could use to solve a new problem. By actively reflecting on such processes in the classroom with the help of a teacher, learners become aware of the mental tools at their disposal, so that when they are alone in a problem-solving situation later, they will be able to make a plan for solution.

A final critical idea is that of mediation, again originated by Feuerstein (1980). Mediation is a special form of teaching, in which the teacher does not directly tell or inform the student, but instead leads, suggests, questions, offers a partial solution, and gives hints. In that way, the learner gradually acquires the strategy for problem solving rather than depending on solutions provided didactically by the teacher.

Cognitive Strategies

Just what do we mean by generic cognitive strategies? They are that set of problem-solving skills that cut across most subject matter content and include

comparing,
categorizing,
identifying patterns,
analyzing,
synthesizing,
explaining,
sequencing,
applying logic,
hypothesizing,
identifying assumptions, and
drawing reasonable conclusions.

It is easy to identify how most of these skills relate to nearly every aspect of the subject matter of the curriculum; for example, we compare things in literature, in history, in science, in mathematics, and so forth. Categorization is done when analyzing characters in a story, identifying different kinds of historical periods, observing phenomena in science, classifying number patterns and patterns in word problems within mathematics, and so forth.

Activities

What would be some examples of thinking skills exercises that could be integrated with the regular curriculum? Nearly 20 different published programs are available that purport to teach various aspects of thinking skills; we discuss later in this chapter how to make quality adoption choices among them.

To give one example, let us suppose that we are interested in relating the strategy of comparison to our study of characters in a literature story in the classroom; thus, the curriculum of the moment in our class is reading and analyzing a work of literature. We would first have the students practice finding similarities and differences between pairs of objects, pairs of pictures, pairs of words, and pairs of symbols using materials that are temporarily outside the content of the literature work that is being studied. Then we would discuss what mental processes we had just used in doing these comparisons (metacognition), listing the strategies as we discuss them. Then we would make a transition and apply that strategy to comparing the characters in the story to each other, reminding ourselves to use strategies similar to those we had just used in comparing pictures and objects.

Another model would be to take an important question such as a policy matter in the federal government—for example, should the United States go to war with a small country that appears to be developing weapons of mass destruction? Students would first identify arguments on both sides of the question, list the assumptions behind each, make tentative positions known, and then take a position and defend it logically; this activity could be done in a controlled debate format. Then the same techniques of identifying assumptions, developing logical arguments, and defending positions could then be applied to a new context in the study of some past event in history.

In both of these examples, the cognitive processes are identified explicitly, and metacognition and application are crucial parts of the process. Published programs are a significant aid to the teacher because these programs have developed specialized materials and teaching techniques to further this process in the classroom. However, it is possible for committed teachers to develop some of their own materials for teaching thinking.

Criteria for Program Selection

The criteria for making an intelligent curriculum decision in the area of thinking skills are particularly important. Some of those to be used in deciding what published curriculum to adopt for teaching thinking would be the answers to the following questions; each question should be answered in the affirmative for any program under serious consideration:

1. Does the program encompass a variety of cognitive skills rather than only one or two?
2. Does the program emphasize a longer process of intervention to achieve results, rather than promise a "quick fix"?
3. Has the program been implemented in other schools, with results available for review?
4. Has the program been tested experimentally and what results were shown?
5. Is the program based on a theory about cognition, rather than only a set of "recipes" for teaching?
6. Does the program require teacher orientation or a series of workshops to be implemented because teaching thinking is a different way of teaching?

When these hard questions are posed, it is easy to imagine that the rather large number of thinking skills programs will narrow down quickly to a few high-quality programs. Among the most important of these criteria is number 2—any program that promises a quick fix for thinking skills will not deal in depth with students' ways of thinking and with teachers' need to teach in a different way (mediation) than the method in which they may have been prepared during their formal preparation program.

Research Results

Extensive research has now been completed on the effects of some thinking skills programs on learners who are deaf and hard of hearing. The results are positive and encouraging. Some of the effects of these programs on deaf learners have included (a) a significant increase in measurable student achievement on standardized tests, (b) acquisition of thinking habits such as finding more than one solution to a problem and not giving up easily, (c) a significant increase in generic reasoning skills, and (d) improvement in sequencing and detail in solving a real-world problem (Jonas & Martin, 1985; Craig & Gordon, 1991). Other researchers have found similar effects (e.g., Keane, 1985; Rembert, 1985). The reader is referred to two edited works that compile research on the effects of cognitive process instruction on deaf learners (see Martin, 1985, 1991), as well as more recent individual studies in the areas of cognition and deafness.

Research on the cognitive development and cognitive strategies of students in general has continued. Martin, Craft, and Zheng (2001) found that with carefully trained teachers, deaf students in both China and England improved measurably after cognitive strategies in the classroom context were applied.

The empirical evidence is clear; now, the will and interest for implementation must evolve widely in deaf education.

General Teaching Techniques

In addition to adopting or adapting one of the published thinking strategies programs and the methodologies embedded in it, teachers also have other techniques to draw upon that are independent of particular published programs. One could summarize all of the techniques as follows:

1. Adopt and localize the concepts from a published thinking skills program and its methods through staff development experiences.
2. Arrange the classroom seating of students to promote interactive dialogue and debate, so that student discussions are not only through the teacher but also in interaction directly with fellow students about significant questions.
3. Employ higher-level questioning whenever questions for discussion are posed to students, for example, not only "when," "who," or "where" questions, but also "why" and "how" questions. Additional teacher requests can include "please explain" and "please elaborate on what you just said."
4. Take advantage of what is known from research about the effects of "wait time," which has shown that after a teacher has asked a high-quality thought question, the longer the teacher waits, the better the chance of a thoughtful response from students. (This technique, however, does not succeed if either the teacher has asked a poorly constructed question or the students have an insufficient knowledge base to even attempt an answer.)

These techniques, when used in combination, prove powerful and effective.

A Recommendation

Based on this discussion, it is recommended that teachers of deaf and hard of hearing students pursue a path toward implementation of explicit cognitive-strategy instruction on a regular basis across all curriculum content areas that are explained in the chapters in this book. The steps to making this decision are first, developing the internal commitment to emphasize higher-order problem-solving strategies; second, identifying a program or approach for adoption or adaptation; third, obtaining the necessary orientation or retraining necessary to understand the methodology and materials; fourth, regularly implementing the program across subject matter content; and fifth, evaluating the effects of the program by collecting before-and-after data. Regular and faithful implementation will reap dividends not only in problem-solving strategies themselves, but also in the depth mastery of the subject matter in which these strategies can be embedded.

References

Brandt, R. (2001). Foreword. In A. Costa (Ed.), *Developing minds* (3rd ed.). Alexandria, VA: Association for Supervision and Curriculum Development.

Craig, H., & Gordon, H. W. (1991). Specialized cognitive function among deaf individuals: Implications for instruction. In *Advances in cognition, education, and deafness*. Washington, DC: Gallaudet University Press.

Dewey, J. (1916). *Democracy and education: An introduction to the philosophy of education.* New York: Macmillan.

Feuerstein, R. (1980). *Instrumental enrichment.* Baltimore: University Park Press.

Gardner, H. (1983). *Frames of mind.* Cambridge, MA: Harvard University Press.

Jonas, B., & Martin, D. S. (1985). Cognitive improvement of hearing-impaired high school students through instruction in instrumental enrichment. In *Cognition, education, and deafness: Directions for research and instruction*. Washington, DC: Gallaudet University Press.

Keane, K. (1985). Application of Feuerstein's mediated learning construct to deaf persons. In *Cognition, education, and deafness: Directions for research and instruction*. Washington, DC: Gallaudet University Press.

Martin, D. S. (Ed.). (1985). *Advances in cognition, education, and deafness.* Washington, DC: Gallaudet University Press.

Martin, D. S. (Ed.). (1991). *Cognition, education, and deafness: Directions for research and instruction.* Washington, DC: Gallaudet University Press.

Martin, D. S., Craft, A., & Zheng, S. (2001). The impact of cognitive strategy instruction on deaf learners: An international comparative study. *American Annals of the Deaf, 144,* (4), 366–378.

Rembert, R. (1985). Philosophical inquiry among hearing-impaired students. In *Cognition, education, and deafness: Directions for research and instruction*. Washington, DC: Gallaudet University Press.

DAVID A. STEWART

Instructional and Practical Communication: ASL and English-Based Signing in the Classroom

WE CAN REACH THE FOLLOWING two conclusions after reviewing the use of sign communication in the classroom during the past 40 years of deaf education:

- American Sign Language (ASL) and English-based signing are here to stay.
- There is more to good teaching than just the way a teacher communicates.

As obvious as it might appear, it took decades of classroom teaching and years of heated debate at conferences and in publications to arrive at a point in time where the field is ready to embrace the implications of these statements. To do so, however, the field's philosophical stance must endorse English and ASL as classroom languages and must present a framework within which both languages can be used to meet instructional and communication objectives. The consequence of this stance is that teachers will possess the skills to use both languages and the understanding of pedagogy to make sound judgments about when to use ASL and when to use English in its print, speech, and sign modalities. Such a philosophy is the basis of the instructional and practical communication (IPC) approach to teaching deaf children.

Instructional and Practical Communication

The most fertile of all learning platforms in the classroom is the interplay of thoughts that occurs when teacher and student draw from their individual portfolios of language and communication skills to negotiate an understanding of one another. This platform is the premise for the IPC philosophy, which is applicable to all school-age deaf children and across all subject matter. IPC allows teachers to make decisions about how they will use ASL and English in their instruction and interactions with deaf students.

For good teaching to take place using the IPC approach, language development must occur in tandem with the growth of subject matter knowledge and skills. To make effective decisions about using ASL and English, teachers must rely on the instructional requirements of the curriculum and the communication needs of their students, which implies that teachers must first have a strong command of both languages in all of their expressive and receptive modalities. For good communication to occur in the IPC approach, students are taught so they will develop the linguistic tools necessary to comprehend communication in both languages.

Instructional Considerations

Learning and language development go hand in hand because deaf students experience language delays in their acquisition of vocabulary and grammar with respect to the reading and language requirements of the curriculum for their grade level. To teach the curriculum in a manner that is suitable to deaf students' learning and communication needs, teachers need to plan lessons that address two main questions:

- What educational activities are important to achieving curricular goals?
- What language experiences will help deaf students best learn from these activities?

In essence, the language experiences associated with instruction are integral to the success of the instruction. For deaf students, the goal is to acquire language skills while they are learning subject matter.

Stewart and Kluwin's (2001) approach to lesson planning makes language experiences an integral part of educational experiences. They suggest that teachers incorporate into their planning the following three principles:

1. Lessons should be grounded in authentic experiences. The authors note that a "series of disconnected sentences in a language book is only as relevant as a child's linguistic and experiential background will make it. In the absence of much real-life experiences, deaf children become restricted in their ability to acquire new vocabulary and formulate new sentences" (p. 9). Experiences also challenge existing understandings and beget new ones—the heart of learning.
2. Vocabulary development should be integrated into lessons. In this respect, words need to appear in contexts that define their meanings. It is not sufficient, for example, to simply list definitions of words that are critical to a social studies or science lesson. Words are best learned when students experience them in a meaningful manner, including classroom discourse and incidental conversations inside and outside of the classroom. With respect to signing, it is incumbent upon teachers to model the use of new words in sentences either in ASL or English or both, using signs and fingerspelling as necessary.
3. Lesson planning should include opportunities for self-expression. Lessons can be designed to include students in conversations with the teacher and one another. An example of the most basic of all levels of teacher-student communication would be a teacher who clearly describes a sequence of activities that she

wants her students to follow and who then asks if the class understands what she has asked of them. A teacher who makes the same description but then calls upon one student to express what he thinks she has just described is moving the linguistic involvement of students to a higher and more intellectually engaging level of communication.

In each of the foregoing principles the role of language is important because it serves to facilitate comprehension as well as to provide linguistic material that will help deaf students make sense of the lesson and assist them in their internalization of meanings. In essence, by embracing these three principles of lesson planning for deaf students, a teacher is acknowledging that deaf students "are not only using language to learn but also learning the language itself" (Mayer, Akamatsu, & Stewart, 2002, p. 488). Given the degree of ongoing language development in a typical classroom of deaf students, it seems unnecessarily restrictive to select a single language that teachers and students can use to express themselves.

Planning for self-expression takes on added significance for teachers who use discourse with their deaf students as a means for analyzing the understanding by a student or group of students. Research has shown that exemplary teachers of the deaf use classroom dialogue to "guide students on a pathway of inquiry and self-expression that leads to a firmer understanding of the concepts they are learning" (Stewart, Mayer, & Akamatsu, 2003, p. 80). These authors discovered that exemplary teachers engage in a process referred to as dialogic inquiry, whereby the student utterances tell the teacher what that student does and does not understand; the teacher then selects a response that is appropriate to the student's needs (Mayer, Akamatsu, & Stewart, 2002, p. 488).

In the IPC approach, the pedagogical considerations relating to facilitating learning should be the major focus in shaping a teacher's response to information gleaned from deaf students' utterances. If switching to another language is deemed the best means to facilitate learning, then the teacher will do so.

Stewart, Mayer, and Akamatsu (2003) offered a model of communicative practice for guiding teachers in their interactions with deaf students:

1. Focus on the content and meaning of what a student is saying.
2. Provide feedback that will help a student be an active participant in the construction of knowledge.
3. Ensure that classroom dialogue engages the student in genuine problem solving (p. 82).

Examples of how this process can be carried out are described elsewhere (e.g., Mayer, Akamatsu, & Stewart, 2002; Stewart, Mayer, & Akamatsu, 2003). Of importance here is that the IPC approach allows teachers to use whichever language will best bring into play different types of teaching strategies.

Practical Considerations

The most practical of all communication questions that a teacher faces is, "Do the students understand what I am saying?" Answering this question is not so simple because of the disparity of language skills found among students in many deaf education programs. This disparity is a common theme found in all classrooms, irrespective of a program's communication philosophy, and is especially pronounced in deaf education programs found in the public school system. The following two guidelines can help teachers address language disparity among their students:

- The communication dynamics of the classroom and learning characteristics relating to deaf students influence how a teacher is going to communicate.
- Different situations may call for different means of communicating.

A visit to a classroom will demonstrate the differences in language skills among students, an example of which is seen in the following description of students who are currently in a local school system:

- Karen is 11 years old and profoundly deaf. She is reading at the third grade level, and her hearing parents do not sign. She uses mostly ASL when signing.
- Chad is a 10-year-old profoundly deaf boy who has deaf parents. He reads at the third grade level and uses ASL and English-based signing when talking in class.
- Dwayne is 12 years old, with a new cochlear implant. He has a fourth grade reading level and uses English-based signing. On his IEP (individualized education plan), his parents indicated that they want him to receive extensive exposure to speech alone or in conjunction with signs.
- Beth is a 10-year-old severely deaf girl who is able to communicate well using speech and speechreading when she wears two hearing aids. She reads at a second grade level. She is a fluent ASL signer, and her parents are considering a cochlear implant for her.
- Tasha is a 12-year-old profoundly deaf girl with deaf parents. She is fluent in ASL and reads at fourth grade level.
- Mandy is a 10-year-old girl who has hearing parents who do not sign. She transferred into this school at the beginning of the school year from an oral program. She reads at first grade level and signs at a beginner's level.
- Deanna is a 9-year-old profoundly deaf girl with hearing parents who have signed to her since she was four years old. She reads at the third grade level and uses ASL and English-based signing.

This list does not cover all combinations of characteristics that might have an effect on student's language and communication skills. It does, however, illustrate that a teacher would be hard pressed to simply use the same type of signing with all of the students all day long. One far too common response to the classroom communication demands illustrated in the previous list would be for a teacher to sign at a level that meets or is close to the lowest common signing denominator of the class. That is, the teacher uses vocabulary and grammatical structures such that the deaf student with the lowest ASL or English skill (Mandy in this classroom) can understand. This "dumbing down" of a teacher's signing is a classroom practice that keeps the complexity of a teacher's language structure at a simple level. Such a practice fails to provide deaf students—Mandy included—with linguistic challenges that will help accelerate their acquisition of language.

Another response would be for the teacher to sign in ASL or English-based signing all of the time. In a classroom where some students exhibit strengths in learning in ASL and others are clearly English-dominant language users, this behavior misses out on opportunities to use the linguistic strengths of the students to enhance learning.

With an IPC approach, the teacher is encouraged to address the linguistic diversity of the classroom through planning and on-the-spot adjustments in the use of language. This process can be accomplished in several ways, including these:

- For some subject matter teaching, the teacher can divide the class into groups and conduct a majority of the lesson in ASL or English-based signing.
- The teacher can conduct a lesson in one language and switch to the other for clarification or emphasis.
- The teacher can provide individual instructional support to those students who might not understand all of the teacher's communication during a group lesson.

In sum, the IPC approach encourages bilingually fluent teachers to meet the demands of teaching by using whichever method of language instruction is called for by the communication dynamics of the classroom.

How IPC Is Different From Other Approaches

When considering the differences among the IPC approach espoused in this chapter and other sign communication approaches practiced in the field, it is helpful to keep the following two points in mind:

- IPC gives equal status to both ASL and English.
- Instructional, situational, and student-based factors dictate the use of either language.

Two types of sign communication approaches presently used in the education of deaf students are Total Communication (TC) and the bilingual-bicultural (Bi-Bi) approach. The TC approach has been around the longest, and various definitions have been used since Roy Holcomb introduced the term to the field in the late 1960s. It promotes both philosophical and methodological positions for the classroom teacher as shown in the following summary:

In theory, total communication reflects an attitude embraced by teachers, parents, and children to allow them to use any available means of communication to express a thought. Thus, it is a philosophy that urges not how one communicates but that one communicates effectively. In practice, total communication calls for parents and teachers to develop their skills, and those of a child, to utilize various abilities of transmitting and receiving information. (Stewart, 1982, p. 139)

In this definition, language is not included, but some TC programs do specify language use. Typically, TC programs endorse English as the primary or only language of instruction, although it would not be hard to find a program where at least one teacher consistently switches to ASL to conduct some aspect of teaching. Studies have shown that most teachers in TC programs use signs and speech at the same time, a method of communication that is known as Simultaneous Communication or SimCom. Sim-Com users rely on English to guide their production of signs (Maxwell, 1990). The IPC approach specifies that ASL and English are to be used for instructional purposes. An IPC program's choice of primary language will reflect factors stemming from the curriculum, learning objectives, and student language skills.

In Bi-Bi programs, on the other hand, guidelines call for teachers to use ASL for instruction and to teach English as a second language (Andrews, Leigh, & Weiner, 2004). In these programs, English-based signing and SimCom in particular are not used. Bi-Bi made its appearance in classrooms during the 1980s, grew in popularity throughout the 1990s and leveled off in use by the turn of the century. As yet, no study has examined how teachers use signs in these programs and whether teachers engage in language mixing (switching between ASL and English-based signing). In contrast to Bi-Bi programs, an IPC teacher faces no programmatic restriction on how to use ASL and English. Moreover, an IPC teacher will rely on student characteristics to determine if teaching English as a second language or some other method is the appropriate approach in any particular situation.

Resolving the ASL and English-Based Signing Controversy

In this section of the chapter, we provide for the bilingual use of ASL and English-based signing in the IPC classroom by revisiting what we know about the way each is used in the classroom.

The Nature of Signing in the Classroom

Directions for the use of signing in the classroom can be summarized with the following two observations:

- ASL is being used by an increasing number of teachers of deaf students.
- The type of English-based signing found in the Deaf community represents a more efficient manner for teaching than English-based signing systems that have been created specifically for use in the classroom.

Although there have been studies that looked at how teachers sign, they have been few and far between and do not offer a realistic picture of what goes on in the classroom today (e.g., Mayer & Lowenbraun, 1990; Stewart, Akamatsu, & Becker, 1995; Woodward & Allen, 1987, 1988). In the absence of empirical research, an understanding of what is presently occurring in many classrooms can be gleaned from information gathered through observations of teachers conducting lessons, discussions at regional and national conferences, and the writings of researchers and educators about the transformation of classroom signing.

During the past four decades, the most visible change in the signing environment of classrooms has been the growing presence of ASL. ASL has evolved from a time when it was not recognized as a language and had no formal role in the classroom to the present when its status as a language is unquestioned. Today, few if any educators question its instructional value for teachers and their deaf students. This point is certainly true in Bi-Bi programs that strive to use ASL as the only in-the-air form of communication. It also applies to other programs where teachers largely use English-based signing and switch to ASL in specific situations to accomplish certain instructional objectives. Further recognition of ASL's role in the classroom is found in university programs that require students to take ASL classes in order to obtain an endorsement as a teacher of deaf students. In some programs, preservice teachers must demonstrate proficiency in using ASL prior to internship placements in classes where ASL is the dominant language for face-to-face teaching. Another potent nod to the importance of ASL is that educators, researchers, and parents routinely acknowledge its value as a first language for many deaf children. In fact, for the past decade or more, fewer and fewer people appear to be opposed to the use of ASL in the education of deaf children.

English-based signing is also enjoying favorable status as a critical part of sign communication in the education of deaf children. Beginning in the late 1960s and through the early 1980s, English-based signing was the driving force when the TC approach was sweeping aside programs that endorsed speech and audition as the primary modes of communication. Acceptance of English-based signing opened the door for ASL. A wide range of English-based signing exists but the overarching characteristic is that English syntax is used to determine the order of signs. Of particular interest to this chapter is the distinction between manually coded English (MCE) systems that were created for classroom use, such as Signed English and Signing Exact English, and the more naturalistic production of English-based signing found in the Deaf community and among many teachers of deaf students.

MCE systems attempt to achieve a high degree of correspondence between signs and English words and morphemes. A detailed description of the articulatory mechanics of producing various MCE systems can be found elsewhere (e.g., Bornstein, 1984; Stewart & Luetke-Stahlman, 1998). MCE systems have been with us for 30 years, but their popularity appears to be dwindling among teachers and researchers. Although they draw heavily from ASL vocabulary, "the style of signing prescribed by manually coded English systems is impractical for the classroom simply because so few teachers use them" (Stewart & Luetke-Stahlman, p. 244).

Different means of articulating English-based signing have long had their place in the Deaf community in general and especially among bilingual deaf adults. In the literature, this type of English-based signing has been variously called Pidgin Sign

English (Woodward, 1973), Contact Signing (Lucas & Valli, 1979), Modern ASL (Bragg, 1990), Sign English (Woodward, 1990; Stewart & Luetke-Stahlman, 1998), and Natural Sign Systems (Fischer, 1998). Others, however, have noted the common use of English-based signing in the Deaf community and have subsumed it under the label "American Sign Language" (Goodstein, 1990; Kuntze, 1990). Moores (2001) noted that "Deaf professionals have provided leadership in making the term *ASL* more inclusive and in embracing varieties of signing within a common core" (p. 227). Nevertheless, for the purpose of the communication approach being espoused in this chapter, from this point forward the definition of English-based signing for this chapter is "a way of signing that is modeled on English grammar but varies in its use of English and ASL linguistic features." This is a broad definition, but it captures the diversity of English-based signing that teachers of deaf students are using.

The Role of Signing in the Classroom

It cannot be easy being a teacher faced with making a decision about which type of signing will provide the best basis for communicating with a deaf child in a classroom at each or all of the grade levels. The historical role of signing in deaf education programs is a rather tiresome picture of contrasts. ASL often has been cast as the preferred linguistic vehicle for the acquisition of a first language. The argument is "learn ASL and deaf children will have a language foundation from which they can draw to acquire English as a second language." The analogy presented is hearing children who pick up a second language after first mastering a first language. In contrast, other educators portray English-based signing as the best means of providing a visual model of grammatically correct English. Their argument is "use English-based signing consistently and deaf children will learn English in a natural manner that is comparable to that of hearing children acquiring spoken English."

Proponents of both arguments push the notion that competence in at least one language is the immediate goal of language learning for young deaf children. They also share the common belief that to attain a quality education, deaf children must acquire proficiency in English, and the sooner this happens, the better. Their differences in opinion about how deaf children can best learn English have produced numerous position papers that espouse one type of signing over the other. But a glance at the claims of either ASL or English-based advocates reveals meager research support for either side (Akamatsu, Stewart, & Becker, 2002). Hence, many programs and more specifically many teachers plow ahead without a high degree of conviction that the way they are signing will best facilitate learning in their deaf students.

What we do know is that deaf children can and do acquire fluency in ASL at a young age if they receive adequate exposure to it. The same case cannot yet be made of young deaf children acquiring proficiency in English just through exposure to English-based signing. At this point, it is tempting to announce that all deaf children should therefore acquire ASL as a first language, which is a conclusion that proponents of many Bi-Bi programs have made.

However, if the case for acquiring ASL as a first language appears so obvious, then why do parents and educators alike not embrace it more readily? The only reasonable answer, given our current research base, is that deaf children who acquire ASL as a first language still face the challenge of learning English: a key barrier to their ability to learn curricular content. Despite two decades of use as the primary language of instruction in a number of deaf education programs, no research evidence shows that on average deaf children whose first language is ASL attain a level of English proficiency that is commensurate with their grade level.

A similar circumstance faces children who are exposed to English-based signing starting at a young age. No studies verify that they have a greater advantage in acquiring proficiency in English than do their deaf peers whose first language is ASL. In fact, there is no classroom-based research to support either position. Some have argued that the reason for the lack of supportive evidence for English-based signing is a result of poor implementation strategies for using MCE systems in the classroom. When MCE was being widely introduced in deaf education programs in the 1970s and early 1980s, teachers were not adequately prepared to use them, the English signing behavior of deaf adults was not explored for ways to improve teachers' signing, and principles of ASL signing were neglected, which in turn reduced the efficiency of producing signs in English word order (Stewart, 1993). Although these reasons may have some element of truth to them, the fact remains that MCE has had a long enough run in the field to rectify any deficiencies that might be perceived as hindering its instructional use.

In contrast, English-based signing other than MCE systems continues to be used in the classroom. One reason for this phenomenon may be the belief that English-based signing can provide a bridge to English literacy. Studies indicate that exposure to English-based signing may facilitate deaf students' acquisition of various English grammatical features such as the use of articles, inflections, and plurals (Akamatsu, Stewart, & Becker, 2000); provides deaf students with a means for reading back stories, which helps the writing process (Mayer, 1999); and may be used as a connection between inner speech and writing (Mayer & Akamatsu, 2000). Similarly, several authors have posited that exposure to ASL helps deaf students develop literacy skills (Hoffmeister, 2000; Wilbur, 2000) and that the more proficient a deaf student is in ASL, the higher level of literacy skills they will demonstrate (Strong & Prinz, 1997). These studies on the connections between signing and literacy development do not provide conclusive evidence one way or the other. Moreover, contradictory studies are found, such as reported by Moores and Sweet (1990), who found, after extensive testing, that ASL did not correlate with reading and writing skills for deaf adolescents.

Perhaps the most telling evidence of the benefit of ASL and English-based signing in the development of English literacy skills is that no research evidence demonstrates that exposure to either type of signing is detrimental in this development. Unfortunately, it is also true that whatever the connections that ASL and English-based signing might have to the development of English literacy skills, the reading level of deaf students upon graduation still lags significantly behind that of their hearing peers.

Thus, the question "What bridging strategies or combination of bridging strategies from the child's communication system to English are most effective?" is more beneficial than asking which sign communication leads to better development of English literacy (Andrews, Leigh, & Weiner, 2004, p. 155). Moores (2001) likewise argues that in signing it is important to address "how to develop English skills and how to bridge the gap between ASL and English" (p. 208).

So what is a teacher to do? And what can teachers do in the classroom that will give parents greater confidence in their decision to endorse ASL and English-based signing either alone or in combination? The answer to these questions lies in developing the IPC perspective in the classroom and using the strengths of ASL and English-based signing. In a review of the influence of signing on the education of deaf students, Akamatsu, Stewart, and Mayer (2002) drew the following conclusion:

> Signing all of the time in ASL or using speech and a form of English signing simultaneously all of the time is an inadequate response to the complex communication needs of deaf students. To focus solely on the signing skills of teachers overly constrains the conception of what a good teacher of deaf students is. It becomes clear that it matters less which language or mode of communication teachers use than the manner in which they use the language. (p. 247)

In the IPC approach, signing is determined by how teachers feel they can best achieve their lesson objectives and by the communication needs related to their discourse with students.

It makes sense to allow teachers to use both ASL and English-based signing, depending upon the instructional and communication demands of a lesson or a teacher-student interaction. Although the precise role of ASL and English-based signing in the education of deaf children still requires extensive investigation, sufficient evidence warrants the following statements:

- ASL gives deaf students an effective means for acquiring a first language.
- English-based signing and ASL provide deaf students with a means for acquiring English literacy skills.

By embracing these two ideas, teachers can devote time and energy to the actual task of teaching, curricular considerations, their pedagogical understanding of teaching content matter, and the learning characteristics of their particular group of deaf students to determine the language and shape of communication that will help them accomplish instructional objectives. Teaching, after all, is the essential responsibility of a teacher, and the role of ASL and English-based signing can only be determined by the goals of teaching.

Instructional and Practical Communication Without Barriers

In truth, no barriers exist for deaf adults who use ASL and English-based signing in any number of settings at home, in the workplace, and in the community. Thus, it seems counterproductive to think that we can place barriers to the use of signing in the classroom.

Furthermore, it is expected that deaf children who use signs will become proficient users of ASL and English. The level of proficiency attained in each language is contingent upon many factors, including language use in the home, exposure to language at school, degree of hearing loss, use of speech and audition, and parental hearing status. Also factored into the language proficiency equation are the intellectual and learning traits of the individual. Eventually, all deaf children who sign will use ASL and English with varying degrees of effectiveness to meet the communication situations they face in their daily lives. These situations are vast and very diverse, and include reading textbooks, websites, magazines, and e-mail messages; writing reports, filling out forms, and conversing in print in the real-time world of instant messaging; talking to parents, peers, teachers, and casual acquaintances; socializing inside and outside of the Deaf community; and, in a manner of speaking, the many thoughts and conversations that take place in the brain as deaf children try to understand and internalize the world around them.

There is no doubt that for deaf children who sign, two languages are better than one. At school, the bilingual student will fare better in the classroom and in the hallway, across all subject matter, within all types of social interactions, and in discourse with all teachers. Being proficient in ASL and English gives deaf students the flexibility to learn and interact better in all types of instructional and everyday situations.

Although the ASL and English competency skills of a teacher are critical to good teaching, an argument can be made that presently not all teachers have reached a level of fluency that will contribute to favorable teaching. This situation is unfortunate, and at some point in our history of educating deaf students, fluency in these two languages must be recognized as a requirement for any teacher attaining an endorsement in this field. This development is already under way in some states that require teaching candidates to pass a basic skills test that includes testing in the area of reading and writing. With respect to signing, some university programs, recognizing the fact that completing courses in ASL or English-based signing does not guarantee sufficient signing skills for teaching, require teaching candidates to achieve specific performance levels in signing as demonstrated, for example, by attaining an advanced level on measures such as the SCPI (Sign Communication Proficiency Interview).

Standards for signing performance need to be broadly implemented and enforced across the country. With a high level of signing skills, teachers are better positioned to focus their instruction on the accomplishment of various curricular and communication goals. This situation contrasts with teachers who have limited signing ability, which constrains how they teach and how they can use two languages to meet their instructional objectives. Improved standards will be attained when schools demand that teachers of the deaf demonstrate proficiency in the use of both ASL and English before acquiring endorsement to teach deaf students who rely on signing as their primary means of communication. When this proficiency is reached, no barriers will face teachers in IPC programs who have the ability to use ASL and English, including English-based signing, for delivering instruction and guiding discourse with students.

Conclusion

ASL and English are a part of everyday communication for deaf students who rely on signing as their primary means of communication. Each language has much to contribute to helping deaf students gain the linguistic tools necessary for succeeding at school, becoming a literate person, and conversing comfortably in ASL or English. The route that each student takes to bilingualism will vary depending upon the language to which they are exposed at home and in early education programs. Variations will also occur because of student characteristics relating to hearing loss, academic aptitude, and other factors. Whatever route a deaf student uses, the ultimate goal is to be proficient in ASL and English.

Thus, it is imperative that teachers of deaf students are able to draw from their own linguistic strengths and use ASL and English in a manner that they feel will optimize learning for their students. They must be able to do so without barriers to the presentation of either language.

The IPC approach recognizes that there is a role for both ASL and some form of English-based signing in the education of deaf children. It therefore provides teachers with a philosophy for making decisions about ASL and English based upon their pedagogical understanding of the subject matter they are teaching and their knowledge of the learning strengths and weaknesses of their students. No constraints on the expression of the two languages must be allowed to interfere with teachers who are bilingually proficient in both languages. Teachers who subscribe to the IPC philosophy will find themselves modeling flexibility in their communication, which is vital for deaf students to see as they strive to acquire the linguistic and academic knowledge necessary to succeed in the bilingual environments that they encounter daily.

References

Akamatsu, C., Stewart, D., & Becker, B. (2002). Documenting English syntactic development in face-to-face signed communication. *American Annals of the Deaf, 145*(5), 452–463.

Akamatsu, T., Stewart, D., & Mayer, C. (2003). Look beyond teachers' signing behavior? *Sign Language Studies, 2*(3), 239–254.

Andrews, J. F., Leigh, I. W., & Weiner, M. T. (2004). *Deaf people: Evolving perspectives from psychology, education, and sociology.* Boston: Allyn and Bacon.

Bornstein, H. (1984). *Manual communication: Implications for education.* Washington, DC: Gallaudet University Press.

Bragg, B. (1990). Communication and the Deaf community: Where do we go from here? In M. Garretson (Ed.), *Eyes, hands, voices: Communication issues among Deaf people.* (pp. 9–14). Silver Spring, MD: National Association of the Deaf, 1990.

Clarke, B. R. (1972). Total communication. *Canadian Teacher of the Deaf 2,* 22–30.

Fischer, S. (1998). Critical periods for language acquisition: Consequences for deaf education. In A. Wiesel (Ed.), *Issues unresolved: New perspectives on language and deaf education* (pp. 9–26). Washington, DC: Gallaudet University.

Goodstein, H. (1990). American Sign Language. In M. Garretson (Ed.), *Eyes, hands, voices: Communication issues among Deaf people* (pp. 47–50). Silver Spring, MD: National Association of the Deaf.

Hoffmeister, R. (2000). A piece of the puzzle: ASL and reading comprehension in deaf children. In C. Chamberlain, J. Morford, & R. Mayberry (Eds.), *Language acquisition by eye* (pp. 143–163). Mahwah, NJ: Erlbaum.

Kuntze, M. (1990). ASL: Unity and power. In M. Garretson (Ed.), *Eyes, hands, voices: Communication issues among Deaf people* (pp. 75–78). Silver Spring, MD: National Association of the Deaf.

Lucas, C., & Valli, C. (1989). Language contact in the American Deaf community. In C. Lucas (Ed.), *The sociolinguistics of the Deaf community* (pp. 11–40). New York: Academic.

Mayer, C. (1999). Shaping at the point of utterance: An investigation of the composing processes of the deaf student writer. *Journal of Deaf Studies and Deaf Education 4*, 37–49.

Mayer, C., & Akamatsu, C. T. (2000). Deaf children creating written texts: Contributions of American Sign Language and signed forms of English. *American Annals of the Deaf, 145*, 394–403.

Mayer, C., Akamatsu, C. T., & Stewart, D. (2002). A model of effective practice: Dialogic inquiry in the education of deaf students. *Exceptional Children, 68*(4), 485–502.

Mayer, C., & Lowenbraun, S. (1990). Total communication use among elementary teachers of hearing impaired children. *American Annals of the Deaf, 135*, 257–263.

Maxwell, M. (1990). Simultaneous communication: The state of the art & proposals for change. *Sign Language Studies, 69*, 333–390.

Moores, D. F. (2001). *Educating the deaf: Psychology, principles, and practices.* Boston: Houghton Mifflin.

Moores, D., & Sweet, C. (1990). Factors predictive of school achievement. In D. Moores & K. Meadow-Orlans (Eds.), *Educational and developmental aspects of deafness* (pp. 154–202). Washington, DC: Gallaudet University Press.

Paul, P. (1998). *Literacy and deafness: The development of reading, writing, and literate thought,* Boston: Allyn & Bacon, 1998.

Stewart, D. (1982). American Sign Language: A forgotten aspect of total communication. *Association of Canadian Educators of the Hearing Impaired Journal, 8*, 137–148.

Stewart, D. (1993). Bi-bi to MCE? *American Annals of the Deaf, 138*(4), 331–337.

Stewart, D., Akamatsu, C. T., & Becker, B. (1995). Aiming for consistency in the way teachers sign. *American Annals of the Deaf, 140*, 314–323.

Stewart, D., & Luetke-Stahlman, B. (1998). *The signing family: What every parent should know about sign communication.* Washington, DC: Clerc Books.

Stewart, D., & Kluwin, T. (2001). *Teaching deaf and hard of hearing students: Content, strategies, and curriculum.* Boston: Allyn & Bacon.

Stewart, D., Mayer, C., & Akamatsu, C. T. (2003). A model for effective communicative practice with deaf and hard of hearing students. *Odyssey, 5*(1), 80–83.

Strong, M., & Prinz, P. M. (1997). A study of the relationship between American Sign

Language and English literacy. *Journal of Deaf Studies and Deaf Education*, 2(1), 37–45.

Wilbur, R. (2000). The use of ASL to support the development of English and literacy. In C. Chamberlain, J. Morford, & R. Mayberry (Eds.), *Language acquisition by eye* (pp. 131–141). Mahwah, NJ: Erlbaum.

Wodward, J. (1973). Some characteristics of Pidgin Sign English. *Sign Language Studies, 3*, 9–46.

Woodward, J. (1990). Sign English in the education of deaf students. In H. Bornstein (Ed.), *Manual communication: Implications for education* (pp. 67–80). Washington, DC: Gallaudet University.

Woodward, J., & Allen, T. (1987). Classroom use of ASL by teachers. *Sign Language Studies, 54*, 1–10.

Woodward, J., & Allen, T. (1988). Classroom use of artificial sign systems by teachers. *Sign Language Studies, 61*, 405–418.

H A R O L D   J O H N S O N

D O N N A   M .   M E R T E N S

New Strategies to Address Old Problems: Web-Based Technologies, Resources, and Applications to Enhance Deaf Education

Tell me and I will forget,
Show me and I will remember,
Let me do it and I will understand.

  —Confucius (n.d.)

THE PURPOSE OF SCHOOL is not more school, but preparation for life outside of school. The Partnership for 21st Century Skills (2003), a coalition of corporate, professional, and governmental leaders, committed their time and expertise to establish a common vision of the essential knowledge, skills, and attitudes that are needed by a 21st century learner who could function successfully upon completion of his or her formal schooling. The resulting vision describes such a person as an effective, efficient, self-directed, technologically sophisticated, lifelong learner who collaborates with others for the common purpose of generating and using knowledge to address problems of value to the communities in which they live. Unfortunately, there is a "profound gap between the knowledge and skills most students learn in schools and the knowledge and skills they need in typical 21st century communities and work places" (Partnership for 21st Century Skills, 2003, p. 3). However, educators have both the opportunity and responsibility to make these skills a reality for all students.

This chapter explores how this vision of a 21st century learning environment can be established within deaf education through a review of scholarly research and the work of the Association for College Educators—Deaf/Hard of Hearing (ACE-D/HH).[1] This exploration first focuses on the most critical component of any learning environment, teachers. The chapter synthesizes the literature concerning the characteristics of effective teachers and the learning environments that they establish for their students, along with the barriers that teachers face as they attempt to integrate technologies into those environments. The final sections of the chapter identify evaluation, instructional, and teacher preparation designs that can be used within deaf education to establish a 21st century learning environment for us all.

21st Century Teachers

The single factor that is most predictive of student performance is the instructional effectiveness of teachers (Garry & Graham, 2004; Hasselbring, Smith, Rakestraw & Campbell, 2000). Effective teachers are those who understand the learning process; the content areas that they teach; the knowledge, interests, and experiences of their students; and their students' existing learning strategies (Bransford, Brown, & Cocking, 1999c; Donovan, Bransford, & Pellegrino, 1999a). Effective teachers motivate their students through use of collaborative, project-based activities that clearly link schoolwork to student lives (Donovan, Bransford, & Pellegrino, 1999b). Such projects serve to establish not only why the targeted knowledge is important, but also when and how the knowledge should be used. Finally, effective teachers use formative assessments to continually monitor both their students' learning and the effectiveness of their own instruction (Hasselbring et al., 2000). Such formative assessments are designed in such ways as to give students increasing responsibility to document and monitor their own learning.

The research on effective teaching suggests a changing role for the teacher: from a "keeper and provider of all knowledge" to "facilitator of information and critical thinking" (Cerf & Schutz, 2001, pp. 2–3). Critical to this emerging role of teacher as facilitator is the design and establishment of a classroom environment that encourages *both* teachers and students to become increasingly effective and efficient learners. The key characteristics of an effective classroom learning environment are provided in the next section of this chapter.

21st Century Learning Environment

The model of teachers as facilitators reflects the new learning environment that is needed for the 21st century (Bransford, Brown, & Cocking, 1999b). The major differences between the traditional and new learning environments have been characterized as follows: teacher-centered vs. student-centered learning, single-sense instruction vs. multisensory instruction, single media vs. multimedia, isolated work vs. collaborative

---

1. ACE-D/HH is a professional organization whose primary members consists of the faculty who prepare teachers of deaf and hard of hearing students in the United States and Canada.

work, information delivery vs. information exchange, passive learning vs. active/exploratory/inquiry-based learning, factual knowledge vs. critical thinking, and artificial context vs. authentic context (PT3, 2004).

Support for this new learning environment is provided by a significant array of research concerning how children learn. That research, summarized by Bransford, Brown, and Cocking (1999a), describes children as

- actively engaged in making sense of the world;
- lacking knowledge and experience but not reasoning ability;
- bringing to school many misconceptions that must be identified and corrected;
- needing to develop learning strategies to assist their planning, monitoring, revising, and reflecting upon what they learn; and
- individuals who inherently seek to both solve and create problems.

To become a reality, the vision of effective teachers preparing 21st century learners requires an additional ingredient—information and communication technologies. If used effectively, such technologies have the potential of changing classrooms from four walls and a door to dynamic, interactive learning portals that are connected to a worldwide community of learners (Partnership for 21st Century Skills, 2003). Unfortunately, as the next section of the chapter reveals, the potential and the realities of technology are often far apart.

Technology Promise and Problems

Since 1990, more than $40 billion have been invested to place computers, software, and the Internet in U.S. schools (Dickward, 2003). Although that has yielded a significant improvement in teachers' and students' access to classroom-based, computer technologies linked to the Internet, inequities persist in terms of access and high-speed connectivity, and inadequacies exist in terms of instructional use. For example, Cattagni and Farris-Westat (2001) reported that 98% of schools and 77% of classrooms were connected to the Internet. However, the rate of home-based computers linked to the Internet was found to vary along economic and minority lines (25% of the poorest households vs. 80% with incomes of more than $75,000 and 32% of Hispanic, 40% of African American, and 60% white households) (Dickward, 2003). Such data reflect more limited access for specific groups with attendant consequences for student achievement (Cattagni & Farris-Westat, 2001). Furthermore, schools' investments in technology were carried out with the clear, albeit poorly defined, expectation that they would result in significant improvements in student performance (CEO Forum, 2001; Heafner, 2004; Neumann & Kyriakakis, 2002). Unfortunately, research has not proven this to be the case.

Although the link between technology integration and student performance has yet to be clearly established (Cradler, 2003a), research has documented that the effective use of technology does increase students' motivation; time on task; amount of work completed; critical thinking, research, and organizational skills; self-confidence; and interest in content (Cradler, 2002; Heafner, 2004). Cradler (2003b) noted that the extent of such effects was determined by two essential factors: how well the technology was applied and in what context it was used. In an earlier article, Cradler (2002) also noted that the effect of technology was the greatest when it was carried out in support of local and state curriculum standards. Cradler (2002) and others (CEO Forum, 2001; Partnership for 21st Century Skills, 2003) have indicated that the actual effect of technology on teaching and learning will only be established once assessment protocols have been developed that measure how, versus simply what, students learn. To date, the needed assessment protocols have yet to be developed.

In spite of the huge investments in computers and Internet access, research indicates that teachers do not feel well prepared to integrate technology into their teaching (Cradler, Freeman, Cradler, & McNabb, 2002; Hasselbring et al., 2000; Web-Based Education Commission, 2000). This reality has led to the conclusion that "learning how to use technology turned out to be at least as challenging as building it" (Cerf & Schutz, 2001, p. 2). Research concerning the reasons teachers do not use more technology within their teaching reveals a consistent pattern: lack of time, support, evaluation, and preparation.

Time is consistently identified as the largest single barrier to the effective integration of technology into teaching and learning (Dickward, 2003; Jacobsen, Clifford, & Frisen, 2002). The following teacher comment illustrates the time conundrum faced by teachers of the deaf and hard of hearing (D/HH) students:

> Although most people feel/hope that using technology will make teaching easier, that is a fallacy. It's a lot more work now that I'm using more technology. For example there's always a learning curve so I'm perpetually learning new technology, it takes more time to set up equipment, and troubleshooting when things don't go as planned. That said, technology has made my teaching more robust, more visual, and I believe more interesting. We are using technology to greater extents to teach deaf students English literacy. (Mertens, 2004a)

Although this teacher sees the value of her time and energy investment, many teachers do not. This position is supported by the fact that although their existing instructional strategies may not be technologically intensive, they are known, consistently available, and they work as good, or better, than the technology alternatives. In addition, the previously quoted teacher makes the point that learning technology is a task never finished. There are differential learning curves associated with each new piece of hardware or software. Thus, lifelong learning is important for teachers of D/HH students.

Teachers identify the lack of support, both technical and professional, as the second largest barrier to their greater use of technology within the classroom (Dickward, 2003). Although technical support may simply involve having a replacement printer cartridge or installing a new piece of software, the frequency with which computer problems occur and the disruptions, delays, and embarrassments that they cause have resulted in a situation in which many teachers do not trust the technology to be there when they need it. This problem could be addressed by providing teachers with more professional development opportunities; however, Bransford, Brown, and Cocking (1999d) determined that schools typically spend between 1 and 2% of their operating budget on such development. Yet, Sivin-Kachala and Bialo's (2000) review of more than 300 research studies concluded: "If we want students to engage in appropriate technology-based learning experiences...then teachers' professional development and support are essential" (p. 7). Unfortunately, the vast majority of existing teachers' professional development opportunities are ineffective as a result of the common use of a deficit model, top-down, one-shot, lecture approach that does not reflect teachers' interests, experiences, knowledge base, or instructional realities (Adsit, 2004; Bransford, Brown, & Cocking, 1999d).

The third barrier to school-based technology integration concerns the lack of consensus among teachers, administrators, and legislators concerning the effect that such integration has on student performance (Dickward, 2003). Adding to this confusion is the lack of assessment protocols that effectively measure not simply what students learn, but how their critical thinking and problem solving skills are enhanced by the use of technology. This confusion, combined with the performance and accountability mandates of the No Child Left Behind Act (U.S. Department of Education, 2002) and the increasing reliance upon state competency tests as measures of educational effectiveness, has resulted in many teachers simply deciding to meet state-mandated standards by focusing on textbooks, not inquiry-based learning (Bransford, Brown, & Cocking, 1999e; NCATE, 2001). This decision, although logical, has the effect of reinforcing the use of traditional learning environments rather than new environments that are inherently more amenable to technology applications.

The final reason for the lack of technology integration is the inability of recently graduated, newly hired, technologically sophisticated teachers to affect the instructional strategies of their more experienced peers. Although the teacher preparation of these individuals is more technologically advanced than that received by most existing teachers, their preparation most often focuses upon knowledge of, as opposed to use of, technology (Jacobsen, Clifford, & Frisen, 2002; Web-Based Education Commission, 2000). Additional research indicates a more fundamental and potentially important reason for the lack of technology integration. Although courses form an important component of teacher preparation, the single largest predictor of how preservice teachers will teach is not the courses they complete, but the instructional patterns of the teachers with whom they are placed for their field and student teaching experiences (Browne & Hoover, 1990; Goodlad, 1990). However, placement decisions are more frequently based on availability than the extent to which the placement provides an opportunity for preservice teachers to see and practice the instructional strategies, curricular resources, and technological tools that are presented within their courses (Wilson, Floden, & Ferrini-Mundy, 2001). Therefore, because preservice teachers rarely have the opportunity to see and use technology within their field/student teaching placements, they rarely include technology within their own instructional design as they begin their teaching careers (Hasselbring, et al., 2000; Kellogg & Kersaint, 2004). This element of teacher preparation programs has the unintended outcome of ensuring that traditional learning environments remain the norm with U.S. schools.

Effective Professional Development

The barriers to K–20 technology integration must be overcome before a 21st century learning environment can be established for the nation's teachers and students. Those barriers can most effectively be addressed through a combination of both initial and ongoing professional development. This section of the chapter presents a synthesis of the literature concerning the essential characteristics of effective professional development programs.

Fortunately, the characteristics of learning opportunities that are needed by teachers are very similar to those that are needed by their students (Cradler & Cradler, 2002–2003; Donovan, Bransford, & Pellegrino, 1999b). As a result, effective professional development opportunities for teachers serve not only to address their ongoing learning needs, but also to model the type of learning opportunities that will benefit their students. Research concerning professional development has determined that the most effective programs are those that

- reduce isolation by establishing peer-support networks;
- increase access to a broad range of instructional and curricular resources (Adsit, 2004);
- provide "just in time" vs. "just in case" learning opportunities;
- provide sustained collaborative activities that address authentic, challenging, and multidisciplinary tasks;
- establish a culture of learning in which risk-taking and knowledge generation are common;
- provide teachers with sufficient time to reflect upon and apply what they have learned and then to both receive and provide feedback concerning the learning (Bransford, Brown, & Cocking, 1999d; Jacobsen, Clifford, & Frisen, 2002);
- incorporate strategies that foster critical thinking;
- establish study groups that share topical interests and goals and that foster sustained and collegial discussions;
- provide specific directions and establish clear expectations and accountability (Garry & Graham, 2004);
- link instructional strategies and technology integration to content-specific local/state standards for student performance;
- use action research projects as the core professional development activity;
- link targeted learning to student performance data (Cradler & Cradler, 2002–2003); and
- align teachers' existing classroom activities and curricular resources with targeted knowledge and skills (Hasselbring et al., 2000).

A critical element of teacher professional development that is rarely available (Adsit, 2004) is the ability to not only hear about a given concept, strategy, technology, or assessment, but to also see and practice its use (Donovan, Bransford, & Pellegrino, 1999b). The importance of being actively engaged in learning and practicing new ideas and tools has been stressed throughout this chapter. Initial and ongoing professional development must be grounded in the most innovative theories and research and provide opportunities to observe and interact with the most innovative and effective teachers. The final sections of the chapter place the preceding information concerning 21st century learning, teaching, environments, and professional development within the context of deaf education.

The Context of Deaf Education

Current Challenges

The primary problem of deafness is not too little hearing but an abundance of isolation from peers, meaningful learning opportunities, and needed learning resources (Dolnick, 1993; Johnson, 2003). During the course of the past decade, the extent of that isolation has increased as parents have elected to place their children who are D/HH in neighborhood schools rather than larger, aggregate programs or schools for the deaf (Dodd & Scheetz, 2003; Ramsey, 1997; U.S. Department of Education, n.d.). Within these schools, educational settings have shifted from self-contained to resource to inclusion placements (Moores, 1995, 2001). This shift has resulted in the increasing use of general education teachers, supported by itinerant teachers, interpreters, and speech pathologists, to meet the educational needs of students who are D/HH. Because of the NCLB legislation, all students are now required to take state proficiency exams and to demonstrate expected levels of academic (mathematics, literacy, and science) performance (U.S. Department of Education, 2002). This will be difficult for many students who are D/HH. Although these students possess the same learning potential as their hearing peers (Rosenstein, 1961), their overall level of academic performance is significantly below that of their peers (Traxler, 2000). The effects of this lack of performance are demonstrated by the fact that although 68% of the 1999–2000 D/HH high school graduates received standard diplomas (U.S. Department of Education, n.d.), only 25% of those graduates that enter postsecondary programs graduate from those programs (Lang, 2002). Preparation of students who are D/HH for life after high school is further complicated by (a) the students' increasing ethnic diversity (Holden-Pitt & Diaz, 1998), (b) the lack of such diversity in their teachers (Moores, 1995, 2001. See also Long, Martin, Moores, and Pagliaro, this volume), and (c) their teachers' lack of adequate academic content preparation (Marschark, Lang, & Albertini, 2002; Pagliaro, 1998; Stewart & Kluwin, 2001. See also Lang, Martin, Moores, and Pagliaro, this volume). A final challenge facing deaf education concerns the number of students who must be educated. During the 2000–2001 school year, 70,767 K–12 D/HH students received educational services within the United States (U.S. Department of Education, n.d.). That number represents an increase of more than 10,000 students since the 1991–1992 academic year. Unfortunately, although the number of students has increased, the rate at which individuals are becoming teachers of D/HH students has remained constant (Johnson, 2003). As a result, there is a persistent and growing nationwide shortage of teachers of D/HH students (LaSasso & Wilson, 2000). The final section of this chapter identifies how computer-based technologies linked to the Internet are now being used to address the many problems facing K–20 deaf education while simultaneously establishing a 21st century learning environment for both students and their teachers.

Deaf Education Teacher Preparation Designs

Emerging Solutions

Sixty-nine colleges and universities in 36 states and the District of Columbia offer degree programs for individuals to become teachers of D/HH students (DeafEd Teacher Preparation Programs, 2004). Within those programs, approximately 220 full and part-time faculty prepare an estimated 2,500 to 3,000 individuals to become teachers of D/HH students. Available data indicate that the programs graduate between 750 and 800 individuals a year (Johnson, 2003). Thirty-eight percent of those graduates are eligible to receive state certification, and 62% are eligible to receive both state certification *and* one or more endorsements from the Council on the Education of the Deaf (CED). All of those graduates must be prepared to address the current deaf education realities while simultaneously enhancing those realities to better prepare students for 21st century life. The ACE-D/HH has established a plan to ensure that this occurs. In 1999, ACE-D/HH was awarded the first of a series of grants by the federal Preparing Tomorrow's Teachers to use Technology (PT3) program. The first grant (1999–2000), "Instructional Effectiveness Through Collaboration and Technological Innovations for the Field of Deaf Education," was designed to promote faculty use of technology to both share and generate instructional materials. The second PT3 grant (2000–2004), "Crossing the 'Realities Divide': Preservice Teachers as 'Change Agents' for the Field of Deaf Education" (Catalyst Deaf Ed. Project, 2000), was designed to enhance deaf education teacher preparation through the development and use of computer-based, Internet-linked technologies to create an online community of learners. One product of the resulting collaborative activities was the design, development, and maintenance of the Deaf Education website (http://www.deafed.net), which disseminates information about exemplary practices in deaf education, publications, events, job announcements, and candidates' resumes.

ACE-D/HH was awarded a third PT3 grant (2003–2006) in October of 2003, "Join Together: A Nationwide On-Line Community of Practice and Professional Development School Dedicated to Instructional Effectiveness and Academic Excellence Within Deaf/Hard of Hearing Education" (Join Together, 2003), designed to link the theories, research, and resources of the teacher preparation programs with the innovative and effective practices of K–12 teachers of D/HH students. The Join Together grant was designed to address the technology application barriers of time, support, evaluation, and preparation by providing evidence of applications that are sufficiently compelling; tying technology support to student performance; recognizing teachers for their efforts; and facilitating the placement of teacher candidates with the best, rather than simply the available, K–12 teachers.

Virtual Professional Development School

Existing home, school, and college and university computers and technologies linked to the Internet can be used to establish a K–20 virtual professional development school (VPDS) for deaf education. The VPDS would serve to reduce isolation, increase collaboration, and enhance the preparation of new teachers by grounding them in the realities and knowledge of existing teachers of students who are D/HH. The VPDS can accomplish these tasks through a four-step process.

Step One: Build an Online Community for Sharing Effective Strategies

The first step in this process is establishing an online community of learners. The grant-supported website http://www.deafed.net provides a forum for community-building activities that reduce the informational isolation frequently experienced within deaf education. This web portal provides the community with an efficient and effective means to search other, deafness-related Internet sites that are recognized for the quality of the information that they possess. In addition, the community can share information about their uses of technology as is illustrated in the section on compelling applications of technology.

Compelling Applications of Technology

People who have experience in the use of technology include faculty who prepare new teachers, practicing K–12 teachers, and the teacher candidates in the preparation programs who have already been surveyed to identify the applications of technology they find to be most useful and to provide ideas for others for using technology to enhance teaching and learning.

Strategies for Using Technology with New and Existing Teachers

As a part of the Join Together grant, a survey of 94 faculty in programs that prepare teachers of D/HH students was conducted in which faculty members were asked to describe how they use technology in their teaching (Mertens, 2004a). Frequently mentioned strategies included the use of presentation software (e.g., PowerPoint), digital images, and partially or fully online courses (e.g., Blackboard, WebCT); communication with students via e-mail and online discussion groups; e-portfolios; collaboration with colleagues; and web-based research projects. Faculty who prepare teachers of D/HH students revealed in more detail the strategies they used to share technology and resources with existing and preservice teachers in the following comments:

- "Increase of power point presentations, assigning students to do web searches on different topics on deafness and reporting that information to their peers, and requiring ALL clinical lab students who were working with DHH students after school to turn in their downloaded visual materials with their lesson plans on a weekly basis. In addition, students writing research papers must incorporate resources which can involve web searches on their topic of discussion, and those students involved in the final clinical lab class must create a Deaf Culture Notebook which gathers information from the different websites in 10 designated areas of deafness."

- "I have required my college level students to communicate with a deaf student through dialogue journaling via e-mail rather than journaling through writing. . . . I have required the college level students to create a power point presentation to the class to share research that has been done via the Internet. . . . The students must complete an Internet Inquiry and present the information in an abstract that requires the use of technology that describes research on the process of teaching language to the Deaf/HH and their opinion of the article. . . . The students and I often communicate during the week with the use of e-mail. . . . The students are encouraged to gather ideas for teaching Deaf/HH from the Internet and incorporate ideas into their 5 hours of practice teaching in a Deaf/HH classroom. . . . Students are directed to things that they should include in their electronic portfolios. . . . The students are allowed to view communication being done through video conferencing. . . . I have located several good videos via the Internet that help to show several kinds of strategies and techniques for teaching language to the Deaf/HH, and I've shown these in my classroom. . . . Showing students' classroom attendance and absences on line."

- "I had had a pretty good background regarding the integration of tech with teacher education. I redesigned our program so that the use of technology. . . is incorporated into coursework as well as into field experiences and other venues. One particularly good implementation involves work at the state level regarding deaf blind children and youth. Students in the program contract to take workshops and to tutor deaf blind kids. I have gotten supplementary grant funds from our state project to provide some tuition and to purchase tech for use in the field. We now have 4 ViGOs and one is connected from the state office to my office where I use our ViaVideo (obtained in the PT 3 Catalyst Grant.) My teaching has changed as I grapple with providing the best supplements to classroom instruction. Our college has periodic workshops in which I have presented a couple simple things. . . . I purchased an Elmo and our own multimedia projector with deaf blind funds and now all of the faculty and myself can use it daily in our graduate quarters where we teach all courses. I also got a Smart Board that has come in handy for students' demonstrations of lessons."

Faculty recognize the benefits of using technology in the teacher training program because it allows for increased access to visual information; sharing of ideas among themselves, their colleagues, and preservice and existing teachers; and improved communications.

Teacher Candidates' Applications of Technology

Teacher candidates constitute the second part of the solution. They are learning to become increasingly valuable resources to their communities. As a result, students are part of the solution to the problems of isolation, sharing, and grounding. As part of the ACE-D/HH initiative, teacher candidates submit their work to compete in "Best of the Deaf Ed Web Site" competition (Best of the Web, 2001). The winners' technological applications are posted to the website and represent an example of how the work of college or university can be designed to benefit the larger deaf education community. The potential of this web portal to enhance deaf education is only limited by the willingness of the growing community to recognize and share their informational resources and collaborative opportunities.

Instructional Strategies of Deaf Education K-12 Teachers

As a part of the Join Together grant, a survey was conducted of 58 exceptional K–12 teachers of D/HH students. These teachers had been recognized by the faculty who place their students with these teachers for internships and student teaching (Mertens, 2004b). When they were asked to describe how they use technology in their teaching, they replied with a broad range of uses, such as instructional strategies that make use of hand-held computers, SMART boards, scanners, digital/video cameras, and Internet access, as well as administrative uses such as preparing and monitoring IEPs and grading reports. The following teacher comments provide a more detailed look at how they use technology:

- "I use a digital camera almost every day. We use it to document results of experiments, take photos of examples of categories (plants, animals, etc.), to clarify concepts. We use the photos on posters, worksheets, and power point presentations. I use digital cameras to record role-plays and to make teaching videos in Health class, and to record science experiments. I also use the digital camera for the students to summarize information they have read in textbooks and have them take notes from the video. I have a wonderful "Teach Cam" which can attach to a microscope or focus in on a demonstration and be projected on the television. The benefits of using it with a microscope are obvious, but I was happy to have it when one of my students was also visually impaired. I use the equipment myself, and teach my students how to hook up and use everything also, saving me time and teaching them new skills in the process."

- "My school (Texas School for the Deaf) is lucky to be participating in a laptop project with Apple computers, in which all freshmen and teachers of freshmen get a free laptop to use in the classroom and at home/dorm for educational purposes. Through this program we are also connected to our network wirelessly with airports around the school. This has helped A LOT! Now all the freshmen have computers to use, homework and projects can be done in the classroom more easily and students are exposed to new computer programs. It's great! It has also helped me because I can take the laptop home or where ever I go to work, grade papers, use my grade book, etc. Another thing that has changed is the use of digital cameras (one of which was bought with tech grant money) that can be used to get pictures of students in a variety of activities. Another BIG benefit is using LCD projectors, connected to a laptop or an ELMO machine. Awesome! I can show PowerPoint presentations, student's [sic] can present projects with it, and we can also use projections with the ELMO instead of overhead projectors. So easy, so effective."

- "I have internet access almost all the time with my laptop at school. I am now able to help the kids do research and answer questions on the internet. Being an Itinerant, one piece of our job is to work on auditory training. With the use of the laptop, we are able to play a variety of games that makes a really boring task fun and interesting. I service 9 buildings. With email I am able to be contacted and also contact teachers all over the district any time any where. Most importantly, with the new technology that I now have, I have been able to help my students become better self advocates. Because of my computer I came up with the idea of having my kids present their needs using PPT. I also had the kids create a movie about hearing loss and being in the classroom that I use for in-services. With the computer, I am able to make effective presentations to staff."
- "Technology has proven to be a great motivator for my students. They enjoy writing, math drills and reading on the computer. Much more motivating than paper and pencil. It has brought the world into the classroom. We can look at a real brain or go on a journey with explorers. Using presentation software (Hyper studio, PowerPoint, Apple works) students can have an end product to research or study that they are proud to show to others. They become much more motivated."
- "I do not claim to be a technology expert, but I have incorporated technology into my teaching recently. I have CD ROMs that match leveled texts I use to teach reading. These programs have many activities related to each book in the set. I also have "Book Builder" CD ROMs used with students to create their own books. I use email to communicate with parents and with students (to encourage writing). I use the internet as a research tool for myself and for students. I use overhead projectors and most of my teacher-created materials for students and parents are done with the use of a computer. Technology is a great tool and it is necessary to prepare our students for the future."

The teachers' use of technology does require extra effort to learn how to use hardware and software; however, the majority agree that the effort is worthwhile in terms of increased access to resources, improved communication, and increased learning and motivation for their students.

Step Two: Cyber Mentor Program

The establishment of a cyber mentor program (CMP) is step two of the VPDS process. The CMP uses e-mail exchanges among deaf education stakeholders to share experiences, ask questions, and search for information. The goal of the exchanges is to reduce isolation, increase networking, and encourage collaboration between the cyber mentor and the individual with whom they are communicating. In February of 2001, ACE-D/HH, as part of their PT3 grant efforts, initiated a CMP (Cyber Mentor, 2001) designed to link individuals in preparation to become deaf education teachers with teachers and parents of children who were D/HH, Deaf adults, and other stakeholders. E-mail exchanges between the individuals and their cyber mentors provided a forum to share information learned in courses, discuss experiences gained from years of working, and collaboratively identify and seek needed resources. As of mid-2004, ACE-D/HH had accepted 237 cyber mentors into this project. They have subsequently exchanged hundreds of e-mail messages with individuals who are preparing to become deaf education teachers. Although such exchanges represent a success, the existing CMP should be expanded to provide mentors for the hundreds of teachers, thousands of parents, and tens of thousands of students who are D/HH and who are geographically isolated from one another and need information.

Step Three: Establish Topical Teams

Step three of the VPDS process entails establishing collaborative topical teams. These teams, drawn from the larger community of learners, use e-mail, mailing lists, bulletin boards, and phone conferences to focus on topics of particular interest and importance to deaf education. Although topics such as meaningful professional development, high-stakes testing, literacy development, science instruction, and parent involvement are almost impossible to address as an individual, or even as a small group of individuals, they can be addressed via a focused, nationwide collaborative effort that includes individuals with a wide range of experiences, expertise, and professional responsibilities. The Join Together (2003) grant created topical teams that focus on building a technology infrastructure; faculty technology competence; teacher diversity; multistate teacher preparation programs; certification; "best practices" in K–12 instruction of D/HH students, and design, development, implementation, and ongoing funding of a nationwide, virtual professional development program for deaf education. These topical teams use a variety of synchronous technologies (video streaming, chat rooms, IP video conferences, phone conferences, and virtual relay services) and asynchronous technologies (bulletin boards, mailing lists, e-mail messages, and downloadable files) to share their work and to invite individuals to join the teams in their efforts. The topical team design provides an effective and efficient mechanism to establish a critical mass of otherwise geographically isolated individuals who collaboratively work on topics or problems of common interest.

Membership on such teams is not limited to adults. Collaborative groups of students, who are D/HH, with or without their hearing peers, could and should be formed to explore topics, address problems, and share knowledge with the larger community of learners. Such topical teams represent both a significant challenge and a significant opportunity for deaf education because their design and use provides an excellent context for the development of 21st century learners.

Step Four: Providing Models of the Best Teachers

The fourth and final step in the VPDS process is the most dramatic and technologically challenging. This task entails the identification, documentation, support, and sharing of the nation's most innovative and effective teachers of students who are D/HH. The VPDS would then use the resulting instructional models to enhance and refine both teacher preparation and ongoing professional development. As such, preparation and professional development would be based on the instructional designs and practices of the most effective teachers, rather than theories, research, and personal beliefs that are often not well supported by actual gains in student performance. In 2003 ACE-D/HH established the Master Teacher Project (Master Teacher Project, 2003). This project solicited nominations from parents, teachers, administrators, faculty, and other stakeholders of K–12 teachers who were locally considered to be the most innovative and effective in their instruction of students who are D/HH. As of mid-2004, 82 individuals had been nominated. Information was requested from each of the nominated teachers, including a biographical sketch, instructional activities, and their solution to an educational problem that they have encountered with their students. The project then conducted research to document the teachers' instructional designs and the effects of those designs on student performance.

In addition, the teachers, their administrators, and technology support personnel were contacted about the use of Internet-based, remote control video cameras in the teachers' classrooms. Half of the cost for the videoconferencing technology is funded via the ACE-D/HH Join Together (2003) grant. The remote control cameras were selected to be compatible with smaller, computer-based, Internet-linked video systems that have been distributed among the faculty of the nation's deaf education teacher preparation programs. The resulting system provides good quality, no-cost, two-way video conferencing not only among teachers, faculty, and their students, but also teacher to teacher and teacher to students for virtual learning opportunities throughout the world. In this way the teachers' classrooms become learning portals, rather than the four walls and a door common within traditional learning environments. The systems also enable the teachers to provide virtual field experiences for deaf education teacher preparation programs. They have the potential to permit faculty to supervise student teaching placements in classrooms across the country. As a result, the systems give faculty the opportunity to use the best rather than simply the available placement for student teachers.

ACE-D/HH had just begun to work on this fourth phase of the VPDS process. Although this phase of the work is both technically and professionally challenging, the potential benefits for deaf education are well worth the effort. The identification of proven models of instructional designs, the technological ability to observe and work with colleagues throughout the country, and the opportunity to demonstrate what students who are D/HH can accomplish have the potential to effectively and efficiently prepare students for the 21st century learning environment they will face in life after school.

Deaf Education Evaluation Designs

An evaluation design is needed to guide the development of a VPDS (or any professional development model) and should be developed in tandem with the development of the VPDS itself. The evaluation framework in education should be based on an understanding of the program theory (what is needed for the desired effect to be achieved), the philosophical assumptions that underlie the choice of evaluation approach, and the principles of good evaluation (Joint Committee on Standards for Educational Evaluation, 1994). The principles of the transformative paradigm of research and its associated philosophical assumptions can be used as a basis for the development of an evaluation framework within the context of technology-based initiatives in deaf and hard of hearing educational settings (Mertens 2001a, 2001b, 2005; Mertens & McLaughlin, 2004).

The role of the evaluator who works within this framework is to raise questions about the involvement of diverse groups in the process of constructing an understanding of what the project should do and actually does, and documenting its accomplishments. In this approach, the evaluation plan calls for involvement of the variety of stakeholders who have diverse professional and personal positions with regard to the preparation of teachers or teaching of students and dimensions of diversity such as preferred communication mode, hearing status, race/ethnicity, rural/urban settings, and socioeconomic status of the faculty, preservice teachers, cooperating teachers, and the students they serve.

A second underlying philosophical assumption is related to the need for an interactive relationship between the evaluator and the stakeholders to develop trust and deeper understandings of diverse perspectives. Therefore, the evaluation design may well include mixed methods, including both qualitative and quantitative data collection. Data collection methods can include web-based surveys to reach all constituencies, participant observation, website collection of demographics and use data, site visits by the evaluator and her assistants, tests of learning, scales to measure attitude change, special case studies on diversity issues, focus groups with faculty and students, a rubric to assess student work, document reviews, personal interviews, and portfolios for students.

The Program Evaluation Standards should also guide the development of the evaluation design (Joint Committee on Standards for Educational Evaluation, 1994). These standards were developed by representatives of many national organizations including the American Evaluation Association, American Educational Research Association, and other organizations for administrators, counselors, and teachers. The main categories of these standards are the following:

- Utility—an evaluation must be useful.
- Feasibility—an evaluation must fit within the resources and time constraints of the project.
- Accuracy—an evaluation must adhere to criteria of rigor that will yield credible evidence.
- Propriety—evaluations must be designed to respect the ethical principles when dealing with human beings.

For each of the project's major goals, the evaluation plan should include specification of objectives, yearly indicators of success, data collection methods and sources, intended uses of the evaluation data, and dates when the evaluation activities would be conducted. For example, a technology project might be designed to improve student learning by using teams to develop innovative approaches using technology. Table 1 contains an example of the components of an evaluation plan that could be developed for such a project.

Table 1

SAMPLE EVALUATION PLAN FOR TEAMS AND INNOVATIVE TECHNOLOGY

Goal 1: Build a model to enrich the educational process for deaf and hard of hearing children by using a "team" approach and innovative technology.

Objectives	Indicators of Success	Data Collection Methods and Sources	Use	Date
Thematic units respond to critical needs of deaf children and their families	Teams are built with teachers, parents, interpreters Consensus is reached on critical needs	Participant observation, conference calls, surveys, focus groups	To determine if the teams are established in a proper time frame with appropriate expertise Modify topics included in thematic units	Participation with project staff and evaluator in biweekly phone calls Needs data assessed prior to the development of each thematic unit
Thematic units use high-quality methods and materials	Experts judge quality of methods and materials	Expert panels Focus groups with teachers and parents Document reviews	Revision of thematic unit materials and methods	Prior to first implementation of each unit and following data collection on effectiveness of each unit
Thematic units improve results for deaf children and their families	Test results for experimental group exceed that of control group Stakeholders express high level of satisfaction	Teacher made tests Observation of selected sites Interviews/surveys with parents, teachers, and interpreters	Demonstrate effectiveness Determine readiness for wider distribution Revisions	Following implementation of each unit

Performance assessments can be included in a number of ways: The evaluator can attend professional development or teaching sessions and gather data both by applying what she learns from the workshop and through observation of participants' applications at the end of the workshops. For example, if a workshop addressed the use of digital cameras and video, as well as the creation of student e-portfolios, then the participants can be asked to make a presentation demonstrating their first attempts at implementing their new technological skills. For workshops that use this demonstration strategy, participants and the evaluator are immediately able to determine the effectiveness of the workshop based on their performance.

Another form of performance assessment is the use of a rubric for scoring a product. One example of a rubric used in a competition for preservice teachers' work that was technologically based used five categories to rate their products: quality of writing, quality of content, educational value of materials, educational use of technology, and inclusion of diversity. This rubric was developed by the program staff and leaders in cooperation with the evaluator to judge the quality of preservice teachers' work (Table 2). (Additional resources are available to guide the development of rubrics. See websites such as http://www.uc.edu/certitest/rubric/rubric.htm and http://

Table 2

RUBRIC FOR EVALUATING STUDENT PROJECTS: CROSSING THE REALITIES DIVIDE IN DEAF EDUCATION

Area of Evaluation	Excellent (3)	Good (2)	Needs Refinement (1)	Score	Weighting	Product
Quality of Writing	No grammatical, punctuation, or spelling errors	A few grammatical, punctuation, or spelling errors	Multiple grammatical, punctuation, or spelling errors		1	
Quality of Content	Demonstrates relevance and depth of information	Demonstrates emerging knowledge of the topic	Demonstrates questionable level of understanding of topic		3	
Educational Value of Materials	Presents information of significant usefulness to relevant audiences	Presents information of some usefulness to relevant audiences	Presents information of limited usefulness to relevant audiences		3	
Effective Use of Technology	Appropriate use of advanced features of selected technology	Appropriate use of basic features of selected technology	Limited or inappropriate use of selected technology		2	
Inclusion of Diversity (If not applicable mark X_____)	Accurate and substantial reflection of diversity*	Moderate reflection of diversity*	Limited or no reflection of diversity*		1	
					Total	

*Diversity includes gender, race/ethnicity, and other cultural dimensions of deaf or hard of hearing communities.

This competition was established as a mechanism for preservice teachers to exhibit their work and earn recognition as being "technologically proficient." Students attending university deaf education programs participating in the ACE-DHH Catalyst Grant were eligible to post their work. (See www.deafed.net.) Those selected received a $500 award and recognition for their product development. This assessment rubric was used as a way to evaluate the projects.

www.rubrics4teachers.com/.) Additional information can be found in Mertens and McLaughlin (2004).

An evaluation plan that is tied to the underlying logic of the program and standards for good evaluation can provide steady guidance with regard to progress, successes, and challenges. A culture of evidence can be created in which the project leadership looks to the evaluation to collect data on important issues and then make decisions based on that evidence.

Summary

The vision of a 21st century learner is that of an individual who is an effective, efficient, self-directed, technologically sophisticated, lifelong learner who collaborates with others for the common purpose of generating and using knowledge to address problems that are of value to the communities in which they live. Technology in the education of D/HH children holds the potential to prepare them to be successful in the future. Tied to the use of technology for this purpose are the preparation of new teachers and the support of existing teachers with an understanding of the complexities that they face in their classrooms. As evidenced in this chapter, educators with experience in the use of technology can share information with their colleagues.

A four-step process for developing a VPDS includes development of an online community of learners to share effective practices, connecting cyber mentors with teacher candidates to increase awareness of lived experiences of people who are D/HH, forming topical teams to investigate and share information about key topics in deaf education, and providing models of deaf education's best K–12 teachers in the preparation programs of new teachers. Careful research and evaluation of the efforts made within this community will add to our understanding of how the applications of technology can improve D/HH student motivation and performance.

References

Adsit, J. N. (2004). A report on technology-mediated professional development programs for teachers and school leaders. American Association of Colleges for Teacher Education. Retrieved June 2, 2004, from http://www.aacte.org/Research/TMPDpaper.pdf

Best of the Web. (2001). Deaf ed. preservice teacher product competition. Retrieved July 11, 2004, from http://www.deafed.net/PageText.asp?hdnPageId=50#2003

Bransford, J. D., Brown, A. L., & Cocking, R. R. (Eds.). (1999a). *How people learn: Brain, mind, experience and school—Executive summary*. Washington, DC: National Academy Press. Retrieved June 2, 2004, from http://www.nap.edu/html/howpeople1/es.html

Bransford, J. D., Brown, A. L., & Cocking, R. R. (Eds.). (1999b). *How people learn: Brain, mind, experience and school—Chapter 6: The design of learning environments*. Washington, DC: National Academy Press. Retrieved June 2, 2004, from http://www.nap.edu/html/howpeople1/ch6.html

Bransford, J. D., Brown, A. L., & Cocking, R. R. (Eds.). (1999c). *How people learn: Brain, mind, experience and school—Chapter 7: Effective teaching: Examples in history, mathematics, and science*. Washington, DC: National Academy Press. Retrieved June 2, 2004, from http://www.nap.edu/html/howpeople1/ch7.html

Bransford, J. D., Brown, A. L., & Cocking, R. R. (Eds.). (1999d). *How people learn: Brain, mind, experience and school—Chapter 8: Teacher learning*. Washington, DC: National Academy Press. Retrieved June 2, 2004, from http://www.nap.edu/html/howpeople1/ch8.html

Bransford, J. D., Brown, A. L., & Cocking, R. R. (Eds.). (1999e). *How people learn: Brain, mind, experience and school—Chapter 9: Technology to support learning*. Washington, DC: National Academy Press. Retrieved June 2, 2004, from http://www.nap.edu/html/howpeople1/ch9.html

Browne, D., & Hoover, J. (1990). The degree to which student teachers report using instructional strategies valued by university faculty. *Action in Teacher Education, 12*(1), 20–24.

Catalyst Deaf Ed. Project. (2000). *Crossing the "realities divide": Preservice teachers as "change agents" for the field of deaf education.* Retrieved June 16, 2004, from http://www.deafed.net/PageText.asp?hdnPageId=117

Cattagni, A., & Farris-Westat, E. (2001). *Internet access in the U.S. public schools and classrooms: 1994–2000* (Report No. NCES 2001-071). U.S. Department of Education, Office of Educational Research and Improvement, National Center for Education Statistics. Retrieved June 2, 2004, from http://nces.ed.gov/pubs2001/2001071.pdf

CEO Forum. (2001). *Key building blocks for student achievement in the 21st century: Assessment, alignment, accountability, access & analysis.* Retrieved June 2, 2004, from http://www.ceoforum.org/downloads/report4.pdf

Cerf, V., & Schutz, C. (2001). Teaching in 2025: Education and technology transformed. In *Visions 2020: Transforming education and training through advanced technologies.* Retrieved June 2, 2004, from http://www.technology.gov/reports/TechPolicy/2020Visions.pdf

Confucius. (n.d.). *Quotes.* Retrieved June 16, 2004, from http://www-cdr.stanford.edu/~baileys/quotes.html

Cradler, J. (2002). How does technology influence student learning? *Learning & Leading With Technology, 29*(2), 46–56. Retrieved June 2, 2004, from http://caret.iste.org/caretadmin/news_documents/StudentLearning.pdf

Cradler, J. (2003a). Technology's impact on teaching and learning. *Learning & Leading With Technology, 30*(7), 54–57. Cradler, J. (2003b). Research on e-learning. *Learning & Leading With Technology, 30*(5), 54–57. Retrieved June 15, 2004, from http://caret.iste.org/caretadmin/resources_documents/30_5.pdf

Cradler, J., & Cradler, R. (2002–2003). Effective integration: Research-based decision making for technology planning and integration. *Learning & Leading With Technology 30*(4), 46–56. Retrieved June 2, 2004, from http://caret.iste.org/caretadmin/resources_documents/30_4.pdf

Cradler, J., Freeman, M., Cradler, R., & McNabb, M. (2002). Research implications for preparing teachers to use technology. *Learning & Leading With Technology, 30*(1), 50-54. Retrieved June 2, 2004, from http://caret.iste.org/caretadmin/news_documents/ProfDev.pdf

Cyber Mentor. (2001). *Cyber mentor project.* Retrieved July 11, 2004, from http://www.deafed.net/Mentor/default.asp

DeafEd Teacher Preparation Programs. (2004). Retrieved June 16, 2004, from http://www.deafed.net/PageText.asp?hdnPageId=120#AL

Dickward, N. (Ed.). (2003). *The sustainability challenge: Talking ed-tech to the next level.* Washington, DC: Benton Foundation. Retrieved June 15, 2004, from http://www.benton.org/publibrary/sustainability/sus_challenge.html

Dodd, E., & Scheetz, N. (2003). Preparing today's teachers of the deaf and hard of hearing to work with tomorrow's students: A statewide needs assessment. *American Annals of the Deaf, 148*(1), 25–37.

Dolnick, E. (1993, September). Deafness as culture. *The Atlantic Monthly,* 37–51.

Donovan, M. S., Bransford, J. D., & Pellegrino, J. W. (Eds.). (1999a). *How people learn: Bridging research and practice—Chapter 2: Key findings.* Washington, DC: National Academy Press. Retrieved June 2, 2004, from http://www.nap.edu/html/howpeople2/ch2.html

Donovan, M. S., Bransford, J. D., & Pellegrino, J. W. (Eds.). (1999b). *How people learn: Bridging research and practice–Chapter 3: Responses from the education and policy communities.* Washington, DC: National Academy Press. Retrieved on June 2, 2004, from http://www.nap.edu/html/howpeople2/ch3.html

Garry, A., & Graham, P. (2004). Using study groups to disseminate technology best practices. *tech*LEARNING.* Retrieved June 2, 2004, from http://www.techlearning.com/shared/printableArticle.jhtml?articleID=17301678

Goodlad, J. (1990). Better teachers for out nation's schools. *Phi Delta Kappa, 72*(3), 181–194.

Hasselbring, T. S., Smith., L., Rakestraw, J., & Campbell, M. (2000). *Literature review: Technology to support teacher development.* Retrieved July 1, 2004, from http://www.aacte.org/Research/EdTechPrep.htm

Heafner, T. (2004). Using technology to motivate students to learn social studies. *Contemporary Issues in Technology and Teacher Education* (CITE). Retrieved June 2, 2004, from http://www.citejournal.org/vol4/iss1/socialstudies/article1.cfm

Holden-Pitt, L., & Diaz, J. (1998). Thirty years of the annual survey of deaf and hard-of-hearing children & youth: A glance over the decades. *American Annals of the Deaf, 143, 2,* 72–76.

Jacobsen, D. M., Clifford, P., & Frisen, S. (2002). Preparing teachers for technology integration: Creating a culture of inquiry in the context of use. *Contemporary Issues in Technology and Teacher Education* (CITE). Retrieved June 3, 2004, from http://www.citejournal.org/vol2/iss3/currentpractice/article2.cfm

Johnson, H. A. (2003). *U.S. deaf education teacher preparation programs: A look at the present and a vision for the future.* Gainesville, FL: Center on Personnel Studies in Special Education. Retrieved June 15, 2004, from http://www.coe.ufl.edu/copsse/pubfiles/IB-9.pdf

Join Together. (2003). *Join Together: A nationwide on-line community of practice and professional development school dedicated to instructional effectiveness and academic excellence within deaf/hard of hearing education.* Retrieved June 15, 2004, from http://www.deafed.net/PageText.asp?hdnPageId=116

Joint Committee on Standards for Educational Evaluation. (1994). *The program evaluation standards: How to assess evaluations of educational programs.* Thousand Oaks, CA: Sage.

Kellogg, M., & Kersaint, G. (2004). Creating a vision for the standards using online videos in an elementary mathematics methods course. *Contemporary Issues in Technology and Teacher Education* (CITE). Retrieved June 3, 2004, from http://www.citejournal.org/vol4/iss1/mathematics/article1.cfm

LaSasso, C., & Wilson, A. (2000). Results of two national surveys of leadership personnel needs in deaf education. *American Annals of the Deaf, 145,* 5,429–435.

Lang, H. G. (2002). Higher education for deaf students: Research priorities in the new millennium. *Journal of Deaf Studies and Deaf Education, 7*(4), 267–280.

Marschark, M., Lang, H. G., & Albertini, J. A. (2002). *Educating deaf students: From research to practice.* New York: Oxford University Press

Master Teacher Project. (2003). *Deaf education master teacher project.* Retrieved July 11, 2004, from http://www.deafed.net/PageText.asp?hdnPageId=71#goal

Mertens, D. M. (2001a). Inclusivity and transformation: Evaluation in 2010. *American Journal of Evaluation, 22*(3), 367–374.

Mertens, D. M. (2001b, August). *PT3 evaluations: Are we closing or widening the digital divide?* Paper presented at the Preparing Tomorrow's Teachers to Use Technology Annual Grantees' Meeting, Washington, DC. Retrieved August 9, 2005, from http://www.deafed.net/activities/PT3MtgDCAug01DM.htm

Mertens, D. M. (2004a). *Faculty join together spring 2004 preliminary report of survey results.* Retrieved August 9, 2005, from http://www.deafed.net/activities/Evaluation/FacSp04.doc

Mertens, D. M. (2004b). *Master teacher spring 2004 preliminary report of survey results.* Retrieved August 9, 2005, from http://www.deafed.net/activities/Evaluation/MTSp04.doc

Mertens, D. M. (2005). *Research and evaluation in education and psychology: Integrating diversity with quantitative, qualitative, and mixed methods.* Thousand Oaks, CA: Sage.

Mertens, D. M., & McLaughlin, J. (2004). *Research and evaluation in special education.* Thousand Oaks, CA: Sage.

Moores, D. (1995). *Placement of deaf children in the most appropriate environment.* Washington, DC: Gallaudet Research Institute.

Moores, D. (2001). *Educating the deaf: Psychology, principles and practices.* Boston: Houghton Mifflin Company.

NCATE. (2001). *Technology and the new professional teacher: Preparing for the 21st century classroom.* Retrieved June 2, 2004, from http://www.ncate.org/accred/projects/tech/tech-21.htm

Neumann, U., & Kyriakakis, C. (2002). 2020 classroom. In *Visions 2020: Transforming education and training through advanced technologies.* Retrieved June 2, 2004, from http://www.technology.gov/reports/TechPolicy/2020Visions.pdf

Pagliaro, C. M. (1998). Mathematics reform in the education of deaf and hard of hearing students. *American Annals of the Deaf, 143,* 22–28.

Partnership for 21st Century Skills. (2003). *Learning for the 21st century.* U.S. Department of Education. Retrieved June 15, 2004, from http://www.21stcenturyskills.org/downloads/P21_Report.pdf

PT3. (2004). *Technology & learning. Preparing tomorrow's teachers to use technology.* Retrieved June 2, 2004, from http://www.pt3.org/technology/tech_learning.html

Ramsey, C. (1997). *Deaf children in public schools: Placement, contexts and consequences.* Washington, DC: Gallaudet University Press.

Rosenstein, J. (1961). Perception, cognition and language in deaf children. *Exceptional Children,* 27(3), 276–284.

Sivin-Kachala, J., & Bialo, E.R. (2000). *2000 research report on the effectiveness of technology in schools.* Washington, DC: Software Information Industry Association. Retrieved July 7, 2004, from http://www.sunysuffolk.edu/Web/Central/InstTech/projects/iteffrpt.pdf

Stewart, D. A., & Kluwin, T. N. (2001). *Teaching deaf and hard of hearing students: Content, strategies and curriculum.* Boston: Allyn and Bacon.

Traxler, C. (2000). The Stanford Achievement Test, 9th edition: National norming and performance standards for deaf and hard-of-hearing students. *Journal of Deaf Studies and Deaf Education,* 5(4), 337–348.

U.S. Department of Education. (2002). *No Child Left Behind Act*. Retrieved June 4, 2004, from http://www.ed.gov/nclb/landing.jhtml

U.S. Department of Education. (n.d.). *Twenty-forth annual report to Congress on the implementation of the Individuals With Disabilities Education Act*. Retrieved June 16, 2004, from http://www.ed.gov/about/reports/annual/osep/2002/index.html

Web-Based Education Commission. (2000). *The power of the Internet for learning: Moving from promise to practice*. Retrieved June 2, 2004, from http://interact.hpcnet.org/web commission/text.htm

Wilson, S. M., Floden, R. E., & Ferrini-Mundy, J. (2001). Teacher preparation research: Current knowledge, gaps, and recommendations. U.S. Department of Education (Research Report). Retrieved January 5, 2005, from http://depts.washington.edu/ctpmail/PDFs/TeacherPrep-WFFM-0202001.pdf

PART FOUR

Final Comments

DONALD F. MOORES

DAVID S. MARTIN

Summary

IT HAS BEEN SAID that the only constant is change. That is certainly true if we look at the fundamental changes in education of deaf children during the past generation. In a way, the title of this chapter is a misnomer; we cannot effectively summarize anything because the world is in a constant state of flux. That is why we, in common with so many other authors, wanted to hold onto the text and continue to modify it as new developments and trends kept appearing, until, finally, it was time to let it go. Although there were clear trends in some areas, no one 20 years ago predicted the effect on the education of deaf children of developments in such disparate areas as human genome research, technology, cochlear implants, the regular education initiative, federal legislation, and statewide standards of learning. Anyone who wishes to predict the future should do so with a large dose of diffidence and humility. It is within this spirit that we offer a few final comments.

Upon reviewing this entire volume and the work of its well-qualified, highly skilled, and insightful chapter authors, it is clear that the forces of change fully operate in the field of curriculum for deaf and hard of hearing students and will continue to do so. Although the fundamental principles of education have not changed—the importance of self-determination, strong subject matter knowledge, and application of contextually appropriate skills and strategies—it is clear that much has changed in terms of expectations for learners who are deaf or hard of hearing. Perhaps the most fundamental change is the clear expectation that these learners will have opportunities to access the general education curriculum, and the concomitant expectations for achievement that accompany that goal. Thus, in-depth examinations of the subject matters of these areas of knowledge, in addition to consideration of the special needs of these particular learners, are the major focus of this volume. Some particular changes in both the general education and deaf education fields have affected the curriculum context in ways that could not have been predicted even a few short years ago. Some of the major changes include the following:

1. The passage of the bipartisan No Child Left Behind Act of 2002 has imposed not only expectations for achievement of all children but also requirements of teacher qualifications—both of which goals are elusive at best. Just a few short years ago, such a law could not have been anticipated. The emphasis on

accountability and scientifically based instruction will continue to have significant influence.

2. The performance of cochlear implantion with very young children in the United States is not as widespread as in some other countries such as Australia and much of western and northern Europe, but has increased rapidly in recent years. Results suggest that the procedure is effective with some, but not all, children. It is clear we will see miniaturization and more efficiency in the devices. Unfortunately, many professionals believe, and many parents have been led to believe, that implants will cure deafness in all children. This is incorrect, and future developments in curriculum will have to address education of children with implants of varying effectiveness. Many of these children should continue to be instructed through some form of manual, as well as oral, communication.

3. More and more deaf children are placed in regular classrooms and, by definition, are exposed to the general education curriculum of a particular school district. For most children, however, mere placement contiguous to hearing peers, even with highly skilled interpreters, itself a relatively rare occurrence in most states, is not sufficient, and the services of a qualified itinerant teacher of deaf students are necessary to support and supplement classroom instruction. It is only through the cooperation of the regular classroom teacher and the itinerant teacher that the curriculum can be implemented effectively.

4. Since the beginning of the massive human genome project, more and more of genes causing a variety of conditions, including deafness, are being identified and located. There already have been attempts at in vitro fertilization to eliminate recessive genes causing deafness in prospective parents. Our field, as so many others, is facing complex moral issues as new breakthroughs are made on a regular basis. Genetic counseling will probably assume increasing importance in understanding and even determining the hearing status of learners.

The lesson to be learned for educators, policy makers, parents, students, and others is that we all must remain adaptable. The pace of change will continue to quicken, and the pressure to remain up to date will be greater than ever. Only when educators are adaptable can the progress of deaf and hard of hearing learners match that which they all can truly perform.

Contributors

BARBARA GALE BONDS is a PhD candidate at Gallaudet University. She has had prior professional experience as a teacher of deaf and hard of hearing students, including the University of Virginia Pre-School Program, the Virginia School for the Deaf and Blind, the Driver Education Program at Wilson Rehabilitation Center in Maryland, Virginia Community College, and Gallaudet University. She currently works with deaf adults employed by federal agencies in eLearning and is a nationally certified sign language interpreter.

CAROL CONVERTINO has been a professional sign language interpreter for the National Technical Institute for the Deaf at Rochester Institute of Technology. Currently she is a research associate at the Center of Excellence for the Study of Sign Language Interpreting. She has a master's degree in secondary education for deaf and hard of hearing students. Her research focuses on communication obstacles and learning strategies of deaf students in science, technology, engineering, and mathematics.

M. KATHLEEN ELLIS is assistant professor and director of the adapted physical education program at the University of Rhode Island. She is a graduate of Michigan State University with a PhD in kinesiology and cognate (an area of specialty) in deaf education. Formerly a physical education coordinator at the Michigan School for the Deaf, she has expertise in the areas of fitness and physical activity of deaf children, Deaf sport, and the influence of parents on their deaf children's physical activity and fitness.

KAREN M. EWING is a PhD candidate and adjunct faculty member at Gallaudet University. Her educational background is in elementary education, special education, and education of deaf students who have multiple disabilities. Her prior teaching experience includes education of students who are deaf-blind and students with multiple disabilities. She has worked extensively with schools and families in the field of autism and advocacy. Her research interests include deaf students with multiple disabilities and online learning.

HAROLD JOHNSON is professor of education at Kent State University and director of the Kent State Deaf Education Teacher Preparation Program; he is also codirector of the federally supported Join Together Nationwide On-Line Professional Development School on Excellence in Deaf/Hard of Hearing Education. He has been a teacher of deaf children and has supervised student teachers in that field. He has done advanced study in rehabilitation, emotional disturbance, and linguistics and has researched the changing patterns of deaf mother-child interactions.

JULIE K. JONES is a consultant in special education who specializes in work with students with multiple disabilities and deaf-blindness. Formerly a public school teacher of children with multiple disabilities (including deafness, deaf-blindness, mental retardation, vision impairment, autism, and cerebral palsy), she is the author of articles on that topic. She has been on the faculty of Texas Tech University and George Mason University and adjunct faculty at the University of Virginia and Gallaudet University. She was associate director for the Virginia Deaf-Blind Project and director of the Migrant Headstart Disabilities Services Quality Improvement Center.

THOMAS W. JONES is professor of education at Gallaudet University; he is a specialist in education of deaf students with multiple disabilities and formerly was a public school teacher in this field. He has authored numerous articles on this topic. Formerly coordinator of the National Council on Accreditation of Teacher Education process for the School of Education and Human Services at Gallaudet University, he has also been director of program evaluation for the Council on Education of the Deaf and is involved in issues related to credentialing of teachers.

DONI LAROCK has worked at the National Technical Institute for the Deaf at Rochester Institute of Technology for many years and is currently manager of interpreting services and a classroom sign language interpreter. He is adjunct instructor for the Liberal Arts College at the Institute with a specialization in American history. He has also been an interpreter at the elementary and secondary levels of education. He is currently working with the Center of Excellence for the Study of Sign Language Interpreting at the National Technical Institute for the Deaf.

HARRY G. LANG is professor in the Department of Research at the National Technical Institute for the Deaf at Rochester Institute of Technology. He has taught physics and mathematics and was chair of the Institute's faculty development program. A visiting professor at Leeds University (England), he has written numerous articles, chapters, and books on the teaching of science to deaf students and the history of scientific invention and discovery by deaf scientists. His educational research has focused on teaching and learning styles and factors contributing to effective teaching, including multimedia and analyses of sign communication. He received Rochester Institute of Technology's Eisenhart Award for Outstanding Teaching.

JOHN LUCKNER is professor and coordinator of the deaf education program at the University of Northern Colorado. He has been a teacher of deaf or hard of hearing infants, children, and graduate students. He is associated with the National Center on Low Incidence Disabilities clearinghouse for research and information on deafness, blindness, and severe disabilities. The author of numerous articles and coauthor of three books dealing with these topics, he also serves on the editorial review board for the *American Annals of the Deaf*, the *Volta Review*, and the *Communication Disorders Quarterly*.

PAMELA LUFT is associate professor in deaf and special education at Kent State University. She worked for 15 years in residential and public schools with deaf and hard of hearing children in West Virginia; Maryland; Washington, D.C.; Florida; and California. She has been coordinator of a teacher preparation program, behavior specialist, and career center coordinator and has worked with a range of students from gifted to those with multiple disabilities. She has directed federally funded projects in educational interpreting, teaching ASL as a foreign language, and transition-focused programs on deaf education and rehabilitation counselor education.

LUCAS MAGONGWA is currently a lecturer at the University of the Witwatersrand in Johannesburg, South Africa; he is also the coordinator of the Department of Deaf Education. His areas of specialization are deaf education, deaf community and culture, and South African Sign Language. He is a candidate for the Master of Education degree in deaf education. He was educated in a school for the deaf as well as in public schools. He has also been a teacher in schools for the deaf and subsequently a principal of a school for the deaf.

MARC MARSCHARK is professor in the Department of Research at the National Technical Institute for the Deaf at Rochester Institute of Technology, where he heads the Center of Excellence for the Study of Sign Language Interpreting. He is also professor in the Department of Psychology at the University of Aberdeen (Scotland), and he is editor of the *Journal of Deaf Studies and Deaf Education*. He has authored and coauthored books on the subjects of educating deaf children, connecting practice with research in education of deaf learners, and sign language interpreting.

DAVID S. MARTIN is professor emeritus and dean emeritus at Gallaudet University, where he taught a variety of subjects including curriculum to teacher-education candidates at undergraduate and graduate levels. He has been a curriculum director in two public school districts and was a curriculum developer at Education Development Center in Cambridge, Massachusetts. He has held positions as a teacher, school principal, chair of a department of teacher education, and dean of education. He has published numerous articles, chapters, and books related to deafness, higher-level thinking, and the teaching of social studies.

DONNA M. MERTENS is professor in the Department of Educational Foundations and Research at Gallaudet University, where she teaches research methods, program evaluation, and educational psychology. She is past president and board member of the American Evaluation Association and is a leader within its Graduate Internship for Evaluators of Color program. She has authored and edited several books and journal articles related to research and evaluation. She serves as evaluator for a federally supported national technology project to improve the preparation of teachers of deaf students; she has also participated in national and international evaluations for projects supported by both private foundations and governmental agencies.

MARGERY MILLER is professor of psychology and coordinator of the Psychology Internship Program at Gallaudet University. A psychologist, school psychologist, speech and language pathologist, and special educator, she has also been acting director of the National Academy, director of the Family Learning Vacation Program, and director of the Northwest Campus Counseling Program at Gallaudet. Prior to coming to Gallaudet she taught at the Maryland School for the Deaf and the Montgomery County, Maryland, program for the deaf. She has authored articles and chapters related to language, communication, conceptualization, assessment, literacy, and social-emotional issues within the family, all related to the lives of deaf individuals. Her research is in sign-adapted assessment, literacy and bilingualism, information-processing, the relationship between language and intelligence for deaf learners, and family issues in the Deaf community.

DONALD F. MOORES is professor of education at Gallaudet University, editor of the *American Annals of the Deaf*, and associate editor of the *African Annals of the Deaf*. He has written numerous articles, chapters, and books related to deafness. He taught deaf students at the middle and high school level for 5 years and has been a dorm counselor, football coach, summer camp director, and adult education director for the deaf. He has conducted research with deaf individuals from early intervention programs to college in more than 40 educational settings and in home environments. Prior to coming to Gallaudet, he was a professor of psychoeducational studies, coordinator of the graduate training program in deafness, director of the University of Minnesota Research Center on Education of Handicapped Children, and chair of the Pennsylvania State University Department of Special Education. He was director of the Gallaudet Center for Studies in Education and Human Development during its 16 years of existence, from 1980—1996.

CLAUDIA M. PAGLIARO is associate professor and director of the Program in Education of Deaf and Hard of Hearing Students at the University of Pittsburgh. She specializes in the teaching of mathematics to deaf learners. Previously she was a teacher of deaf students at the elementary level. She currently teaches deaf studies, deaf education, lesson design, and methodology of teaching mathematics to deaf and hard of hearing students. Her current research interests include mathematics instruction and the learning of deaf and hard of hearing students, with a focus on problem solving and the influence of a visual language.

DAVID S. STEWART was professor of education and director of the Deaf Education Program at Michigan State University. His expertise encompassed numerous areas, including language development and physical education in deaf learners. He was also interested in best teaching practices to enhance language development and educational attainment across grade levels. His work on Deaf sport addresses the effects that sports have on the Deaf community and culture. He previously held a faculty position at York University in Toronto and was a member of the Board of Trustees at Gallaudet University.

CLAUDINE STORBECK is senior lecturer in education at the University of the Witwatersrand in Johannesburg, South Africa. She was the founder and until recently the coordinator of both the Department of Deaf Education and the Centre for Deaf Studies at the university. She developed the first curriculum for teachers of deaf students in South Africa at the honors and certificate levels, and was a teacher of deaf students and a teacher trainer for 7 years. She was also involved in the development of the curriculum and unit standards for South African Sign Language as a first and second language and is involved in both academic and community work within the South African Deaf community. Active in international conferences related to deaf education, she was the recipient of a Fulbright Fellowship at Gallaudet University in 2005.

Index

OC